THE FATE
OF WAR

THE FATE
OF WAR

Fredericksburg, 1862

Duane Schultz

WESTHOLME
Yardley

Frontispiece: Buildings in Fredericksburg, Virginia, destroyed by a Federal artillery barrage in December 1862. (*Library of Congress*)

Westholme Publishing, LLC
904 Edgewood Road
Yardley, Pennsylvania 19067

ISBN: 978-1-59416-145-2

Printed in the United States of America.

Book Club Edition

The men anticipated what many of them termed "a gay and happy winter in Dixie's land." But alas, poor fellows, hundreds never left the place. Such is the fate of war.
—*Pvt. Bill McCarter, the Irish Brigade*

It is the night before a battle. The moon is shining through the soft haze with brightness almost prophetic. For the last half hour I have stood alone in the awful stillness of its glimmering light gazing upon the strange, sad scene around me striving to say, "Thy will, Oh God, be done."
—*Clara Barton*

I saw battle-corpses, myriads of them,
And the white skeletons of young men, I saw them,
I saw the debris and debris of all the slain soldiers of the war.
—*Walt Whitman, When Lilacs Last in the Dooryard Bloom'd*

A Note to the Reader

This is not an academic history. It focuses on individuals, not armies; on people, not plans and positions drawn on maps. It is a narrative of how soldiers and civilians react to the stress of war; a record of triumph and failure, courage and cowardice, compassion and cruelty. It is about what people can force themselves to do in the name of duty, patriotism, and dedication to a cause, or in the face of the ultimate fear of letting down their friends or betraying their own sense of who they are.

Although I write histories, I am foremost a psychologist, which may explain why I focus more on people than on the structure of an event. I am interested in the motivations, passions, and emotions of the people who fought on both sides at Fredericksburg on December 13, 1862. Based on careful research, this book is not a detailed reconstruction and recounting of the battle, a task which has been done in many other books; rather, it is the story of the people—the ordinary and high-ranking, soldier and civilian, men and women—who came together one terrible day.

CONTENTS

Prologue: Waiting Their Turn to Die

On Saturday, December 13, 1862, Sgt. Thomas Plunkett of the 21st Massachusetts Infantry lost his arms. Only minutes before, the regiment had calmly dressed ranks and formed a straight line, prepared to charge the Confederates. The Northerners knew what they were facing. They had watched wave after wave of their fellow soldiers attempt to dislodge the rebels from their heavily defended position at Fredericksburg's stone wall. Each successive attack had failed. Now it was up to the men from North Oxford, Massachusetts.

Not far away, near enough to have witnessed the slaughter, forty-year-old Clarissa Harlowe Barton, who preferred to be called Clara, saw the men of the 21st prepare to advance. She knew many of the soldiers—North Oxford was her hometown— and she wondered whether they would survive even the next ten minutes. Clara Barton had already seen more of war than had many soldiers. Just that morning a rebel shell fragment had torn her skirt.

The North Oxford men moved out. Rebel artillery opened fire. A Confederate shell decapitated one man. His body remained upright for an instant while blood spurted from his neck; his head bounced to the ground like a ball.

As wounded men fell, those remaining closed ranks, surging toward the Confederate line with Sergeant Plunkett waving the regimental banner. A shell exploded overhead, killing three men near him. Plunkett's arms were crushed, mangled, and he swayed on his feet, clinging to the flagstaff. To drop the colors would be to dishonor them. He anchored the base of the wooden pole on the ground, propped it against one of his feet, and held the banner aloft with the bleeding stump of his right arm.

"Don't let it fall, boys!" he shouted. "Don't let it fall."

Straight as a ramrod amid the rain of shells and bullets, Plunkett held the flag high until another soldier eased it from him. When that man was hit seconds later, a third man grabbed the flag before it could touch the ground. The regiment rushed ahead leaving Plunkett sprawled in the dirt until, finally, there was no one left standing to carry the colors.

The men of the 21st Massachusetts Infantry lay dead or dying, or flattened against a slight rise in the ground trying to stay alive until rebel fire shifted from them to the next line of Union soldiers preparing to march forward.

And so it went, hour after hour, throughout the day.

The field that these Union troops were attempting to cross was a half mile long. At the far end, protected by a thick wall of stones that stretched five hundred yards, Gen. James "Pete" Longstreet's Confederate soldiers watched them come on. Standing four deep, three of the rebels would load muskets while the point man fired, thus reloading the weapons so rapidly that a continuous hail of bullets poured forth.

The hill above the stone wall was lined with Confederate cannon, their muzzles aimed at overlapping points to blanket the oncoming Yankee troops. A Southern artillery officer assured General Longstreet that once they opened fire, a chicken couldn't live on that field!

For three weeks, the soldiers of Gen. Ambrose Burnside's Army of the Potomac, 141,000 strong, remained encamped on the northern bank of the Rappahannock River while Gen. Robert E. Lee's Army of Northern Virginia, at 74,000 troops—slightly more than half the strength of the Yankees—fortified its defenses.

The Union soldiers were well aware that they would soon have to brave musket and cannon fire to cross the barren field and then march uphill to attack the rebels at the stone wall. They also knew that many of them would die there because no army could cross an unprotected expanse and take the heights against a strong defensive position. If only their generals knew it as well.

When the attack was launched, evasive action was not part of the plan. The men did not dart across the terrain, dodging and weaving to reduce their chances of becoming targets. That was not proper military procedure. Instead, the Union soldiers marched in formation at "trail arms," holding their muskets at their sides by the middle of the barrel, maintaining a steady 160 steps per minute, each man elbow-to-elbow with the man beside him. When Confederate shells tore huge bloody gaps in the line, the men halted, dressed right, and closed ranks, calmly and orderly as if on the parade ground.

By the time the Yankees neared the stone wall, their lines had grown much shorter but they never faltered. Soldiers fell by the scores, the hundreds, then the thousands, but the rest kept marching up the hill at the same measured, steady pace.

"Straighten up! Close ranks!" Once within firing distance, the northern troops raised their muskets, fired their single shots, and ran forward together, yelling to bolster their courage, and offering a silent prayer that the sight of wild-eyed Yankees bearing down on them would cause the rebels to flee. But none did. And the Union soldiers were cut down like wheat at harvest time. Not one man came within twenty-five yards of Lee's position.

After the initial assault failed, wave after wave of perfectly aligned Union troops followed relentlessly until daylight faded. The men waiting in each new line watched the troops ahead of them fall, their bodies shattered by Confederate shells and bullets. With so many casualties, the grass soon became slippery with their blood. The Northerners formed and re-formed, stepping resolutely over the corpses of those who went before them, waiting their turn to die.

When darkness finally halted the killing, 8,789 Union troops lay scattered on the frozen ground below the stone wall. A Union general later referred to the field at Fredericksburg as "a great slaughter pen. They might as well have tried to take Hell."

Murat Halstead, correspondent for the *Cincinnati Commercial* newspaper, wrote, "It can hardly be in human nature for men to show more valor, or generals to manifest less judgment, than were perceptible on our side that day."

When President Abraham Lincoln got the news, he remarked, "If there is a worse place than Hell, I am in it."

And Ambrose Burnside, the Union general responsible for the disaster, for one of the bloodiest days of the war, was heard to cry out, "Oh, those men, those poor men over there. I am thinking of them all the time."

Even the Confederates felt pity for the enemy's terrible losses. A soldier of the 17th Virginia Infantry wrote: "All that day we watched the fruitless charges with their fearful slaughter until we were sick at heart. I forgot they were enemies and only remembered that they were men, and it is hard to see in cold blood brave men die."

ONE

ALAS FOR
MY POOR COUNTRY

Ambrose Burnside firmly believed he was not competent to lead the Army of the Potomac. He was right. But someone had to take command of the largest of all the Union armies. Its existing general, George McClellan, was running out of time and excuses to explain his continuing failure to pursue Robert E. Lee. And Abraham Lincoln was running out of patience. If McClellan did not attack the Army of Northern Virginia soon, he would have to be replaced.

It was mid-September 1862. Lee had invaded Maryland in an attempt to carry the war north into Pennsylvania. McClellan's forces had stopped him at Sharpsburg, along Antietam Creek. More than 13,000 Confederate troops and 12,000 Union soldiers were dead, wounded, and missing by the time Lee led his army back to Virginia.

Lincoln expected McClellan to pursue the Confederates while they were on the run and destroy their army before Lee had a chance to regroup and establish a strong defensive line in northern Virginia. The president cajoled, pleaded, and threatened, but McClellan always offered an excuse—he needed to reorganize the army, to appoint new officers, replenish his supplies, rebuild transportation lines, or give the troops time to rest. Meanwhile, the rebels continued to put more distance between themselves and the Union army.

October came and McClellan was still at Sharpsburg even though Lincoln told him he was weary of excuses and disgusted with his lack of progress. The president spent three days at Sharpsburg in person in early October to urge McClellan to take action. McClellan smiled politely and listened earnestly but gave no indication that he was ready to pursue Robert E. Lee.

One morning Lincoln arose early and climbed to the top of a hill, accompanied by Ozias M. Hatch, an old friend from Illinois. The two men stood in silence, gazing at the sea of white tents stretching far into the distance—the mighty Army of the Potomac, then 100,144 strong.

"Do you know what this is?" Lincoln asked his friend, gesturing at the camp.

"It is the Army of the Potomac," Hatch answered.

"So it is called," Lincoln said, "but that is a mistake. It is only McClellan's bodyguard."

Lincoln returned to Washington, having failed to budge McClellan. Noah Brooks, a reporter for the *Sacramento Daily Union* who had known Lincoln in Illinois before the war, was shocked at how defeated the president looked on his return from Sharpsburg. "The change in his personal appearance was marked and sorrowful," Brooks wrote. "His eyes were almost deathly in their gloomy depths, and on his visage was an air of pronounced sadness. His face was colorless and drawn."

On October 6, Lincoln issued a peremptory order to McClellan to "cross the Potomac and give battle to the enemy or drive him South. Your army must move now while the roads are good." But the Army of the Potomac stayed rooted in place while McClellan offered more reasons why he could not march south just yet.

On October 13, Lincoln tried again. He wrote a letter reminding McClellan of a previous conversation in which the president suggested that McClellan was being overly cautious when he had informed Lincoln that the army could not operate like Lee's army because it did not have sufficient supplies and food.

Lincoln noted that Lee's ragged men were marching twenty miles a day without adequate food or supplies. If Lee could do it, why couldn't McClellan? Lincoln urged McClellan to move immediately to interpose his forces between Lee and the Confederate capital at Richmond so that Lee would have no choice but to fight out in the open. That was the only way the rebel army could be destroyed.

Two more weeks passed with McClellan's forces still at Sharpsburg. The latest excuse was that the horses were exhausted. That was one excuse too many for Lincoln. He knew that the quartermaster general had recently sent 10,254 fresh horses and a large number of mules to McClellan at a cost in excess of $1 million. Lincoln sent a sharp retort to McClellan: "Will you pardon me for asking what the horses of your army have done since the battle of Antietam that fatigues anything?"

McClellan finally marched his men across the Potomac River on November 1, but he moved so slowly that Lee had ample time to position part of his army around Culpeper Courthouse, blocking the Yankees' path to Richmond. In addition, Lee placed Stonewall Jackson's troops in the Shenandoah Valley where they could menace the Union army's flank. McClellan, who believed he was the only man who could save the nation, was too late. Lee had outmaneuvered him again, and Lincoln had had enough.

On November 5, Lincoln sent an executive order to the War Department:

> By direction of the President it is ordered that Major-General McClellan be relieved from the command of the Army of the Potomac, and that Major-General Burnside take command of that army.

Catharinus Putnam Buckingham had been a West Point cadet with Robert E. Lee; they graduated in 1829. Lee was first in the class, Buckingham a close fourth. Now Buckingham was a Union brigadier general, the confidential assistant adjutant-general to Secretary of War Edwin Stanton.

On the night of November 7, Buckingham was the only passenger on a train from Washington, DC, bound for the Army of the Potomac headquarters at Rectortown in northern Virginia. He carried with him War Department General Orders Number 182, officially announcing the replacement of George McClellan by Ambrose Burnside. Buckingham knew that it might not be so simple to effect this change in command; Burnside might refuse the commission.

Burnside had told Lincoln on two previous occasions that he was unfit to lead the army, and Buckingham did not know whether Burnside had changed his mind. Stanton had told Buckingham to use every argument he could think of to persuade Burnside to accept the job. Buckingham knew of one argument in particular that he thought would work, no matter how reluctant Burnside seemed.

Buckingham reached Burnside's tent in the dark of night in the midst of a swirling snowstorm. He handed Burnside the orders. Burnside insisted that he had not changed his opinion; he was not prepared to lead the army. Burnside maintained that McClellan was perfectly competent to continue in command, and that it was too risky to change commanders once a campaign was under way.

Following Stanton's instructions, Buckingham played his final card. He said that McClellan was going to be replaced anyway, even if Burnside refused the command, and if Burnside did not take the job it would most likely be offered to Fighting Joe Hooker. If there was anyone the genial Burnside despised, it was Hooker, whom he was convinced would lead the Army of the Potomac to its ruin.

Burnside summoned two of his staff officers and advised them of the situation. For more than an hour they argued that Burnside had no choice but to accept the command. It was his duty, they said, and he could not refuse to obey a presidential order. Burnside repeated his belief that he was unfit for such a great responsibility,

General Ambrose E. Burnside and two of his staff officers at Warrenton, Virginia, in November 1862, soon after being named to replace General George McClellan as leader of the Army of the Potomac. (*Library of Congress*)

but finally he relented and agreed to accompany Buckingham when he called on his old friend George McClellan.

McClellan was expecting them, having been notified by a friend in the War Department that Buckingham was on his way by special train, bringing important dispatches. McClellan was certain that those dispatches contained orders relieving him of command. He wrote in his memoirs:

> Late at night I was sitting alone in my tent, writing to my wife. All the staff was asleep. Suddenly someone knocked upon the tent-pole, and upon my invitation to enter there appeared Burnside and Buckingham, both looking very

solemn. I received them kindly and commenced conversation upon general subjects in the most unconcerned manner possible. After a few moments Buckingham said to Burnside: "Well, General, I think we had better tell General McClellan the object of our visit." I very pleasantly said that I should be glad to learn it.

Buckingham handed McClellan the orders that ended his military career. McClellan forced himself to smile as he read them. He was not about to give his audience any degree of satisfaction. "I am sure," he later wrote to his wife, "that not a muscle quivered nor was the slightest expression of feeling visible on my face. They shall not have that triumph."

"Well, Burnside, I turn the command over to you," McClellan said, with all the cheerfulness he could muster.

Burnside accepted dutifully but with obvious reluctance. When offered congratulations on his new command, he replied, "That, sir, is the last thing on which I wish to be congratulated."

After Burnside and Buckingham left his tent, McClellan continued the letter he had been writing to his wife. "Poor Burn feels dreadfully, almost crazy," he wrote. "I am sorry for him." But McClellan also made clear his view that Lincoln was committing a tragic blunder for the Army of the Potomac and for the Union as a whole by relieving him of command. "They have made a great mistake," McClellan told his wife. "Alas for my poor country."

Burnside's appointment was not well received by the Army of the Potomac. "He is very slow," McClellan wrote to his wife, "[and] is not fit to command more than a regiment. If I treat him as he deserves, he will be my mortal enemy hereafter. If I do not praise him as he thinks he deserves, and as I know he does not, he will be at least a very lukewarm friend."

Other military leaders also viewed the change in command as a mistake. "The army is filled with gloom and greatly depressed," Gen. George Meade wrote to his wife on hearing the news. "Burnside, it is said, wept like a child, and is the most distressed man in the army, openly says he is not fit for the position, and that McClellan is the only man who can handle the large army."

When a group of generals met with Burnside the day after his appointment to offer their congratulations, he replied candidly, as was his nature, that he was not fit to command but would do his best. Some of the officers found his guileless comments touching. The German-born general Carl Schurz wrote: "One could not help feeling a certain tenderness for the man. But when a moment later the generals talked among themselves, it was no wonder that several shook their heads and asked how we could have confidence in the fitness of our leader if he had no such confidence in himself."

It was a question that would haunt the Army of the Potomac in the weeks to come. It was not only the generals who were uneasy about Burnside. Discontent spread down the line. Capt. Francis Adams Donaldson of the 118th Pennsylvania Infantry recorded his sorrow in his diary:

> How can I describe it, how can I tell the utter despondency of the soldiers, at the loss of their idolized commander? The news broke upon us like a thunderclap. Our general [McClellan] removed during an active campaign, taken from the head of the army when about to engage the enemy. Who ever heard of such a thing? Does history point to a like occurrence? The whole army was in tears, there were no exceptions.
>
> And now to the man who will succeed Genl. McClellan, I will do him justice to say that we all think he had no hand in it. But we do not think he can command this army. I have no confidence in our future success. I believe the next battle will witness a terrible and bloody defeat for this army.

On November 10, the Army of the Potomac assembled in ranks almost three miles long to honor its departing commander. That day may have been the closest any United States army ever came to mutiny. Before the review, most of the officers of the 1st Minnesota Volunteers submitted their resignations in protest of

McClellan's dismissal. They were persuaded to change their minds—to resign in the face of the enemy could be viewed as an act of cowardice—but the fact that they even considered resigning their commissions showed the depth of their shock and anger.

The review was a sad and stirring occasion for the men. Many wept unashamedly as "Little Mac," as the men adoringly referred to McClellan, passed by on his horse, taking his hat off to honor his troops. "Today we have been on review," wrote Capt. Robert Carter of the 22nd Massachusetts in his diary. "We took leave of McClellan, and the whole army is discouraged and sad."

"The army is in mourning," Gen. Marsena Patrick remarked, "and this is a blue day for us all."

Captain Donaldson of the 118th Pennsylvania had more to say:

> A sadder gathering of men could not well have been assembled. Our corps was reviewed in the morning, and as General McClellan passed along its front whole regiments broke and flocked around him, and with tears and entreaties besought him not to leave them, but to say the word and they would soon settle matters in Washington. Indeed it was thought at one time that there would be a mutiny, but by a word he calmed the tumult and ordered the men back to their colors and their duty.
>
> At one point during the slow, painful final ride, the men of the Irish Brigade broke ranks and crowded so closely around McClellan and his entourage—which included a solemn Burnside bringing up the rear—that the procession came to a halt. The brigade commander, Brig. Gen. Thomas Meagher, ordered the colors to be thrown down in the dirt for McClellan to ride over as a gesture of contempt for the War Department. McClellan refused. He told Meagher to take up the colors and carry them with pride.

As the troops continued to cheer themselves hoarse for their beloved Little Mac, Captain Donaldson overheard Gen. Andrew Humphreys talking to another officer. "I heard [Humphreys] say,"

General "Little Mac" McClellan, accompanied by General Burnside, waves his hat to the troops as he takes leave of the Army of the Potomac. (*Library of Congress*)

Donaldson wrote, "that he wished to God General McClellan would put himself at the head of the army and throw the infernal scoundrels at Washington into the Potomac." That night, a group of drunken young officers tried to beat up a reporter from a New York newspaper that had been urging the army to go after Lee. They were led by a young aide to McClellan by the name of Custer.

The next morning, McClellan and his staff boarded a train bound for Washington. An honor guard of 2,000 troops lined the railroad tracks, standing stiffly at attention as a final salute was fired. Suddenly, spontaneously—no one was heard to give the order—they broke ranks, surrounded McClellan's car, and uncoupled it from the train.

As they shoved the car back from the rest of the train, they shouted for McClellan to stay. Curses were screamed at the War Department and Abraham Lincoln for dismissing McClellan. One officer described the tense scene as a moment of "fearful excitement."

One word [from McClellan], one look of encouragement, the lifting of a finger, would have been the signal for a revolt against lawful authority, the consequences of which no man can measure. McClellan stepped upon the front platform of the car, and there was instant silence. His address was short. It ended in the memorable words "Stand by General Burnside as you have stood by me, and all will be well."

In silence the honor guard rolled the railroad car forward, recoupled it to the train, and watched it move away. The incipient revolt was over. McClellan changed trains in Washington and went home to New Jersey, bearing with him a bitterness that lasted the rest of his life.

The army was Burnside's now, and he felt even more discouraged than usual after witnessing the outpouring of emotion for the man he had just replaced. He knew the troops would never care so deeply about him, and he was well aware of the military challenges he was facing. The experiences that awaited him were later accurately recounted by Lincoln's private secretaries, John Nicolay and John Hay: "It can be safely said that from the hour when in that blinding snowstorm he accepted the command of the Army of the Potomac to the hour when he laid it down in discouragement and despair, [Burnside] did not see a single happy day."

TWO

Marked for Greater Things

People liked Ambrose Burnside—at least, before he was given command of the Army of the Potomac. Those who knew him before then described him as affable, genial, friendly, courteous, affectionate, and trusting. He was well mannered and charming and made everyone in his presence feel at ease. One historian wrote that Burnside was a "simple, honest, loyal soldier, doing his best even if that best was not very good, never scheming, or conniving or backbiting."

He cut a fine figure: six feet tall, handsome, and heavyset, with a bushy set of distinctive whiskers reaching halfway down his cheeks. They would later be known as "side-burns," a play on his name. He typically wore a high-crowned hat with a wide, turned-down brim; a double-breasted knee-length coat; large buckskin gauntlets; and a revolver on his hip. The soldiers of his early commands always cheered heartily whenever he rode past.

He had been an excellent officer with smaller commands and a good subordinate. "He seemed dashing and brave, and he was. He also seemed to be very intelligent, but he was not." This is a blunt assessment, but accurate. Burnside had been correct in his own estimation of his abilities; he was not competent to command a large army.

Gen. George Meade, writing two months after Burnside had taken over the Army of the Potomac, observed that Burnside lacked "knowledge and judgment, and was deficient in that enlarged mental capacity which is essential in a commander. The command was too much for him." Once he had decided on a plan, he would not change his mind. Burnside once told a friend that "when once convinced of the correctness of my course, all the influence on the face of the earth cannot swerve me from pursuing it."

Gen. William F. "Baldy" Smith wrote about Burnside's "intense stubbornness which sometimes takes hold of weak minds." Smith noted how appalled he was when he learned that Burnside spurned the advice and counsel of his staff officers, preferring to consult someone a bit less qualified instead.

"Burnside turned to me," Smith recalled, "apropos of nothing and said: 'Do you know what I do when you fellows get away from here at night?' I admitted ignorance, and he said: 'I call Robert in here and have a long talk with him, certain that I shall get honest opinions.'"

Robert was Burnside's servant and cook. A slave Burnside had purchased before the war, Robert was devoted to his master. Baldy Smith wrote that Robert "would have willingly laid down his life for Burnside. I did not doubt but that Robert's advice was always honestly given, but I never after that entered into competition with him in the bestowal of it." The implication was clear as far as Smith was concerned, and he no doubt passed it on to others: The commanding general valued his servant's opinion more than that of his senior generals.

Burnside had another fault that manifested itself shortly after he took command and quickly grew more apparent. Within two days of taking over the army, he worked himself to the point of exhaustion. Unable to delegate authority or assign tasks to others, he spent hours on details that his staff should have been handling for him. He worked all day and half the night and soon wore himself down to the point where his judgment and decision-making ability were clouded by lack of sleep. Burnside's staff offered to help with the routine tasks that keep an army running, but Burnside insisted on attending personally to almost every aspect of daily operations.

His personal physician, Dr. William Church, had told the general weeks before the change of command that he needed rest. He had reminded Burnside that he had not taken so much as one day's leave in well over a year, since the summer of 1861. Dr. Church bluntly told his weary patient and friend that he showed signs of imminent collapse. "But for your great powers of endurance you would probably have broken down before this."

Many in the Army of the Potomac wondered openly why Lincoln had chosen Burnside for the job, even after conceding that the president had little choice. Joe Hooker was the only other likely candidate. Hooker yearned for the job, which he believed was his due, but he was junior in rank to Burnside. In addition, Hooker was thought too politically ambitious and was strongly opposed by both Secretary of War Edwin Stanton and General-in-Chief Henry Halleck. All of the other generals Lincoln had considered for the position had serious flaws of character or performance.

Also, Burnside had the strong support of powerful Abolitionists in Congress, and his military record was, if not brilliant, at least acceptable. Lincoln was impressed by what he considered to be evidence of Burnside's noble character because Burnside twice refused to replace his good friend McClellan as army commander. Lincoln interpreted this as a supreme act of loyalty and admired Burnside for it.

Finally, Lincoln knew how popular McClellan was with the soldiers of the Army of the Potomac. He hoped that by appointing someone who was such a close friend of McClellan, the other generals would be more accepting of him. The president also knew that if Burnside did not live up to his expectations, he would have to give Hooker the chance for which he had been scheming. But for the moment, Lincoln hoped that Burnside would become the military leader he had been searching for since the war began. It cannot be said that Lincoln was overly optimistic, however. He commented to a friend after selecting Burnside: "We shall see what we shall see."

Ambrose Burnside had come a long way from the log cabin on his father's farm near Liberty, Indiana, where he was born on May 23, 1824. At birth, it appeared that he might not survive. He did not draw a breath until the frantic doctor who delivered him tickled his nose with a chicken feather. Ambrose was the fourth of nine children in a family of modest circumstances; all the children were expected to take on daily farm chores as soon as they were able.

The Burnside family valued education. Young Ambrose became a diligent, faithful, and hardworking student who did well enough in school, but the family was too poor to send him or any of the other children to college. Their financial situation worsened when Ambrose's mother died. At seventeen, he was forced to earn his own living and decided to become a tailor.

He moved fifteen miles away from Liberty to Centreville to become an errand boy and apprentice to a tailor. He worked hard during the day but at night led quite a different life. One biographer called him the "leading beau" in all of Centreville. Gregarious, courteous, and charming, Burnside loved the company of young women whom he courted at dances, quilting bees, and church prayer meetings. He managed to get by on only two or three hours' sleep a night.

Despite his late hours, he became a highly skilled tailor, though he found little satisfaction in the work. To satisfy his intellectual curiosity, he turned to reading, drawn especially to biographies of military leaders and stories of famous battles. He also listened intently to the tales told by local veterans who had fought in the Indian wars and the War of 1812.

After a year of apprenticeship, Burnside returned to Liberty and opened a shop in partnership with John M. Myers. Myers & Burnside—Merchant Tailors was located in a small one-story building in which Burnside slept at night, turning his cutting table into a bed. The business was successful, but Burnside did not like the work any better than he had as an apprentice. He passed the hours discussing military strategy and tactics with his partner, who had had some prior military experience. They planned imaginary troop maneuvers on the cutting board, using buttons to represent the hundreds of soldiers who could be moved in various formations.

Burnside saw himself as trapped, with no way out of small town life, wedded to a job that brought neither challenge nor fulfillment, while dreaming of military glory.

His situation changed abruptly one day when a visiting congressman campaigning for reelection tore his coat. The Honorable Caleb Smith sought out a tailor and found young Burnside stitching up a jacket while reading a book on military tactics.

The congressman was intrigued and began asking Burnside about himself. "You should be a cadet at West Point!" the congressman said. Burnside happily agreed.

Burnside received his first demerit on his third day as a cadet. He sat down at the breakfast table before the order was given. Two days later he showed up late for drill and received another in what turned out to be a long string of demerits that brought him perilously close to being expelled. Fun-loving and given to staging elaborate pranks and jokes, he broke as many rules as he thought he could get away with.

As a result, he was immensely popular with his fellow cadets, but by the end of his first year he had accumulated 198 demerits. Two more would mean expulsion. Of 211 cadets in the corps in that year of 1843, Burnside ranked 207th in general conduct. The four students who ranked lower did not return for a second year.

Burnside found many ways to defy authority. He was often late for breakfast, having been carousing late the night before. He played practical jokes, smoked, and went absent without leave. He was one of the regulars who left the post at night for Benny Havens, the notorious off-limits tavern. Burnside soon became one of Benny's favorite cadets.

Benny Havens's bar was in nearby Highland Falls on the banks of the Hudson River, a location that allowed Benny and his wife to easily restock their large stores of wine, whiskey, and tobacco. Mrs. Havens was beloved by the cadets for her buckwheat cakes and roast turkey. The young men could have all the food and whiskey they wanted on credit. For many of them, the riotous evenings there were the only escape from the bleak rigors of their training.

Burnside often led his fellow cadets in round after round of drink-fueled song. He knew more than fifty verses of "Benny Havens, Oh!" sung to the tune of "The Wearing of the Green."

> *Come, fill your glasses, fellows, and stand up in a row,*
> *To singing sentimentally, we're going to go;*
> *In the army there's sobriety, promotion's very slow,*
> *So we'll sing our reminiscences of Benny Havens, oh!*
> *Oh! Benny Havens, oh!—oh! Benny Havens, oh!*
> *So we'll sing our reminiscences of Benny Havens, oh!*

Despite his continual rule-breaking behavior, Burnside was promoted to cadet captain in the fall of his senior year. By spring, however, he had been demoted to the ranks for being absent from the post without permission, one of the more severe infractions with which a cadet could be charged. Yet he managed to graduate eighteenth in his class of thirty, a respectable finish to a checkered cadet career. At the completion of the two-week period of oral examinations Burnside was pronounced by the faculty to be the "finest looking and most soldier-like of the corps."

Not only had he become a well-regarded second lieutenant, but his country was at war and he was off to Mexico to fight. A new graduate of the military academy could ask for no better first assignment than the chance to prove himself in battle.

Burnside lost all his money on his way to war. Riverboat gamblers on the Mississippi cheated him out of it in one of the oldest confidence games of all. While en route to New Orleans, Burnside was asked by a passenger to join a game of euchre, a popular card game played with the thirty-two highest cards in the deck. The passenger also asked another man to join their "friendly game."

The two men were, of course, cronies. They let Burnside win most of the games when the stakes were small, but when the young lieutenant agreed to their request to up the ante, he began to lose. Burnside persisted, stubbornly, as was his nature, despite mounting losses. Only when he went broke did he stop playing.

Burnside was traveling with Egbert Viele, a West Point classmate, who had been paying their travel costs. As a result of Burnside's wagers, Viele was almost out of money too. They had a long way to go before reaching New Orleans, where the army paymaster would reimburse them for their travel expenses.

While Burnside and Viele were trying to figure out how they would manage, another stranger approached them. He told Burnside that he had watched as the two cardsharps had cheated him at euchre. He introduced himself as John Gill and offered to lend them enough money to get to New Orleans. Once there, Burnside was able to pay Gill back before embarking on an army transport headed to the war in Mexico.

The ship docked at Vera Cruz, where Burnside and Viele joined a large detachment of recruits marching inland. On the way they passed several battlefields that bore grisly reminders of the fighting. On December 9, 1847, they arrived at Mexico City only to learn that the war was over. Instead of opportunity for glory and promotion, there was only the tedium and boredom of garrison duty.

Burnside spent much of his time in Mexico City in gambling casinos. The owners welcomed him warmly, once it became known that he had a habit of upping the stakes repeatedly until he lost all his pay. One biographer commented that Burnside lacked "sufficient self-denial to stop until he had been regularly plucked." He apparently was so addicted to gambling that he soon found himself in debt for all of his pay for the next six months. It looked as though he would be forced to resign in disgrace; it was considered unseemly for an officer and a gentleman to accumulate such heavy gambling debts. A senior officer saved Burnside by loaning him enough money to pay off his obligations. Ambrose Burnside was not a lucky man.

Burnside was removed from further temptation when he was transferred to Fort Adams, near Newport, Rhode Island, where no gambling casinos were available. His next post was an isolated and dreary spot on the Santa Fe Trail near the present-day town of Las Vegas, where his job was to escort the US mail through hostile Apache Indian territory. He also served as post commissary and quartermaster, which got him into financial difficulty again. This time, however, it was not entirely his fault.

Because he had to be absent for weeks at a time while riding with the mail, Burnside had signed blank requisition forms and left them with Capt. Alexander Reynolds, chief quartermaster for that department. Those requisitions, often for thousands of dollars, were Burnside's way of ensuring that the Las Vegas post would be able to purchase sufficient food and supplies during his long absences. Once again he was unlucky, this time in trusting Captain Reynolds.

Either Reynolds was extremely incompetent in dealing with financial affairs or he was a thief. In the end, Burnside was charged with failing to account for a sum in excess of $6,000—a debt that "remained a blight on his reputation for more than a decade." Reynolds was dismissed from the service for fraud, but that did not fully erase the stain on Burnside's name.

Burnside was also reputedly unlucky in love. The story goes that during a leave back home in Indiana in 1851, he met Lottie Moon, a beautiful, accomplished, and charming young woman. He fell madly in love and proposed marriage. She accepted. All went well until that portion of the wedding ceremony when Lottie was asked if she took Ambrose to be her lawfully wedded husband. She said no, quite emphatically, and ran out of the church.*

Burnside's second attempt at marriage was more successful. In 1852, while stationed again at Fort Adams in Rhode Island, he

*Another tale is told about Lottie Moon, which may or may not be true. A few years later she agreed to marry someone else. While on their way to the church for the wedding ceremony, the groom pulled out a revolver and told her that he would either marry her or shoot her; the choice was hers. That wedding went ahead as planned.

met twenty-four-year-old Mary Bishop, known as Molly. They were married in April of that year. They never had children, but Burnside always called her "Mother," perhaps because of the strong influence she had in curbing his high spirits and softening the excesses in his behavior.

One day a delivery boy broke a bottle of wine Burnside had ordered for an afternoon party. He was furious at the boy and let loose a string of profanities that would have surprised no one who had known him at West Point. Molly was greatly offended by his coarse language.

"My dear," she said calmly, "you have shocked me by swearing so. Don't, I beg of you, ever let me hear you use profane language again."

Burnside was rarely heard to swear after that, even though he soon had ample reason to. He was about to lose every cent he had.

A year after marrying Molly, Burnside resigned from the army and moved to Bristol, Rhode Island, twelve miles from Fort Adams, to set up a factory he was certain would make his fortune. Since his days out west he had been working on the design of a new breech-loading rifle. He had obtained several patents on his design for a weapon that would not overheat during rapid fire. The gun was waterproof, simple to operate, and more accurate than any other rifle then in use by the army.

In comparative tests of eighteen weapons conducted at West Point, Burnside's carbine was judged to be the best of the lot. Confident of the success of his new weapon, Burnside borrowed money from friends to establish the Bristol Rifle Works. He planned to manufacture as many new rifles as the army would buy. He expected an order for $90,000 worth of firearms—the total government appropriation for new weapons.

But it was not to be. Secretary of War John B. Floyd bought only a few of Burnside's carbines, placing the major order for new weapons with a friend of his, even though that rifle had been judged inferior to Burnside's. Burnside had been offered the chance to win the full contract if he paid a $5,000 bribe to an unnamed War Department official.

"I met a man tonight," Burnside told a West Point classmate, "and he informed me that if I would pay five thousand dollars I would get the award, otherwise not. I at once indignantly refused. There is but one thing I regret, and that is that I did not fell him to the ground."

Burnside was ruined financially. He could have declared bankruptcy, leaving his investors—the friends who had loaned him money—with no way to recoup their losses, but he refused to do that. He was determined to pay them back; an honorable man could do no less.

Burnside distributed his few assets, including his patents for the rifle, to his creditors and promised to repay the remainder as soon as he was able. He sold his military uniforms and sword for thirty dollars in a secondhand clothing store in the Bowery in New York. He mailed half of that money, plus twenty dollars, to Molly, whom he had sent to live with relatives.

With no more assets, property, or job, Burnside wrote to old army friends asking for help in finding employment. One of these letters went to George McClellan, who had recently resigned from the army to become vice president of the Illinois Central Railroad. McClellan offered Burnside a job as cashier at the railroad's land office in Chicago.

Burnside gratefully took the job, and he and Molly lived with McClellan for two years, paying room and board and living as frugally as possible. Every month, Burnside sent the bulk of his salary to his investors and eventually repaid them all in full. In 1860, Burnside was promoted to treasurer of the railroad, in the New York office, and he and Molly were finally able to afford a home of their own.

Ironically, while Burnside was paying off the last of his debts to the people who had invested in his business venture, the company's new owners were making a substantial profit from manufacturing the weapon he had designed. A few years after Burnside failed to secure the government contract for his rifles, the War Department began purchasing them. The new owners got rich, eventually selling 55,000 of the guns during the war that was about to begin.

Shortly after Fort Sumter was fired upon in April 1861, Rhode Island's governor appointed Burnside a colonel and placed him in command of a regiment of ninety-day volunteers. Most Northerners expected the rebels to be defeated in no more than three months, and so they saw no need for longer enlistments for the volunteers. The Union's staggering defeat at Bull Run in July—when Burnside's men endured the same humiliating retreat to Washington as the rest of the army—proved the optimists wrong. It would take a lot longer than ninety days to crush the rebellion.

In late July, Burnside brought his volunteers home to Rhode Island and resumed civilian life, although he was eager to return to the war. A week later he was surprised to read in the local newspaper an announcement that the president had appointed him, Ambrose Burnside, to the rank of brigadier general. He was ordered to report to his commanding officer in Washington: Maj. Gen. George McClellan.

Once there, Burnside formulated a plan for an independent operation, an amphibious campaign to capture the North Carolina ports. This action would deny points of entry to Confederate blockade-runners bringing critical supplies to the South and would also present the rebels with a new Union threat. Burnside proposed recruiting experienced sailors to man a small fleet of ships that could survive in the open sea yet have the shallow draft necessary to operate close to shore.

The plan was deemed ambitious; nothing like it had ever been tried before. The War Department gave its approval, and Burnside began to gather ships and men. He traveled to New York and the New England states to assemble a force of 12,000 troops, many of whom had seafaring and mechanical backgrounds. His force would have to operate independently, so he needed men who not only could fight, but also could sail and repair the ships.

Burnside personally inspected every boat to make sure it was safe and suitable for his operation. Eventually he had a motley collection of vessels—canal barges, coal scows, and passenger ferries—some fashioned into gunboats. They hardly looked like a proper battle fleet, but Burnside was convinced that his force could survive the open sea passage to the North Carolina coast and come near enough to shore to offload the troops who would capture the vital ports.

Although Burnside had assembled a competent staff, he quickly demonstrated his need to attend to every detail personally, no matter how inconsequential it might seem to others. He habitually worked well into the night. One of his two secretaries, Daniel Larned, a thirty-three-year-old banker from Rhode Island, feared that Burnside was pushing himself to the point of exhaustion. "The General is a man of action," Larned observed, "and is on the go the whole time."

Late one night Larned brought a letter for Burnside to sign. He handed it over, stood by the desk, and watched as the general fell asleep while signing his name. That same night, Larned came back to ask Burnside a question and found him upright against a wall, sound asleep while still standing. Burnside never seemed to be able to rest. Nothing escaped his attention, and his staff realized that the rebels and the sea were not the only problems they would have to contend with. An exhausted commander could easily make mistakes in judgment that could lead to disaster.

This time, however, Burnside made no mistakes. The expedition was a great success. And Burnside's men learned early on that their general was devoted to their welfare, which was not always the case with officers in the Union armies. It was precisely Burnside's obsessive attention to detail that endeared him to the men.

Burnside also knew how to lead by example. He could be counted on to share the dangers and privations the ordinary soldiers endured. Some of the men expressed anger at being assigned to the oldest, least seaworthy of the boats. Dying at the hands of the enemy was one thing, but they had not volunteered to drown in leaky boats. Burnside defused that protest immediately by transferring his headquarters and his staff from a new large steamboat to the smallest, least safe boat of the lot.

The ships left on January 8, 1862, from Annapolis, Maryland, and the voyage south almost ruined the operation. Gales, fog, and

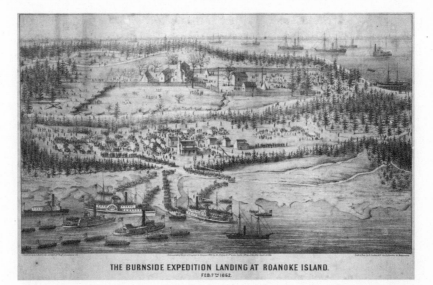

THE BURNSIDE EXPEDITION LANDING AT ROANOKE ISLAND.
FEB.7TH 1862.

A contemporary illustration of Ambrose Burnside's capture of Roanoke Island on the coast of Virginia, one of the first Union successes in the Civil War. (*Library of Congress*)

high seas threatened to sink three of the ships, including Burnside's. The vessels were scattered, all order lost. When they finally arrived off the coast of Hatteras, North Carolina, another severe storm kept many from reaching land, confining the men aboard ship for two weeks, miserable with seasickness, wet clothes and food, and the fear of drowning within sight of shore.

The weather finally eased and a grateful army staggered ashore, happier to face the rebels than the savage sea. On February 7, Burnside sent them against their first objective: Roanoke Island— ten miles long and two miles wide, which was defended by 3,000 Confederate troops. The garrison on Roanoke Island protected several southern ports, including Elizabeth City and Plymouth. Burnside's gunboats quickly drove off the smaller boats that guarded the island, and then his steamers towed landing barges through raging surf to offload 7,500 Union troops.

The battle lasted only a few hours. The Union flag was hoisted over the island, and the following day Burnside's forces captured

Elizabeth City and several other ports, effectively closing them to blockade-runners. The operation was the first major Union success in ten months of defeats and setbacks. Overnight, Burnside became a national hero. Hundreds of Northern citizens wrote to him to express their thanks for boosting the morale of the Union. One man said he named his newborn son after Burnside.

Over the ensuing weeks, Burnside's name reappeared in news-paper headlines as his men captured the remaining North Carolina ports, including New Bern and Beaufort. Lincoln pro-moted Burnside to major general. Oliver Wendell Holmes sent Burnside a handwritten poem, and the Rhode Island legislature voted to purchase an elaborate sword from Tiffany's for Burnside. Daniel Larned, Burnside's secretary, composed a piece of music that he entitled "Burnside's Grand March." It was performed for the general by the band of the 24th Massachusetts outside his New Bern headquarters.

"By Jove," Burnside said, when Larned presented him with a copy of the score, "I'll send one of these to my wife." He knew that Molly Burnside hated music of all kinds. Ambrose teased her in his letter, insisting that she play the piece on the piano for him the next time he came home.

In July 1862, some five months after his victories on the North Carolina coast, Burnside was first offered an opportunity to com-mand the Army of the Potomac. The president invited him to Washington, ostensibly to question him about his recent cam-paign, but Lincoln had another reason as well. He wanted to form his own judgment about Burnside's character, and he plied the general with questions. Burnside's voice was hoarse by the time he left the White House to rejoin his staff at Willard's Hotel, a few blocks away. Burnside said that the president made a highly favor-able impression on him. "If there is an honest man on the face of the earth," he told his staff officers, "Lincoln is one."

At Burnside's second meeting with Lincoln, the president asked Burnside if he would replace McClellan and lead the Army of the Potomac. McClellan's much-vaunted Peninsular campaign, in which he transported an army of more than 100,000 troops,

25,000 horses and mules, and tons of equipment and supplies by water down the Chesapeake Bay to Fortress Monroe, had failed dismally that spring.

The idea had been to attack Richmond by moving up the narrow peninsula between the York and James rivers. But McClellan's excessive caution, his inflated estimate of the size of the enemy force, and his wariness of Robert E. Lee, along with continuing heavy rainfall, forced McClellan to return to his starting point. Lincoln then ordered McClellan's army back to northern Virginia.

It was clear to the president that he needed a new leader for the Army of the Potomac. Used to bragging, boastful generals scheming for personal advancement, Lincoln was surprised when Burnside turned down the offer. Not only did Burnside insist that he was not qualified to lead such a large army, he also vociferously defended his old friend McClellan, calling him by far the better officer.

Lincoln was disappointed, but he was also pleased with Burnside's principled stand in favor of McClellan evidenced by his not taking advantage of the situation. Burnside left Washington and traveled for about a month, stopping first to see Molly, who was then staying in Baltimore. He was often recognized on the city streets, as he had been in Washington, by large crowds of cheering soldiers. When he went on to New York to take care of some railroad business, he was greeted and sometimes mobbed by soldiers and civilians.

In late July, Burnside was given command of the 9th Corps, which consisted of three divisions, and was ordered to take the force to the small town of Falmouth, Virginia, on the Rappahannock River, fifty miles south of Washington. He set up his headquarters in Lacy House, a brick mansion that overlooked the larger, more prosperous town of Fredericksburg across the river.

Burnside had been to the area before. In his bachelor days, not long after his return from Mexico City, he and West Point classmate Jesse Reno went to Fredericksburg for the wedding of Dabney Maury, another West Pointer, who would later become a

Confederate general. Burnside stayed a week for the festivities, and Maury later said it was probably the most fun Burnside ever had.

At the beginning of September, Burnside and his men left Fredericksburg, slogging north to Aquia Landing over roads turned to thick mud by dreary rains. At the landing, on the night of September 4, Burnside and the men of the 9th Corps boarded boats for the return trip to Washington. The following day, Burnside arrived in Washington in time to hear the news that Lee's Army of Northern Virginia had crossed the Potomac River into Union territory near Edwards Ferry, fewer than forty miles from the capital.

Lincoln summoned Burnside to the White House that day and asked once more if he would take command of the Army of the Potomac. Burnside refused again, repeating the arguments about his own lack of competence for the job. The president persisted, but so did Burnside, and Lincoln finally gave in and dismissed him.

McClellan, meanwhile, chose to reorganize his army into three wings—left, center, and right—and placed Burnside in command of the right wing, the largest of the three. This gave Burnside his biggest command of his career—approximately 12,000 men. The force consisted of two corps—his old 9th Corps and a larger corps once led by Joe Hooker. As the Army of the Potomac moved into western Maryland to try to stop Lee's advance, Burnside was greeted with cheers and acclaim whenever the men of the 9th Corps saw him.

On September 12, Burnside led his men into Frederick, Maryland. The residents, who had been under Confederate occupation for a week, welcomed them with bands, applause, and singing. American flags hung from almost every window. As the general rode through the crowds, "a pretty young woman asked if she could kiss him. Never one to refuse a lady, Burnside freed a stirrup for her foot, drew her up, and steadied her with one arm about her waist while offering his bewhiskered face."

The campaign was off to a good start. The soldiers were optimistic that this time the rebels were about to meet their match.

Antietam Creek did not look like much of an obstacle to the army. It was about fifty feet wide and so shallow for much of its length as it wound through the town of Sharpsburg, Maryland, that a soldier could wade across in many places and still keep his powder dry.

In the middle of September 1862, McClellan placed three corps at the right end of his line and positioned Burnside's 9th Corps along the left end. Hooker's corps was temporarily removed from Burnside's command and assigned elsewhere. No matter. Burnside knew that his 9th Corps was more than enough for the assignment McClellan had given it. While McClellan would attack Lee from the Union right, Burnside would cross Antietam Creek, forcing Lee to keep troops on the far end of the line instead of defending against McClellan. Once across the creek, Burnside was supposed to roll up the flank of Lee's line so that the Confederates would be forced to retreat.

But both McClellan and Burnside made serious errors of judgment in executing the plan. McClellan's attack occurred in three successive waves instead of a single massed assault, thus giving Lee's men time to regroup between each attack. Also, Lee was able to shift troops from the more secure parts of his line to reinforce the section under attack. When the Yankees managed nonetheless to breach the Southerners' defenses, McClellan failed to send in his ample reserves. Because the Union breakthrough was not supported, it collapsed.

As for Burnside, instead of crossing Antietam Creek wherever it was shallow enough to be forded easily, he ordered his men to assemble at a stone bridge so narrow that the troops had to approach in a column of fours instead of spread out in a line. Furthermore, the approach, and the bridge itself, provided little cover from the rebel troops that were dug in on the far side.

For whatever reason—perhaps Burnside had exhausted himself again by his obsessive attention to every detail of the operation—he apparently made no attempt to check the depth of the water to see where else the men might wade through. It was the bridge or nothing.

McClellan was becoming impatient with Burnside. He kept sending couriers to 9th Corps headquarters, repeating his orders, increasing the pressure on Burnside to cross Antietam Creek.

Finally, under withering enemy fire, two regiments bridged the creek and began to push back the rebel defenders. Other regiments followed, and it seemed as if they would breach Lee's line. But Burnside then committed another error of judgment.

He did not attack the rebels with his full command. If he had done so, he surely would have overwhelmed the fewer than 3,000 Confederate troops opposing him. Instead, Burnside permitted one of his divisions to rest and replenish its ammunition supply. He held yet another division in reserve behind the lines. And a third was several hundred yards away, looking for someplace else to ford the river. As a result, he was making his attack with only 3,000 of the 12,000 men at his command.

Ironically, shortly after Burnside's forces cleared the bridge, McClellan's main assault ground to a halt. Unless McClellan renewed his attack, Burnside's 3,000 troops would be left on their own. Burnside sent a courier racing to McClellan's headquarters requesting more troops immediately. McClellan replied that he had no infantry to spare, despite the presence of nearly two divisions close by. Neither general was willing to commit additional manpower, although it was obvious to both that Burnside's troops were making steady progress against the enemy despite the heavy return fire.

By midafternoon, the rest of Burnside's men were closing in on Sharpsburg and would soon be in position to take the road leading to the only ford across the Potomac River. If that road were held by Union troops, then Lee's Army of Northern Virginia would be cut off from any possibility of retreat as well as from replenishing their supplies. Lee had good reason to be concerned.

Suddenly, salvation was at hand for the Confederates. With a great cloud of dust to mark its triumphant arrival, Gen. Ambrose P. Hill's division attacked Burnside's flank. Hill had left half of his men by the roadside, fatigued from their brutal seventeen-mile forced march from Harpers Ferry. But the troops that remained

Several regiments of Ambrose Burnside's 9th Corps stormed across a stone bridge over Antietam Creek on September 17, 1862. Had Burnside and his commanding officer, George McClellan, committed more of their forces to the battle early on, the Union may have carried the day; instead they lost the advantage and ended up retreating. (*Library of Congress*)

with Hill, many wearing captured blue uniforms, caught the Union soldiers by surprise.

Confused by the sight of the uniforms, the Northerners thought at first they were being attacked by their own side. By the time they figured out that those were rebels dressed in blue, it was too late. Burnside's assault was over, and so was the entire Union operation. McClellan and Burnside had more than enough fresh troops to renew the battle, but they believed they had been beaten and so gave up the fight. The battle of Antietam was over.

When Lee returned to Virginia, McClellan proclaimed victory. But the Army of Northern Virginia, although diminished in size by heavy casualties, was still intact. McClellan had failed to carry out Lincoln's instructions to destroy Lee's army. He had let the rebels get away and did little to pursue them despite the president's insistent prodding. In despair, Lincoln gave up on McClellan and turned to Ambrose Burnside—for the third time.

Now the Army of the Potomac was his, and the pressure from Washington to use its might to end the war was intense. And so Burnside devised a new plan, the success of which depended on the same thing that had caused him so much trouble at Antietam—getting his troops across a bridge.

THREE

He Was Simply
Elegant

Henry W. "Old Brains" Halleck, general-in-chief of all the Union armies, was not happy with Ambrose Burnside. Not that he was happy with most of his generals, or with much of anything else for that matter. But on November 12, 1862, the major target of his unhappiness was the new commander of the Army of the Potomac. Burnside was proposing to change the plan of operations from the one Lincoln had given to McClellan. Halleck had assumed that Burnside would continue with the original plan, but here he was, planning to do something else.

That was why Halleck, who hated to leave his comfortable office in the War Department to go into the field, was in Warrenton, Virginia, to meet with Burnside. Not that he was happy in Washington, either. He detested the capital and found it nothing short of a "political Hell." Still, it was better than Warrenton's nondescript hotel where he spent the night. It was all Burnside's fault, for insisting on a new plan.

The supreme military commander of all the Union armies did not look like much of a soldier. He stood five feet, nine inches tall, weighed a robust 190 pounds, and sported a large double chin and a prominent bald spot. Gen. James Wilson remembered Halleck's "bulging eyes, his flabby cheeks, his slack-twisted figure, and his slow and deliberate movements, and his sluggish speech lacking in point and magnetism."

In short, Halleck was not likable, charismatic, or attractive. In an age when it was fashionable for high-ranking officers to leave the top few jacket buttons undone, "Halleck was buttoned up tight, from his double chin to his fat paunch, but he appeared slouchy rather than neat. He had a stooping posture and walked with his hands held behind his back or thrust into the pockets of his trousers. No initiative lurked behind his surly face, with its big, bulging bug eyes."

It was hard to find anyone who liked Henry Halleck, but there were many who feared him.

Young Henry Wager Halleck attended the military academy at West Point to escape the drudgery of his father's farm in upstate New York. He did well, graduating third in the class of 1839. He was invited to stay on for a year to teach French to the cadets and then was posted to New York City to work as an engineer on the forts in the area. He wrote a paper on coastal defenses, which so impressed Gen. Winfield Scott, hero of the Mexican War and then commanding general of the army, that Scott sent Halleck to Europe to study military tactics.

Halleck was an ambitious young man, and when he returned to New York, he published a book entitled *Elements of Military Art and Science*, based on his study of the armies of several European countries. Drawing on examples from the Napoleonic Wars, Halleck discussed the design of fortifications; the organization of military units; and the most effective ways to use cavalry, infantry, artillery, and support units. He devoted a long section to the construction of bridges for military use. His work had an immediate influence on US military thinking and was adopted as a standard textbook at West Point. Lincoln read it during the war, as did many Union army officers.

When the war with Mexico began in 1846, Henry Halleck was stationed in California and missed the war entirely. Garrison duty offered few opportunities for a man as ambitious as Halleck, so he chose to study law. He also took a position as secretary of state to the military governor. This gave him easy access to land titles, which allowed him to acquire several large plots of land, along with their mineral rights.

By 1850, the thirty-five-year-old Halleck, though still serving in the army, founded a law firm that rapidly became one of the best known in the state. After four years, the firm was so successful that Halleck resigned his commission to devote all of his time to his legal and business interests. The following year he married Elizabeth Hamilton, granddaughter of Alexander Hamilton. By the time the Civil War broke out, Halleck was serving on the board of directors of a bank and two railroads, owned a considerable amount of land, and was part owner of the world's second-richest quicksilver mine. His net worth was calculated at a half million dollars—a huge sum at the time.

War interrupted Halleck's financial pursuits. When he heard the news about Fort Sumter he knew it would be bad for business. Five months later, General Scott appointed Halleck to the rank of major general. He proved to be a good administrator for the army, albeit not a very audacious or daring leader in the field. It was Halleck's good fortune that some of his subordinates—notably Ulysses S. Grant—won stunning victories early in the war, which reflected well on Halleck. Largely for that reason he was ordered to Washington in July 1862 to take charge as general-in-chief of all the Union armies.

Unfortunately, he was no more an inspiring leader in Washington than he had been in the field. He soon antagonized most of the people with whom he came in contact. As an alleged expert in the art and science of military tactics, he failed miserably. He hounded his generals with unwanted advice, fussed about petty administrative details, and had little to offer in the way of tactical or strategic planning. The theoretical expertise he had displayed in his influential book did not translate into practice. He gave vague, indefinite, even conflicting orders and was often derelict in responding to urgent requests from his field commanders.

He was seen as "a typical old-line government-service hack, to whom the tidy operation of an office is an end in itself, infinitely more important than anything the office can conceivably do."

Gideon Welles, then secretary of the navy, loathed Halleck and detested the man's habit of rubbing his elbows with his hands in a slow, methodical manner when he was deep in thought. Welles noted in his diary that whenever someone asked Halleck a question, "he rubbed his elbow first, as if that was the seat of thought."

Commodore Andrew Foote, one of Welles's top naval officers, recorded his assessment of Halleck more bluntly and caustically, describing him as "a military imbecile, though he might make a good clerk."

Such was the man who met with Ambrose Burnside on November 12.

Halleck had come to Warrenton to persuade Burnside to continue with McClellan's plan—keeping the army heading in a southerly direction. Burnside had vetoed that idea on the grounds that the farther south his army ventured, the more vulnerable his supply line would be to attack by Jeb Stuart's cavalry.

The meeting between Halleck and Burnside did not begin well. Before Halleck could insist that Burnside carry out the original plan, Burnside told him what he had told so many other people— that he did not even want the command.

"I am not fit for it," he said to Halleck. "There are many more in the army better fitted than I am; but if you and the President insist, I will take it and do the best I can."

Halleck did insist, and Burnside did not object further, turning instead to his proposal for defeating the Confederate army: He planned to shift the whole of the Army of the Potomac forty miles east to Falmouth, on the Rappahannock River, an area he knew well. From there Burnside would cross the river to Fredericksburg, using pontoon bridges, before Robert E. Lee even knew the Union troops had left Warrenton.

Burnside would then drive south toward Richmond, only fifty miles away. Lee would be forced to try to intercept the Union army before it threatened the Confederate capital. The entire maneuver,

Burnside said, would happen so fast, and take Lee by such surprise, that he would have no time to prepare a strong defensive position. Thus the two armies would meet in the open rather than fighting a battle with one side behind prepared defenses. Given Burnside's numerical superiority, victory would be assured.

In addition, taking the army to Fredericksburg would position it better to protect Washington, should Lee try to menace the capital. It would also provide a more secure supply line from Washington. Steamboats sailed directly from the capital city to Aquia Landing. A railroad line ran the two miles from Aquia to Falmouth, on the bank of the

Henry W. "Old Brains" Halleck was general-in-chief of the Union armies and ordered Ambrose Burnside to take command of the Army of the Potomac. (*Library of Congress*)

Rappahannock opposite Fredericksburg. Once Union soldiers occupied Fredericksburg, army engineers could rebuild the railroad bridge the rebels had destroyed. Burnside's huge supply train of hundreds of wagons with ammunition and twelve days' rations, as well as a large number of beef cattle, would cross the pontoon bridges and follow the army south.

Halleck objected, and he also apparently misunderstood a key part of Burnside's plan. Whereas Burnside told Halleck he would cross the Rappahannock from Falmouth to Fredericksburg on pontoon bridges, Halleck later claimed that Burnside said he would ford the river *before* reaching Falmouth. That way the pontoon bridges would not be needed in order for the army to cross. Instead, they would be used later to bring supplies over until the railroad bridge could be rebuilt.

This was a crucial difference and a critical misinterpretation. In Burnside's plan, the drive south from Fredericksburg would not begin until the pontoon bridges—then located at Berlin, Maryland, forty-five miles up the Potomac River from

Washington—could be brought to Falmouth. In Halleck's version, there was no urgency in getting the pontoon bridges to Falmouth because Burnside's army would already have crossed the river without them.

Nevertheless, in response to Burnside's insistence, Halleck ordered the pontoons to be sent from Berlin, even though he didn't like anything about Burnside's plan. When Halleck left Warrenton the next morning, November 13, he promised only to discuss the plan with Lincoln but made it clear that he was not in favor of the idea himself. The final decision, of course, would be Lincoln's.

Burnside received his answer the following day. Although the president was not enthusiastic either, he gave his consent. He also issued a warning to Burnside, delivered by Halleck in a terse telegraph message: "It will succeed, if you move rapidly; otherwise not."

Burnside made big changes in the organization of the Union forces under his command. The Army of the Potomac had comprised seven corps, with each commanding general reporting directly to McClellan. Burnside replaced the seven corps with three "grand divisions," which meant that only three generals reported directly to him.

Two of the key generals he selected had commanded wings at Antietam. For his third choice he selected a man he disliked professionally and personally but who had previous experience leading a corps.

Burnside's choices may not have been the wisest or the best, but his options were limited, as Lincoln's had been when seeking a new commander for the Army of the Potomac.

Maj. Gen. Edwin Vose Sumner, picked to command the Right Grand Division, was, at sixty-five, the oldest of the division commanders, and the only one to not have attended West Point. Born in 1797, Vose had joined the army in 1819, apparently influenced by childhood tales of war. His uncles had fought in the American

Revolutionary War, only twenty-one years before Sumner's birth, and many of his relatives had served in the War of 1812.

Sumner began his military career as an earnest second lieutenant. Throughout his career he held to one belief above all: "The first duty of a soldier is to obey his orders."

A tough and demanding leader, he quickly demonstrated his courage in skirmishes with the Indians in the West and in the major battles of the Mexican War. Lt. Richard Ewell, who would later become a general in the Confederate army, thought Sumner was a martinet. He added that many men who served under Sumner who had never been addicted to prayer before, suddenly learned to pray hard.

It was at the battle of Buena Vista during the Mexican War that Sumner received the nickname "Bull," which, as he got older, became "Old Bull." "His soldiers used to tell with great relish, the story that a bullet which struck [Sumner] square in the forehead fell flattened to the ground without breaking the skin, as a hunter's ball glances from the forehead of a buffalo." True or not, the story, along with Sumner's bravery under fire, brought him glory, citations, and promotion to lieutenant colonel of the 1st Dragoons by 1848.

Fort Leavenworth, Kansas, was Sumner's next duty station, where his reputation as a hard, no-nonsense, but fair leader was enhanced.

> He seemed to be always on the defensive with both subordinates and superiors. Some found him cantankerous; others admired his blind obedience. There was no middle ground with Sumner. You fought him or you loved him, but you were never indifferent about him.

Because of his ambition, it was inevitable that Sumner would make enemies on his way up through the ranks, but his men soon learned that behind that gruff, stern façade was a leader who cared about their comfort and welfare. As a commander he did whatever was necessary, including bending regulations, to get better food, tents, uniforms, and blankets for his troops. There were fewer desertions in Sumner's commands than in others, despite his reputation as a strict disciplinarian. The enlisted men, as well as the majority of the officers above and below Sumner in rank, came to respect him.

And so did the high command in Washington. In 1855 he had been chosen, along with other officers who showed promise—officers including George McClellan—to observe and report on European army tactics in the Crimean War. When Sumner returned, he was promoted to colonel and given command of the 1st Dragoons, renamed the 1st Cavalry, at Fort Leavenworth. His commanding officer there, Col. William S. Harney, whom Sumner had once challenged to a duel, ordered the 1st Cavalry to undertake a hazardous trek to Fort Laramie in Wyoming Territory. The outfit was to remain there through the winter to prepare to strike the Indians in the spring.

Sumner carried out his orders without question initially, even though he doubted their wisdom. The farther he drove his men, however, the more he came to believe that such a trek followed by a winter with little forage for the horses would leave them in no shape for a hard-riding campaign come spring. They had already traveled four hundred miles from Fort Leavenworth when Sumner decided the orders were unjust. He turned around and led his troops back, disobeying orders for the first and only time in his long career.

As Sumner expected, Harney ordered a court-martial, charging him with willful disobedience. The War Department did not agree, siding with Sumner. This action earned him the further respect of subordinates and superiors for holding firm to his convictions. Sumner had demonstrated again that he was a man to be reckoned with.

The Cheyenne Indians learned that lesson in 1856 in Kansas when three hundred of their warriors confronted Sumner's 1st Cavalry. The Cheyenne believed they were invincible. Their medicine men had told them that the white man's bullets would not kill them, because their guns would refuse to fire. What they did not know was that Sumner had no intention of using rifles against the Cheyenne. He was going to lead the charge with sabers. As Sumner later explained, he planned to punish the Indians for their depredations against white settlers, not to annihilate them.

"Draw sabers!" Sumner bellowed to his men, who were as amazed as the Cheyenne that they were not going to shoot. "Charge!"

Taken by surprise, the Cheyenne turned and ran, with the troopers of the 1st Cavalry in pursuit. As might be expected, the Indians had faster horses, so most of them got away, but a few of Sumner's officers caught up with the slower ones. Lt. Jeb Stuart, who said he learned everything he knew about cavalry tactics from Old Bull, sustained a chest wound, but the wound was not fatal.

Major General Edwin Vose "Bull" Sumner was born during George Washington's presidency and was the oldest of the division commanders at Fredericksburg. (*Library of Congress*)

As the threat of war among the states grew more serious, Sumner made it clear where his loyalties lay. On January 5, 1861, three months before the onset of war, the sixty-four-year-old soldier wrote to Gen. Winfield Scott, general-in-chief of the army, pledging his allegiance.

> I have belonged to the general government over forty years. I consider it my government, and so long as it lasts, the only government to which I owe fealty. As I view this obligation, I feel bound in honor to devote myself to the preservation of the Union.

Sumner was later to be greatly embarrassed when two of his sons-in-law, both West Point graduates, chose to fight for the Confederacy.

When Abraham Lincoln was elected president of the United States in November 1860, Old Bull was commander of the Department of the West, stationed in St. Louis. As Lincoln embarked on his long train journey from Springfield, Illinois, to Washington, DC, making many stops along the way, General Scott selected Sumner to accompany the president as military escort. It was a singular honor and a measure of the esteem Scott felt for Old Bull.

Alan Pinkerton, the famous detective, was also aboard the train. He raised an alarm, reporting news of a plot to kill the president-elect as he passed through Baltimore. Pinkerton urged Lincoln to don a disguise and change to a special train. Old Bull was irate at this suggestion.

"It is a damned piece of cowardice," he thundered. "I will get a squad of cavalry, sir, and cut our way to Washington, sir."

Pinkerton and the other civilians in Lincoln's retinue decided they would leave the bombastic Sumner behind while they quietly smuggled an incognito Lincoln into the capital city. At a stop at Harrisburg, Pennsylvania, Lincoln, Ward Lamon (the president's bodyguard), and Sumner entered a waiting carriage. Someone called Sumner away on some pretext. As soon as the old soldier stepped out of the carriage, it drove off quickly, leaving him fuming, cheated of his chance to protect the new president.

One of Lincoln's first acts as president was to promote Sumner to brigadier general. Early in the war, after the Union debacles at First and Second Bull Run, Lincoln commented that "Sumner at least was one man we could always rely on." Soon promoted to major general, Sumner was given command of the 2nd Corps, which he led in the series of battles in McClellan's ill-fated Peninsular campaign, and then at Antietam. His men recalled him as always leading the way, waving his sword, and shouting encouragements.

"Steady, men, steady! Don't be excited. When you have been soldiers as long as I, you will learn that this is nothing. Stand firm and do your duty."

They also remembered that he removed his artificial teeth before a battle; he claimed they were too troublesome during a fight. He would raise his eyeglasses to his forehead so he could see better at a distance, shout orders to his subordinates, and gallop fearlessly toward the enemy.

He was still as vigorous and energetic at age sixty-five when he arrived at Falmouth, Virginia, on November 17, 1862. Henry Villard, a reporter for the *New York Tribune*, described him as the "very picture of a veteran soldier—tall, slender, erect, with a fine head thickly covered with white hair, and a noble face fringed with a white beard. He was polished in speech and manner, and seemed almost too full of kindliness for his stern profession."

However, for all his fine qualities, Sumner had not demonstrated any great distinction in the war thus far and was considered a competent, though no better than average, field commander. "Like many officers in this army, he was known for persistence rather than brilliance. Also, like many of his contemporaries, he had risen beyond the station for which his experience and capacity had fitted him."

The same was said of Burnside's choice to lead the Left Grand Division, Maj. Gen. William Buel Franklin. The thirty-nine-year-old Pennsylvania native had graduated from the military academy at West Point in 1843, at the head of his class. (A classmate of Franklin's with a far less distinguished record as a cadet was Ulysses S. Grant.) Based on this sterling performance, Franklin seemed destined for a brilliant career, except for one thing—he "lacked the boldness or creativity to be a successful commander."

Franklin was briefly exposed to combat during the Mexican War at the battle of Buena Vista in February 1847. Gen. Zachary Taylor sent the young topographical engineer on a lone reconnaissance mission to scout out the enemy's strength. Franklin rode to within 1,000 yards of the Mexican troops, counted the number of squadrons, and reported back to Taylor. For his actions, Franklin was given the brevet rank of first lieutenant and sent back to West Point to join the faculty. There, in 1852, he married Anna Louisa Clark.

He was transferred from one engineering and survey job to the next, moving from North Carolina to upstate New York to Portland, Maine, where he served as inspector of coastal lighthouses and superintending engineer of the Custom House. Franklin found the work tedious and dull, and by 1856 he considered resigning from the army to take advantage of the many lucrative and challenging opportunities available for West Point–trained engineers. "I have thought so much of leaving the Army," he wrote to a friend. "My wife too is willing to go."

Major General William Buel Franklin, a division commander at Fredericksburg, was a West Point classmate of Ulysses S. Grant but proved to be a far inferior leader. (*Library of Congress*)

But the pull of duty to the army and to his country was too strong. Franklin was promoted to captain in 1857 and assigned to the most prestigious and visible engineering job in the nation: He was made chief engineer in charge of constructing the dome of the US capitol building in Washington, DC.

When war came, Franklin was promoted to colonel and placed in charge of an infantry regiment. This was the first time in his seventeen years of service that he had ever commanded a body of troops.

In July 1861, he led his regiment out of Washington toward Manassas, Virginia, and the creek called Bull Run, although he did not seem to be in any hurry to get there. "I was kept back by Franklin who moved very cautiously and slowly," his commanding officer wrote. This observation would prove to be prophetic of Franklin's record throughout the war.

Franklin fought in every major battle with the Army of the Potomac during the first two years of the war without achieving any distinction. He was considered a capable officer, although not aggressive, bold, or imaginative. Franklin was "skillful at following his commander's orders, but making decisions as an independent commander was a talent he [had] failed to develop during those many years of reading construction drawings." And he would not drive his men any faster than he had been ordered to.

After two years of fighting, all that could be said of William Buel Franklin was that he was a "stubbornly methodical commander." Faint praise, and entirely accurate.

Sumner and Franklin were neither inspired nor inspiring choices to lead the divisions of the Army of the Potomac, but Burnside's selection for the Center Grand Division commander was the most controversial. It was Fighting Joe Hooker, who certainly did not lack boldness, dash, or imagination. He made no secret about the fact that his sole ambition was to command the Army of the Potomac. The primary way he went about this was to go over the heads of his superiors and point out their flaws and defects to others.

Perhaps matching his ambition was his vanity. At West Point he was known as the "beautiful cadet," and at the time of the Civil War, a newspaper reporter described him as "a model of a war-god." Hooker stood over six feet tall, erect and muscular, with long wavy blond hair. In an age of whiskers he was conspicuously clean-shaven. He had blue-gray eyes and a striking pink complexion, which some people implied was the result of heavy drinking.

Hooker entered West Point in 1833. Like Burnside, he came close to being expelled for a variety of offenses, including late-night carousing, lack of respect for superiors, violation of academy rules, and failure to pay attention in class. Still, he graduated in 1837, twenty-ninth in a class of fifty cadets. He was sent to Florida to fight in the Seminole Wars and then to Tennessee to help subdue the Cherokee.

He returned to West Point in 1841 for a short tour of duty as adjutant. During that time he made an inspection trip to Fort Adams in Newport, Rhode Island, where he made quite an impression. "What a handsome fellow he was!" one observer

wrote, "polished in manner, the perfection of grace in every movement and with all the courtesy of manner we attribute to the old-
time gentleman. He was simply elegant."

Hooker not only looked the part of the dashing soldier, he
demonstrated his audacity and bravery in the Mexican War. He
served as a brigade chief of staff and adjutant to a division commander and saw enough action to win promotions and bring glory
to his name. During the attack on the Mexican fortress at
Chapultepec, he received permission from his division commander
to lead a regiment in the assault.

It was at Chapultepec, in fact, that most of the future military
leaders of both Union and Confederate forces gained their battle
experience, a list that includes Robert E. Lee, Ulysses S. Grant,
Stonewall Jackson, James Longstreet, George Pickett, John
Magruder, A. P. Hill, Richard Ewell, Joe Johnston, and P.G.T.
Beauregard. By the time the war ended in Mexico City, Hooker
had received three brevet promotions to the rank of lieutenant
colonel and prominent mentions in Gen. Winfield Scott's reports.

But then came peace and the tedium of life in Sonoma,
California, where Hooker's army pay seemed to pale in comparison with the fortunes being made in the gold boom. Local wages
were so high that a domestic servant earned a higher monthly
wage than a lieutenant colonel in the army. Bored, Hooker
descended into a life of dissolution—drinking, whoring, and gambling at the notorious Blue Wing Tavern. Two years later he
requested and received a two-year leave of absence. He set out to
make his fortune. The result was a disaster.

Hooker acquired some five hundred acres of land a few miles
outside of Sonoma, built a house, and tried cultivating grapes to
make wine. When that failed, his next crop was potatoes, but that
did not work out either. He gave up farming and hired men to cut
cordwood from the trees on his land while he staged elaborate fies-
tas, drank and gambled at the Blue Wing, and hunted. On one trip
he was mauled by a bear and escaped only by climbing a redwood
tree and remaining hidden until a search party came looking for
him.

In 1853, Hooker was hauled into court for nonpayment of a gambling debt. Fortunately for him, the judge dismissed the case on the grounds that a marker for a gambling debt did not constitute a legal obligation. Hooker resigned from the army, sold his ranch, went into politics, and was elected road overseer for Sonoma County.

He also borrowed money from Henry Halleck and William T. Sherman, who at that time were businessmen in San Francisco. There is some question as to whether Hooker paid them back. During the Civil War years both men did little to conceal their dislike of Hooker, which lends credence to the story that the loans were never repaid. In 1864 Halleck wrote to Sherman that Hooker "is aware that I know some things about his character and conduct in California."

"Fighting" Joe Hooker, leader of the center division at Fredericksburg, earned a reputation for bravery during the Mexican War but also was known for drinking, womanizing, and gambling. (*Library of Congress*)

In 1858, Hooker wangled a job as superintendent of military roads in Oregon. A year later he returned to California and was appointed a colonel in the state militia. At the outbreak of war he wrote to Winfield Scott asking to be reinstated in the army but received no reply. Concerned that this great opportunity for advancement and fame might pass him by, Hooker knew he had to get to Washington to make a personal appeal for a command. But he had no money for the trip.

One day he was passing the time in a San Francisco saloon when the owner, Billy Chapman, noticing his low mood, asked what the problem was. Hooker explained that he was a West Pointer who had fought bravely in the Mexican War and wanted the chance to fight again, but he had no money to pay his debts and finance his trip east. Chapman asked how much he needed.

Seven hundred dollars was the reply. Chapman went to his safe and returned with a pile of cash.

"Here's a thousand, Captain," he said. "Take it and go to the front. I wish I could go with you, but I am not quite willing to be a private, and they wouldn't give a commission to a faro dealer. The steamer sails day after tomorrow. I'll be at the wharf to see you off, and you needn't buy any liquor or cigars to keep you cheerful on the way. There will be a few necessaries of that sort in your stateroom." And so, thanks to the generosity and patriotism of a saloon owner, Hooker got his chance to go to war.

If Hooker had been under the impression that it was going to be easy to get a commission in the Union Army once he arrived in the capital, he was mistaken. He wrote to and called on every political and military contact he knew, but no one was able or willing to help him. His credentials eventually made their way to President Lincoln, who forwarded them to Winfield Scott, but nothing came of that, either. It was apparent that no one wanted Joe Hooker back in the army. Frustrated and angry at seeing West Point classmates and officers once junior to him obtaining promotions and important commands, Hooker had made up his mind to return to California when he got another lucky break.

It was July 1861. Hooker rode out to witness the battle of Bull Run, along with several thousand other spectators from Washington. Many believed this would be their only chance to see combat because surely it would be the first and last battle of the war. How could all those smartly uniformed, high-spirited Union troops who had been camped in Washington for weeks possibly fail to roust a ragged bunch of rebels?

Hooker joined the disastrous retreat of the routed Union army back to the capital. A few days later, he met an old friend from the Mexican War who took him to the White House to meet Abraham Lincoln. This was Hooker's last chance to get into the war, but the president seemed preoccupied and, after a perfunctory greeting, was about to turn away. Hooker immediately spoke up and told Lincoln that he had been a lieutenant colonel in the regular army and had tried to offer his services to the government but had been ignored. He intended to return to California but had one more thing he wanted to tell the president.

"I was at the battle of Bull Run the other day," Hooker said, "and it is neither vanity nor boasting in me to declare that I am a damned sight better General than you, Sir, had on that field."

That got Lincoln's attention. He gave Hooker a quick appraising glance and apparently liked what he saw. They talked for several minutes and finally Lincoln told Hooker what he had been longing to hear: He would be made a colonel and given command of a regiment.

Soon Hooker had another bit of good fortune. Some political cronies had been active on his behalf and on July 31, a list of eleven names was sent to the US Senate as nominees for the rank of brigadier general. On the list were Grant, Franklin, and Hooker.

Before long, Joe Hooker was leading a division in a sweep through southern Maryland, clearing it of rebel spies and provisions. His outfit, meanwhile, was developing a reputation for its heavy drinking. In fact, Hooker's fondness for liquor led his men to coin a new lyric for a popular tune, "Marching Along."

"Joe Hooker is our leader,
He takes his whiskey strong."

Hooker also became known as a womanizer, carousing with ladies of easy virtue who congregated around his camp. Because these women were referred to as Hooker's—meaning they were with Hooker and his troops—some historians have suggested that this was the origin of the word "hooker" as a slang expression for prostitutes.

Hooker developed another, more savory, reputation—as a fighting general praised for his courage and aggressiveness in battle. In one New York paper, a story about Hooker was intended to be headlined "Fighting—Joe Hooker." The dash was accidentally, or deliberately, dropped and Hooker became known forevermore as "Fighting Joe."

He claimed to loathe the nickname and pleaded with reporters not to use it, but he knew they would continue to do so. The press was looking for heroes. These larger-than-life figures sold papers, and Hooker often gave the press the opportunity to write about his deeds as a fearless, indomitable general. Indeed, Hooker himself soon gave that impression after he was wounded in the foot at Antietam.

He had been in the thick of the fighting for three hours, leading from the front as usual and not bothering to seek cover when a rebel sharpshooter hit him. He rapidly lost blood from the wound, but before he let himself be borne away on a stretcher, he barked out a series of commands, ordering his units forward. Later that day, in a letter to his brother-in-law, he implied that had he not been wounded he would have destroyed Lee's army.

Two days later his letter was conveniently printed in a number of Union newspapers. It soon became a popular notion that the war might have ended at Antietam if only Hooker had not been wounded and forced to withdraw from the fighting. Even McClellan endorsed that view, writing to Hooker that the entire rebel army would have been doomed had Hooker been able to stay in the battle.

Newspapers praised Hooker once more as the fearless hero of the Union. He reveled in the accolades and in the numerous expressions of gratitude he received from all over the country. In San Francisco business leaders raised two thousand dollars to present him with a ceremonial sword.

Scores of the well-connected and powerful came to call while Hooker recuperated from his injury at the Washington Insane Asylum, one of many buildings converted to hospitals for the thousands of wounded Union soldiers. President Lincoln stopped by for a visit, and members of the cabinet came to consult Hooker about the future conduct of the war.

High-ranking army officers paid their respects, expressing the view that Hooker was eminently qualified to lead the Army of the Potomac, a point Hooker himself reinforced at every opportunity. He also freely criticized McClellan for being timid and hesitant in battle, downplaying the general's value as army commander. Hooker's implication was clear. The Army of the Potomac needed a new leader, and Hooker did his best to convince everyone of consequence that he was the only choice.

By the fall of 1862, when a desperate Lincoln repeatedly tried to force McClellan to pursue Lee aggressively, the talk increasingly focused on Hooker as the favorite to replace Little Mac. No one was more startled or disappointed than Hooker when Lincoln selected Burnside for the job. But Hooker was convinced that Burnside would lose his first battle as commander and, when that happened, Hooker would have another chance. He knew he would be called on to save the Union.

"I suppose we shall have one more blunder," a soldier in the Army of the Potomac said prophetically, "and then at last they will put 'Old Joe' in the right place."

But that came later. In mid-November 1862, Burnside had succeeded in reorganizing the army, selecting its three primary commanders, and securing the president's consent for his new plan. All that remained was to move the army from Warrenton to Falmouth without alerting Robert E. Lee. And when he reached Falmouth, so Burnside had been led to believe by Halleck, the pontoon bridges would be waiting. His army would cross the Rappahannock River to Fredericksburg and continue on to Richmond. The war would be over in days.

Members of New York's 69th Regiment, New York State Militia, the "Irish Brigade," pose at a camp in Virginia in 1862. (*Library of Congress*)

FOUR

No Pontoons, No Crossing

Clonmel County, Ireland, 1848: The jury's decision in the case of twenty-five-year-old Thomas Francis Meagher was swift and brutal. The presiding Lord Chief Justice solemnly read the pronouncement:

> You [will] be hanged by the neck until you be dead, and that afterward the head shall be severed from [the] body, and the body divided into four quarters, to be disposed of as Her Majesty shall think fit.

Meagher, along with three other men, had been sentenced for a role in the rebellion against British rule. The son of a wealthy Irish merchant, Meagher had no apologies to make before the sentence was read. Instead, in his characteristic impassioned and flowery prose, he had moved spectators and jurors alike to tears and applause.

> I am here to regret nothing I have ever done, to retract nothing I have ever spoken. I am here to crave with no lying lips the life I consecrate to the liberty of my country. Pronounce, my lords, the sentence the law directs; I am prepared to hear it.

But he was not hanged, drawn, and quartered as the law directed. Otherwise, he would not have become a general in the Army of the Potomac, leading the fabled Irish Brigade toward Fredericksburg on the morning of November 17, 1862. The British parliament had commuted Meagher's sentence to life in exile in faraway Tasmania.

Meagher found life in Tasmania quite pleasant, even for convicted criminals. If an exile promised not to escape, and reported all travel away from home to the police, he was granted relative freedom. Only three years after sentence had been passed on him, Meagher owned a house on a lake, several riding horses, and a sailboat, thanks to money provided by his father. He had also found a wife, Catherine, the daughter of a local farmer, and she was expecting their first child.

But Meagher grew restless. In isolated Tasmania he had no cause to fight for, no useful occupation, nor any intellectually exciting friends. The dull, provincial nature of his situation quickly made him discontent. "Worst of all," a biographer wrote, "[Meagher] had no audience. His natural vanity and expressive ambition found little outlet, and he was perfectly convinced that in his absence Irish society suffered a real loss. The English had been quite correct in their assumption that to silence an Irish orator is a far greater cruelty than to hang him."

And so he escaped, taking care to inform the local magistrate by letter that he was rescinding the terms of his parole. In this roundabout way he could claim that he was legally free to escape. Catherine was to stay with her family until he notified her that he had succeeded in getting away. Then she was to go to Ireland to live with Meagher's father.

Meagher's escape caused a sensation in Ireland and England but nowhere was there more excitement than among the sizable Irish population in the United States. The community was eager to show its support for anyone who fought for freedom from the English. So when Meagher arrived in New York City on May 26, 1852, he was already a celebrity.

A crowd of seven thousand cheered him in Brooklyn. Invitations to speak poured in from around the country. Meagher clubs were formed in major cities, and several Irish militia companies changed their name to the Meagher Guards. Fordham University awarded him an honorary degree, and a local musician composed the "T. F. Meagher Polka."

"He is a fine, military looking young gentleman," a writer for the *New York Herald* noted, "stoutly built, handsome, and always a favorite with the ladies." Lady Jane Wilde, who would one day have a son and name him Oscar, remembered Meagher as "handsome, daring, reckless of consequences, wild, bright flashing eyes, glowing colour and the most beautiful mouth, teeth and smile I ever beheld."

Meagher was wined and dined, hailed as a hero, and admired by a great many young women. Meanwhile, Catherine gave birth to their son, but the infant lived only a few days.

Meagher became an American citizen and embarked on a triumphant speaking tour from coast to coast. He was soon the best known and most idolized Irish American of his day. Catherine went to Ireland, as arranged, to live with Meagher's father. The following year, the two of them came to New York, but Catherine stayed only four months. Meagher was preparing for another lecture tour and thought it best that she return to Ireland to await the birth of their second child. Catherine Meagher died in childbirth, but the baby boy survived. Meagher never saw him.

A year and a half later Meagher married Elizabeth Townsend, daughter of a wealthy Protestant merchant. Her father was decidedly not happy at the prospect of an Irish-Catholic son-in-law or having his daughter convert to a religion he detested. Strong prejudice against both Catholics and the Irish was common in the United States at the time. Elizabeth's father promptly disinherited her, but eventually the well-spoken, persuasive Meagher won him over. The couple moved in with Mr. Townsend at his Fifth Avenue mansion. Meagher had achieved the American dream; the future held nothing but promise.

And then came war, and Thomas Francis Meagher had another opportunity for fame and glory. It was one thing to lecture about the Irish fight for freedom, but by joining the Union army, he believed he could hasten the time when the British occupation would be broken. Training Irish-American soldiers and leading them in combat would be valuable experience for the inevitable day when thousands of trained and well-armed Irish Americans would go to Ireland to force the British out.

Meagher wrote,

> It was a moral certainty that many of our countrymen who enlist in this struggle for the maintenance of the Union will fall in the contest. But even so, I hold that if only one in ten of us come back when this war is over, the military experience gained by that one will be of more service in a fight for Ireland's freedom than would that of the entire ten as they are now.

By fighting for the United States, then, they would be fighting for Ireland as well. He posted notices calling for recruits in New York:

> YOUNG IRISHMEN TO ARMS! TO ARMS YOUNG IRISHMEN! IRISH ZOUAVES. One hundred young Irishmen—healthy, intelligent and active—wanted at once to form a Company under command of THOMAS FRANCIS MEAGHER.

Meagher got his hundred men in three days. Within one week, he claimed to have trained them to be soldiers, drilling in a large room at a billiards hall. Off they went to Washington, DC, to join the 69th Regiment, New York State Militia, an all-Irish outfit.

The men of the 69th were a mixed lot. Most were from the working classes and made their living through their brawn. They included day laborers, hod carriers, porters, canal diggers, and highway workers, as well as a number of waiters and bartenders.

Many of the men had prior military experience. Some had served with the British army in India; others had fought at the battle of Balaclava in the Crimean War. One contingent had formed part of the Papal Brigade—the Battalion of St. Patrick that fought for the pope at Spoleto and Ancona. Others had seen action in the Austrian army and the Hungarian Hussars.

Some of the Irish Brigade soldiers had been educated in a variety of professions, including schoolteachers, college professors, newspaper reporters, civil servants, business leaders, and attorneys. One company boasted seven members of the New York Bar. But the most colorful characters of the 69th could be found at Meagher's headquarters—wealthy young men much like him. Dressed in gold-bordered, well-tailored uniforms, they were described as "fox hunters; a class of Irish exquisites good for a fight, card party, or a hurdle jumping."

Despite their varied backgrounds, all were Irish to the core, and none were more eager to fight than those in Meagher's Zouaves. Their bright red uniforms made them stand out in reviews, although apparently no one foresaw how conspicuous those uniforms would be in battle, how well they would mark the men as targets. War for them was still parades and pageantry and good times.

Thomas Francis Meagher led a regiment of Irish-American soldiers at Fredericksburg. (*Library of Congress*)

That thinking changed in July 1861 at Bull Run, when the Northerners learned how wrong they had been about the rebels. Union forces were shattered, and Meagher's red-clad Zouaves paid a terrible price. Capt. David Conyngham, who would later serve on Meagher's staff, described how the men "suffered desperately, their red dress making them a conspicuous mark for the enemy."

But, Conyngham went on, "when Meagher's horse was torn from under him by a rifled cannon ball, he jumped up, waved his sword, and exclaimed, 'Boys, look at [the colors]! Remember Ireland.'"

When the bright green colors were brought down by enemy fire, a second man grabbed them and raised them high. He was shot. A Confederate soldier tore the flag from his hand. The Zouave shot the rebel, recaptured the colors, and took a rebel flag before Confederate soldiers overwhelmed him. Bleeding from his wound, he pulled out a concealed pistol, shot the two rebels who were escorting him behind the enemy line, and retrieved the colors.

But there was no stopping the Confederates. The commander of the 69th, Col. Michael Corcoran, a former postal clerk, was taken prisoner. His second-in-command, Lt. Col. James Haggerty, once a carpenter, was cut in half by a cannonball. That left brevet Major Meagher in command, but he became separated from the outfit when a shell exploded and knocked him senseless. He lay on the ground, helpless, until a Union cavalryman picked him up and took him a few hundred yards behind the rapidly crumbling front lines.

Meagher joined in the retreat, having no idea where his men were, and climbed aboard an artillery wagon. As the wagon started across Bull Run Creek, a band of rebel cavalry swooped down. They shot one of the horses, which caused the wagon to overturn, dumping Meagher into the stream. He pulled himself out and rejoined the flood of retreating soldiers. After stumbling along some thirty-five miles in disarray—many of the men had discarded their weapons and become separated from their outfits—the exhausted, hungry, and defeated Union army reached the safety of the defenses around Washington.

Meager was not happy about his first experience in battle. Worse, he faced public humiliation when he was described in the *New York Daily Tribune* as having disgracefully abandoned his men and fled the scene of combat. Two days later, the newspaper printed a retraction, saying that Meagher "bore himself with distinguished gallantry." Still, his considerable pride and ego had been damaged.

In February 1862, Lincoln appointed Meagher a brigadier general of volunteers and placed him in command of the Irish Brigade. But in early September of that year, at Antietam, Meagher was thrown from his wounded horse and carried off the field unconscious while his men again suffered horrendous losses. More than five hundred were killed or wounded, and two of the regiments lost close to two of every three men.*

Meagher's Irishmen fought hard, and they drank and played hard as well. Their camp was generally a lively place, with John Flaherty, one of the enlisted men, playing the violin while his father picked out Irish jigs on the warpipes. The men's canteens rarely contained water; the supply of whiskey appeared endless. Pvt. Bill Dooley wrote, "It is as well to keep up our spirits by pouring spirits down, for sure, there's no knowing where we'll be this night twelve months."

Meagher kept up with the best of them. A few nights before the brigade left Warrenton for Fredericksburg, he got so drunk he almost killed himself. Pvt. Bill McCarter, from Derry, Ireland, chosen as Meagher's adjutant because of his outstanding penmanship, had great admiration for the general. But he also wrote candidly about Meagher's "sad, most unfortunate, intemperate habits. Sad indeed, for he was a whole-souled and perfect gentleman, this weakness excepted, I saw at last the evil effects of liquor upon him while on guard duty that night."

McCarter's rounds periodically took him past Meagher's tent, where once he noticed someone standing in the opening, grasping a tent pole and swaying back and forth. When he returned a few minutes later, he recognized the figure as Meagher's.

> He was very drunk, looked strangely wild and only prevented himself from falling down by his grasp of the center pole. His position was a dangerous one. Only a few

---

*By the end of the war, the Irish Brigade would have a casualty rate of 85 percent. Out of the approximately 7,000 men in the brigade initially, when hostilities ceased only 1,000 returned home unhurt.

yards in front of him on slightly descending ground burned an immense fire. He would undoubtedly have tumbled headlong into the blaze if he let go of the pole.

McCarter watched carefully, unsure of the proper course of action for a private to take. There were other officers inside the tent, but they were also drinking and paid no attention to their commanding general. McCarter did not want to create an alarm that would draw others to notice that Meagher was drunk. And if Meagher found out that McCarter had seen him in that humiliating state, what might he do to the hapless soldier? McCarter waited in the darkness, trying to decide how to handle this delicate situation. Suddenly, he no longer had a choice.

"Three minutes later, to my horror," McCarter recalled, "Meagher suddenly let go of the pole. He ran or rather plunged toward the fire." McCarter lunged forward and broke Meagher's fall by pushing him back with the flat of the bayonet affixed to the end of his musket. Meagher toppled backward, away from the campfire and yelled, "My God," which got the attention of the other officers. They helped the general to his feet and led him into the tent. One of them pointed to McCarter and told Meagher, "General, you owe your life to that man."

But McCarter's adventures were not over. In trying to help the officers get Meagher to his feet, McCarter dropped his musket into the flames, causing it to fire a shot. The sound awakened the entire camp. Soldiers came running, ready to repulse what they assumed to be the rebel attack, demanding to know why McCarter had fired. He made up some story about his clumsiness and retrieved his burnt and useless weapon from the flames.

When he appeared at Meagher's tent the following morning for his usual duty of copying orders, Meagher said nothing about the incident. Neither man ever spoke of it, but before McCarter finished his paperwork that morning, Meagher presented him with a shiny new musket and bayonet. McCarter remained Meagher's adjutant until he was wounded at Fredericksburg.

On the morning of November 15, Meagher led the Irish Brigade out of Warrenton for the forty-mile march to Fredericksburg. The brigade was part of Old Bull Sumner's Right Grand Division, which made the trek in two-and-a-half days—record time for the Army of the Potomac. Their pace averaged fifteen miles a day, hard going for men used to McClellan's leisurely five to six miles per day.

Lt. Col. William Teall, a lawyer from Syracuse, New York, had married Old Bull's daughter Sarah and served on his staff. In a letter to his wife, he described the first day's march.

> The line of march was seven miles long including the wagons. The scene at night after the campfires were lighted was magnificent. The tent occupied by your father and I was nearly in the center of the arc formed by the encamped troops, so that we could see the entire corps.

Sumner's 40,000 men proceeded eastward in three wide, parallel lines. One marched along a hard-surfaced road; the others made their way through fields and woods alongside the road, leaving a wake of destruction. Bill Teall wrote: "It makes my heart ache to see the devastation caused by an army. The men are hardly halted before they begin tearing down the fences for firewood."

Farms and lives were ruined as the Union soldiers tramped through like a biblical plague of locusts. Corp. Fred Pettit of the 100th Pennsylvania Volunteers recalled that everything edible was taken—turkeys, chickens, ducks, hogs, corn, even beehives—leaving the families with nothing. Pettit wrote:

> There are but few able bodied men left. The suffering of the women and children this winter must be very great. The soldiers have taken everything, and the inhabitants will have neither property nor money. An order came this morning against this wholesale robbery, but it is too late. Everything is taken almost and the men will not stop now even if the penalty is death.

Pvt. Bill Child of the 5th New Hampshire Volunteers was both awed and dismayed at the sight of the huge army trampling the countryside:

> This vast army, with its three heads pushing out, and out, and out, through field and forest, swept over the country. Fences and forage, mules and horses, hogs, cattle and fowls disappeared before this moving monster. Compact, elastic, winding in and out through a wood, over a stream, around a bog, through a swamp, with feelers in every direction, they pushed into every dwelling and barn, down into every well, up into every loft, and through every smokehouse and spring-house. On they pushed, covered with dust or mud.

Some officers tried to stop the looting. Others encouraged it or went along with it, pretending not to notice. One officer of the 6th Wisconsin pointed to a group of farmhouses, announced that he was going to take a nap, and warned his men that he did not want to see or hear of any thievery from the rebel farms. An hour later, he casually joined his men in their feast of ham and eggs. When he asked where the food had come from, they said that some kind Southerners insisted that they take it. The officer sighed in mock relief. "That's all right," he said. "I was afraid you had stolen them."

Sumner's men reached Falmouth on November 17; Burnside and the rest of the army arrived two days later. Burnside was pleased to learn that the town of Fredericksburg across the river was defended by only a handful of Confederate troops. They had no more than a few batteries of field artillery, a small cavalry unit, and a few hundred infantrymen. Burnside had succeeded in outfoxing the fox: Lee did not know where the Army of the Potomac was.

There was no way those scattered, small Confederate units in Fredericksburg could stop Burnside's mighty army from capturing the town, occupying the hills beyond it, and marching south toward Richmond. All the Union forces had to do was cross the river, which was precisely why Burnside had insisted a week earlier, on November 12, that Halleck order the pontoon bridges to be sent from Berlin, Maryland, specifically so they would be ready for this situation.

The bridges, however, could not be found. Burnside had successfully brought the Army of the Potomac to where it was supposed to be, but the pontoon bridges were not there.

Bull Sumner was not a patient man. He knew that Lee's Army of Northern Virginia could appear at any moment on the far side of the river. And when they did arrive, they would dig in on those all-important hills and there would be hell to pay to move them out. Sumner wanted to cross on the seventeenth, as soon as he arrived, particularly after a battery of rebel artillery had opened fire on him. He ordered his own guns to return fire, and in less than fifteen minutes the enemy artillerymen abandoned their guns and fled. Sumner later wrote:

> My orders were to advance and hold Falmouth, not to cross [the river]. But the temptation was so strong to go over and take those guns the enemy had left that at one time I actually gave the order to cross the ford at all events and seize the guns and occupy the city. But on reflection I concluded I was too old a soldier to disobey a direct order.

He quickly penned a note to Burnside asking permission to cross the river. He had noticed several places above the town where his men could ford with ease. Old Bull had watched a cow wade across at one spot and estimated the water to be no more than three feet deep.

The men could cross on foot. Then the engineers could lay an underwater roadway of stones for the wagons. By God, he could have his whole Grand Division over the river and into the hills before the sun set on another day. Let Lee come then. Old Bull would have the high ground and Lee would have to pay a heavy price to take it away from him.

Sumner pleaded with Burnside to issue the orders for his division to cross the river while there were so few Southern defenders on the other side. Burnside said no. His plan called for moving the entire army across on bridges, and he would not deviate. It was like a repeat of Antietam, where Burnside was resolutely focused on the bridge as the only way to cross. "His mind had been made up to cross the river on pontoons, and in no other way, so—no pontoons, no crossing."

"No, Sumner," Burnside told a disgruntled Old Bull. "Wait for the pontoons."

Sumner chafed at the delay, as did many others in the Army of the Potomac. They all knew that each day, each hour, increased the chances that Lee's men in gray would overrun Fredericksburg. And who knew when the bridges might arrive? The next day? The next week? Sumner's 40,000 troops could quickly construct strong defenses in the hills beyond Fredericksburg if allowed to cross on foot. Some officers argued that while Sumner's men were digging in there, the burned-out railroad bridge that once spanned the river could be rebuilt strongly enough to allow reinforcements and supplies to be sent over—all before Burnside's pontoons arrived.

Burnside watched dark clouds race across the sky. A storm was developing. Everyone who had ever fought in northern Virginia knew that winter storms could last for days. If that happened, the Rappahannock would become a raging torrent that could rise as much as six feet in less than twenty-four hours.

Burnside thought that if he let Sumner cross with a storm threatening, he and his men could be trapped on the other side. It would be as impossible to rebuild the railroad bridge in foul weather as it would be to lay the pontoon bridges. No food or ammunition could be supplied to Sumner's troops if they came under attack. Worse, they would have no escape route, no way to retreat. Burnside could lose a third of his army. He decided, therefore, that the risk was too great.

And the rains did come. Heavy, unrelenting sheets of rain fell for three days. Men watched the Rappahannock rise, as Burnside had predicted. The rain did not stop Fighting Joe Hooker's persistent scheming to take charge of the Army of the Potomac, however. He was not about to be outdone in any bid for glory by the likes of Bull Sumner, so Hooker proposed his own crossing at a place some ten miles west of Fredericksburg.

Given the weather, the condition of the river, and Burnside's refusal of Sumner's request, Hooker surely could not have expected his own request to be granted. But perhaps all he wanted to do was show Burnside's superiors how daring and audacious he was in comparison to Burnside. So Hooker made certain that his bold plan to march on Richmond was known at the highest level.

On the same day that Hooker submitted his request to Burnside, he wrote a highly irregular letter to Secretary of War Stanton, in violation of the chain of command, setting forth the same proposal. Hooker told Stanton that he had enough rations on hand for three days. Beyond that, his men could find ample food in the rich farmland between Fredericksburg and Richmond, thus far untouched by the war. Further, Hooker told Stanton that his 40,000 troops would destroy railroad lines and supply depots, thus interrupting the Confederates' communications system.

According to Hooker, Lee would then be forced to rush his army south to protect Richmond, leaving Burnside free to cross the Rappahannock unopposed—whenever his pontoon bridges might show up. Of course, by then, Hooker might already have won the war by his aggressive and capable actions.

By November 20, the day after Hooker submitted his plan to Burnside and forwarded his letter to Stanton, the Rappahannock River had risen dangerously. Fords were impassable, roads were quagmires of mud, and the rains continued. Both Hooker and Sumner may have been relieved that they were not on the Fredericksburg side of the river with no way to get back. The Army of the Potomac would not be moving anywhere until Burnside's bridges appeared.

The pontoon bridges were still a long way from Falmouth. All the boats, floorboards, planks, heavy wagons, and other equipment for assembling the bridges were under the command of Maj. Ira Spaulding of the 50th New York Engineers. A diligent, conscientious officer and a knowledgeable engineer, Spaulding, like Burnside and the entire Army of the Potomac, was the victim of ineptitude, incompetence, and sloth on the part of the command structure in Washington.

The day Burnside arrived in Falmouth expecting to find the pontoons and equipment waiting, they were only then just leaving the Washington area. Why had Halleck's orders not been carried out with more alacrity? The movement of the pontoons, which should have been accomplished in three days, took all of thirteen.

The chain of errors and miscues began even before Burnside took command and decided that he needed pontoon bridges for the crossing. McClellan, in one of his last acts as commander of the Army of the Potomac, had ordered the equipment moved from Berlin, Maryland, to Washington, DC, so they would be closer in case he needed them. For some unknown reason, the order from the War Department to Major Spaulding was sent not by telegraph but by mail. Spaulding did not receive the orders until November 12, six days after they were sent.

By November 14, the energetic Spaulding had dispatched two trains—thirty-six boats in one and forty in the other—on their way to Washington by canal. In addition, he soon had a long column of his awkward, oversized wagons on its way overland to the capital. Spaulding himself went to Washington to meet with his superior, Brig. Gen. Daniel Woodbury, commander of the engineering brigade.

Woodbury expressed surprise at the maneuvers Spaulding had arranged. This was the first he had heard that the pontoons had been ordered to Washington for possible use by the army. Even more puzzling was the receipt of two telegrams from Burnside's headquarters that day referring to the urgent need for the pontoons to be sent to Falmouth.

Woodbury intended to find out what was going on, but it was late in the day and so he told Spaulding to come back in the morning after Woodbury had had a chance to clarify the situation with Halleck. There is no record of the conversation between Halleck and Woodbury, but apparently Halleck did not emphasize any need for haste in moving the pontoons south for Burnside's use. Consequently, Woodbury instructed Spaulding to store the boats and wagons in the engineering depot, which was located on the Anacostia River in southeast Washington, and to set up camp nearby.

That night, for reasons not clear, General Woodbury issued new orders to Major Spaulding. He was now to send two groups of twenty-four boats each by water to Aquia Landing. As far as Woodbury knew, that was where the pontoon bridges were needed, not farther south at the Rappahannock. As a result, no wagons accompanied the boats, which meant there would be no way to transport them the twelve miles from Aquia Landing to Falmouth.

A pontoon bridge of similar construction to that built across the Rappahannock at the onset of the battle of Fredericksburg. (*Library of Congress*)

After Spaulding got those boats on their way, Woodbury then ordered him to assemble a wagon train to convey forty boats by land from Washington to Falmouth. That task took considerable time. First, Spaulding had to requisition two hundred horses from the quartermaster, along with two hundred sets of harnesses. However, all the harnesses were still in their original boxes. They had to be unpacked and fitted together before they could be put on the horses.

Then Spaulding's men learned the hard way that many of the horses had never been in harness before and did not seem to like the idea now, judging by their excessive bucking and kicking. Spaulding also had to requisition drivers for the wagons, plus sufficient rations for the men and forage for the horses for the journey.

It was not until the afternoon of November 19, the day Burnside reached Falmouth expecting to see the pontoons, that the long line of wagons started to make its way across the Long Bridge (now the 14th Street Bridge) over the Potomac River into

Virginia. The rain that thwarted the army in Falmouth was just as heavy in northern Virginia, bogging down the wagons on roads turned to mud. By that evening, the wagon train had covered no more than six miles, and the rain showed no sign of letting up.

When the story of the delayed pontoons later became public, the senior officers were incensed. Maj. Gen. Oliver Otis Howard, in Bull Sumner's command, expressed his opinion in his autobiography written years later.

> As it required thirteen days to do a piece of work which could easily have been done in three days, it would be a marvelous stretch of charity to impute it to mere bungling.
>
> Had Woodbury and Spaulding in the outset been properly instructed by Halleck, those bridges would have been near at hand on the 19th on our arrival. Spaulding would have reported to Sumner at once and in less than an hour would have been pushing out his boats from our front.

As it was, Burnside could do little but wait in the pouring rain and hope that the bridges arrived before Robert E. Lee did.

FIVE

THE MAN WHO
COULD DO NO WRONG

No one was calling him "Granny Lee" anymore, the way some had in the early days of the war. Back then, it seemed that Robert E. Lee was not going to be much of a soldier for the Confederacy, despite his thirty-three years of army service. Also, there were some Southerners who considered Lee a traitor to the noble cause.

In the heady early months of war, while other Confederate generals earned victory and glory at Bull Run in Virginia and Wilson's Creek in Missouri, Lee worked twelve-hour days in a tiny room in a Richmond office building. His collar bore the single star of a brigadier general, but his duties as chief military adviser to Jefferson Davis were more like those of a clerk.

He fought the war with government forms, memoranda, and requisitions as he labored to create an army from virtually nothing. He was responsible for training and equipping thousands of eager recruits with uniforms, weapons, and the other materiel of war— all of which were in perilously short supply.

More important to Lee, in his opinion, he had to curb the new soldiers' bravado as well as temper their belief that one Confederate was worth ten of those no-good Yankees. The prevailing attitude was, Why bother training to be a proper soldier when everyone knew the war would be over in a matter of weeks?

Lee knew better. He knew the conflict would last a lot longer, and he said so publicly. He argued that the soldiers of the new Confederate army should be required to enlist for the duration of the war—however long that might be—rather than signing on for only the twelve months of service authorized by the Confederate States Congress. As a result, people began to question Lee's loyalty. Surely there was something wrong with a general who expressed such a negative view of the outcome and who contended that the Yankees would be hard to beat in battle. "At heart Robert E. Lee is against us; that I know," wrote one Confederate diarist. "General Lee will surely be tried for a traitor," said another.

Lee's restlessness and discontent increased as the first summer of the war wore on. He continued to try to create a fighting force that was fit for a modern war but could not even procure enough bullets for target practice.

At the end of the summer of 1861 Lee was ordered into the field for his first operational command. He failed dismally; his reputation sank even lower. Jefferson Davis had sent him to the mountains of northwestern Virginia to deal with three feuding Confederate officers, political appointees with no military experience who were more intent on vanquishing one another than defeating the enemy.

On Lee's arrival, the situation deteriorated. His efforts to get the generals to cooperate in a joint military action were rebuffed. Unfortunately, Lee was too polite to issue direct orders, which, as military adviser to the president, he had the authority to do. Instead, he made suggestions to the generals, which were ignored. This impossible situation was made worse by problems of logistics, terrain, and foul weather.

There were no railroad lines in the area to move men and supplies, and few roads through the rugged mountains, and after twenty days of continuous rain, what roads there were had turned to mud. The troops had little training and were totally lacking in military discipline. Their officers were hardly better. A cold snap settled over the hills and valleys. The men had no warm clothing and before long succumbed to measles and diarrhea.

Then the Union forces attacked, and although they were equally poorly trained and equipped, those troops easily swept the Confederates away. The three rebel armies, with their feuding generals in the lead, retreated in disarray. Within only four days, Yankee forces occupied the region. Its grateful pro-Union inhabitants promptly voted to secede from Virginia and form a new state, which they called West Virginia.

Lee returned to Richmond, roundly condemned by the Confederate congress and the Southern press. Because of his overly cautious behavior in this operation, it was then that reporters dubbed him "Granny Lee" and "Evacuating Lee." Devastated by the criticism and scorn, he questioned whether he had any further role to play in the war for Southern independence.

He was saved from disgrace by Jefferson Davis, who still believed in him, although not enough to give him a combat command. Instead, Davis ordered him to Charleston, South Carolina, to strengthen coastal fortifications there and at Savannah, Georgia. To Lee's shame, the military and civilian leadership of both cities did not want him. They organized petitions protesting Lee's presence and forwarded them to Davis. The opposition grew to the point where Davis felt compelled to write letters in support of Lee. It was unprecedented for the president to plead with city officials to be permitted to make a military appointment.

Lee was well aware of the shame attached to his name. John Jones, a War Department clerk and a sharp observer of activities in the Confederate capital, wrote in his diary about Lee's circumstances: "General Lee in the streets here bore the aspect of a discontented man, for he saw that everything was going wrong."

Lee went to Charleston and performed his job efficiently, but there was a lot of grumbling among the troops about having to dig coastal defenses and undertake other forms of manual labor. They were not sorry to see him leave after four months. And while other Confederate generals continued to win victories, Robert E. Lee was back at his desk in Richmond watching the war pass him by.

A Yankee bullet and a piece of shrapnel from a Yankee shell changed Lee's prospects, but it was not until May 30, 1862, more than a year after the war began, that he got his chance for glory. As part of his Peninsular campaign, General McClellan was advancing cautiously on Richmond. Although he moved slowly—as always—against a vastly inferior force, by late May it looked as if he might succeed in capturing the Southern capital.

The situation was so serious that Jefferson Davis sent his family farther south to safety. That decision led hundreds of other civilians to evacuate the city. The cabinet fled, and the gold reserves were packed aboard a train and shipped away. Then, on May 30, when Gen. Joe Johnston, commanding the Confederate defense line, was wounded by a Union shell and musket ball, Richmond appeared to be doomed.

Lee and Davis were visiting the front when Johnston was carried off the field. Johnston's second-in-command, Gen. Gustavus Smith, was deemed incapable of handling such a great responsibility, and there was not time for a capable officer to be transferred from another theater of operations. Someone had to assume command immediately if there was any hope of stopping the Union advance.

Reluctantly, Davis appointed Lee to the position. Even after more than a year of Lee's faithful service as Davis's military adviser, the president was still not convinced that Lee would be up to the task of leading the Confederacy's largest army. The troops of that army weren't convinced either.

They bristled at Lee's first order as commander of the newly named Army of Northern Virginia. He put them to work with picks, shovels, and spades instead of rifles, ordering them to dig an elaborate system of trenches and rifle pits. To the soldiers, that was work for slaves. The nickname "Granny Lee" resurfaced, along with "King of Spades."

The rebel soldiers wanted to attack the enemy, not cower in trenches waiting for the Yankees to come. Lee wanted to attack as well, but he also wanted to deceive McClellan into thinking that the Southerners were preparing for a siege. Lee bided his time, drawing the Yankees in before he struck. When he finally unleashed his impatient troops, nearly a month later, he commenced a daring series of battles that came to be called the Seven Days.

After the smoke cleared, McClellan's far larger army was in full retreat. Richmond was safe from capture and Robert E. Lee was hailed as the savior of the Confederacy. Six months later— after Second Bull Run and Antietam— he was being summoned to save it once more, from whatever that new Yankee commander, General Burnside, was up to.

Robert E. Lee, commander of the Army of Northern Virginia at Fredericksburg. (*Library of Congress*)

Lee was sorry to see McClellan go. "We always understood each other so well," he told General Longstreet. "I fear [the Yankees] may continue to make these changes till they find some one whom I don't understand."

Longstreet thought that the change in Union commanders would work to the Confederate advantage. He believed, unlike Lincoln, that McClellan was in the process of becoming a better officer. If left in command long enough, Longstreet suggested, McClellan would eventually pursue Lee's army more tenaciously.

Others in high positions in the Army of Northern Virginia agreed that the change of command would benefit the South. They argued that Burnside was not as capable as McClellan. In addition, the replacement of McClellan was sure to demoralize the Union troops who held him in such high regard.

Speculation about Burnside's abilities as an adversary was soon replaced by concern about his intentions. Would he continue McClellan's push south or formulate some other strategy? By November 12, two days after Lee learned that McClellan had been replaced, he began to worry that Burnside would try something new.

Lee had to be prepared to move his forces from his headquarters at Culpeper Court House to counter an attack someplace else. But where? He decided to retain Longstreet's corps at Culpeper but notified Stonewall Jackson in the Shenandoah Valley to be prepared to shift his forces due east, should the need arise.

By November 14, Lee learned that Burnside was moving eastward. Lee wrote to the secretary of war, George Randolph, "It is plain that the enemy is abandoning his position around Warrenton, and does not intend to advance in the direction first assumed [due south]." But if Burnside was heading east, what was his destination?

In his letter to Randolph, Lee suggested three possibilities. The Yankees might be planning to advance on the Orange & Alexandria Railroad line with a view to threatening the road junction at Gordonsville, south of Culpeper. Or they might be planning to bring the Army of the Potomac back to Alexandria and send it by ship to Fortress Monroe, advancing on Richmond from there. That was what McClellan had tried in his disastrous Peninsular campaign, giving Lee his first victory in battle.

The third possibility was that "those people," as Lee habitually referred to Northerners, would head for Fredericksburg, only fifty miles from Richmond. Lee had only a cavalry regiment, an artillery battery, and four companies of infantry there. Such a small force would never be able to defend Fredericksburg against the Army of the Potomac. Acting on this particular assessment of Burnside's strategy, Lee dispatched another artillery battery and a regiment of infantry to Fredericksburg, hoping at the same time that Jeb Stuart's cavalry would bring him more definite information on the whereabouts of the Union army.

On November 17, Lee learned that Bull Sumner's corps was moving along the Rappahannock River toward Falmouth. Lee ordered Longstreet to send one of his divisions to Fredericksburg and to have the rest of his troops ready to follow the next morning if it became clear that Fredericksburg was Burnside's destination. Jackson was also alerted to move part of his corps closer to the bulk of the Confederate army at Culpeper Court House.

At nine o'clock on the morning of November 19, Lee wrote to Jackson about a report he'd just received from Stuart. The cavalry leader was certain, Lee said, "that Burnside's whole army had marched for Fredericksburg. Genl. Halleck had been to Warrenton on a visit," Lee added. "I shall wait to hear again from Stuart today and will then start for Fredericksburg if circumstances warrant."

Circumstances did warrant. On November 20, Lee sent a terse telegram to Jefferson Davis: "I think Burnside is concentrating his whole army opposite Fredericksburg."

Lee did not want to fight at Fredericksburg; it was the last place he would have selected to make a stand. He believed that the range of hills just beyond the town did not offer sufficient depth for a strong defensive position. These hills formed a natural barrier and could be easily entrenched and fortified, but if the Union forces broke through the line, the terrain beyond was open and flat. In addition, if the Yankees fought at Fredericksburg, they would have a short and easily defended direct line of supply by rail from Aquia Landing, fewer than ten miles away.

At first Lee decided to withdraw some twenty-eight miles south of Fredericksburg and establish a defensive line along the North Anna River. Meeting the Yankees there would leave them with a long supply line that could be easily interrupted by Stuart's cavalry raids. In addition, the open terrain along the river would allow Lee room to maneuver and to attack the Union army, rather than waiting behind fixed defenses for the attack to come, as would be the case at Fredericksburg.

Accordingly, Lee ordered one of Longstreet's divisions to head for the North Anna River. Then he changed his mind and decided to hold the line at Fredericksburg after all. What brought about this change was a report from Stonewall Jackson—which turned out to be false—that other Union troops were planning to march down the Shenandoah Valley. If this were true, then Lee would have to send reinforcements to Jackson, which could be done more quickly from Fredericksburg than from the North Anna. Also, Lee realized that if he retreated to the North Anna, he would lose access to the rich farmland south of Fredericksburg, which had not yet been picked clean by scavenging Yankee armies.

Lee's men needed all the food they could get. They were thin and starving when they began the trek to Fredericksburg. Their rations had been cut in April, seven months before, and had not been restored, even through the growing season and harvest. Food production had been reduced throughout the South because of bad weather and the fact that so many farmhands were serving in the army. The supply of beef and pork was low, the corn crop had failed in Tennessee and Georgia, and wheat production was only half of what it had been the previous year.

To make matters worse, only some of the available food ever reached the troops anyway. Southern railroads were notoriously inefficient and had improved little since the onset of war. Monetary greed was a factor too: Some farmers did not bring their grain to be threshed that year, hoping for higher prices if they waited. Farmers with surplus food to sell refused to accept Confederate money, insisting on payment in gold or Union green-backs.

As a result, Lee's men subsisted on an official daily ration of one pound of cornmeal bread and four ounces of meat that winter, though most men did not receive even that much. There was an ample variety of foods available in Richmond for those with the money to pay for it, but not for the freezing men on the line. Many soldiers contracted scurvy. When Lee complained to the War Department about the lack of fruits and vegetables to prevent the disease, he was advised to "send a daily detail to gather sassafras buds, wild onions, lamb's quarters, and poke beans."

A Virginia woman wrote in her diary:

> Quiet days interrupted only by soldiers begging for food, poor fellows, my heart aches for them. Their privations are terrible. They frequently go all day, sometimes longer, without a mouthful of anything.

In addition to being hungry, the Army of Northern Virginia was ragged and cold. One-third of Lee's men had no shoes. Some, in desperation, had fashioned what they called "Longstreet slip-pers"—flat pieces of rawhide folded over their feet and tied in place. But as the weather turned colder, ice formed on the cow hair on the soles of the slippers, making them slick; the men felt as though they were wearing ice skates. Until the Southerners could kill some Yankees and take their boots, they would have to trudge through the ice and snow barefoot.

The Confederate army was running out of everything. Besides the lack of shoes, warm clothing, and blankets, there were not even belts to hold cartridge boxes in place. Instead, the men had to use ropes to fasten them around their waists. There were no proper leather harnesses for the artillery horses; the animals were lashed to the caissons with odd lengths of rope and rawhide strips. Nor did the horses and mules have enough forage. And many a hungry soldier had dipped his hand into the meager supply of corn feed for the horses.

It pained Lee to see his men in such condition, so poorly fed and provisioned. He wrote to the secretary of war: "I fear that our men with insufficient clothing, blankets, and shoes, will suffer much, and our ranks be proportionately diminished."

The Army of Northern Virginia looked like a band of starving ruffians as it headed east toward Fredericksburg. They were defi-cient in everything a modern army needed to wage war except an indomitable spirit, and the reason they were able to maintain that spirit was their trust and confidence and love for Robert E. Lee, who'd pushed back the Union troops so handily during the battles of the Seven Days.

He had successfully outrun the spectre of "Granny Lee." Now in hushed respectful tones they called him "Marse Robert," and "Old Marse," and reached out gingerly to touch his horse or bri-dle or stirrup when he passed, as if these were holy objects. One veteran soldier later recalled, "Anything that Lee had was sacred to us fellows." A biographer noted, "Lee commanded the souls of his men as no other commander in history ever did. God marches in the ranks of the Army of Northern Virginia. He could not do oth-erwise when the leader was Marse Robert."

The newest recruits who doffed their hats, if they were lucky enough to have any, and stood in silence in a state of grace whenever Lee rode by, would have agreed. God was with the Army of Northern Virginia. Marse Robert was akin to God; he could do no wrong.

In fact Lee's whole life had been defined, proscribed, and directed by the belief that he could not, he must not, he would not, do anything wrong. From childhood on he had been driven by the need to be perfect in order to atone for the sins of his father, and to try to erase the shame and dishonor the elder Lee had left on the family name. At one time it was thought that Maj. Gen. Henry Lee, known as Light Horse Harry, a hero of the Revolutionary War, would surely become president one day, just like his good friend George Washington.

Harry Lee had been elected to the Continental Congress, the Virginia House of Delegates, and the US Congress, and served three terms as governor of Virginia. There seemed to be no limit to his future, except that imposed by his own dark nature. This unfortunate tendency showed itself two weeks after his wedding.

He'd married an extremely wealthy cousin, Matilda Ludwell Lee, who died eight unhappy years later, her fortune long since squandered by one ill-advised scheme after another. Lee made questionable currency transactions, purchased interest-bearing bonds of dubious quality, bought coal mines and ore fields, and invested in grandiose plans to build huge cities. Every financial venture lost money until there was no more to lose. In the end, the financial hardship was so extreme and future prospects so bleak that Lee tried to cheat George Washington with a fraudulent bank note.

After his first wife died, Harry married well again, this time to Anne Hill Carter, daughter of the richest man in all Virginia. By the time his new bride was eight months pregnant, Harry had sold off almost all her property, and their once stately home, Stratford Hall, was in shambles.

The garden was overgrown with weeds, the fields untilled, the barns empty. Creditors had taken most of the furniture. Harry even sold the massive exterior staircase that led to the great hall on the main floor and chained the doors shut to keep out the growing parade of bill collectors.

When his wife gave birth to the boy she named Robert Edward Lee, their fifth child, there was barely enough coal to heat one room and not enough money to pay the doctor for delivering the baby. Her fortune was gone, and so was her husband, off to Richmond, one step ahead of his creditors, hunting for people to back his latest scheme.

The Lees were financially ruined and socially disgraced. Harry Lee was sent to debtor's prison. A few years later—being in the wrong place at the wrong time—he suffered a severe beating when a mob in Baltimore overran a political rally. He never recovered from his injuries yet managed to spend five years living on various Caribbean islands in an attempt to regain his health. Young Robert and his mother were all but abandoned. Harry decided to return to Virginia in 1818, when the boy was eleven, but died on the way and was buried on a barren island off the coast of Georgia.

Robert E. Lee barely knew his father, but he was painfully aware of his scandalous behavior and the legacy of shame he left behind. It was the disgrace associated with that legacy that drove Lee to seek perfection in his own behavior. One writer called the stain of Light Horse Harry Lee a "birth defect," from which the young Robert suffered all his life.

The boy grew up in Alexandria, Virginia, in a series of homes provided by extended members of the Carter family. He matured quickly, assuming responsibility at an early age for his mother's well-being. By the time he was twelve, he took charge of the grocery shopping, supervised the servants, and kept the keys to the pantry, traditionally the job of the head of the household, which he essentially was.

In addition, because his mother's health was poor, Robert became her primary caregiver, mixing and administering her medicines, and carrying her to their carriage for afternoon rides.

During the winter months the boy methodically and dutifully stuffed newspapers into the cracks of their dilapidated carriage to keep out the cold. He was a serious boy at an age when other children had few obligations or concerns. When Robert was thirteen, another scandal broke, another blot on the Lees' family honor. Henry Lee, Robert's half-brother by his father's first marriage, was carrying on an affair with his wife's teenage sister and stealing money from her inheritance. Virginia society was shocked. For the rest of his life, Henry was known as "Black Horse Harry Lee."

It was all too much for Robert's mother. But although she was ill and poor and the family name had been sullied, she found lessons from these sufferings to teach Robert. She drilled into him the need to practice self-denial and self-control. The future honor of the Lee family could be redeemed only if he stayed on the right path, under control at all times. Otherwise, he might end up like his father.

It was decided that the boy should attend West Point, a school fit for a proper Virginia gentleman. In truth, he had no choice; there would be no money or land for him to inherit and no way to afford a private college. Lee was sent first to a local preparatory school, where he excelled in his grades and his deportment. He never broke a rule or disobeyed an instruction and was always respectful and unobtrusive. His behavior was the same at West Point.

Always at the top of his class in every class, in four years he did not accumulate a single demerit. His buttons gleamed. His sword was spotless. He was never late for formation, never had his bed made up in less than perfect fashion, was never guilty of a sloppy salute, missed no bed-check, was not cited for abusing a horse or for folding his towel incorrectly.

And if that were not enough, he was also handsome, charming, and well mannered. He excelled at swimming, skating, dancing, and riding, and managed to be liked, admired, and respected by the other cadets.

When he graduated in 1829, Lee returned home to Alexandria to nurse his mother, rarely leaving her bedside until the day she died, a month later. For the rest of his life he extolled her virtues and insisted that all his achievements were due to her influence. He did not ever mention his father.

From being a model cadet Lee grew to become a model officer, serving as an engineer at Fortress Monroe, Virginia; St. Louis, Missouri; the North Carolina coast; and New York City. He spent those early years of his military career surveying boundary lines and supervising the construction of coastal fortifications. Promotions in the peacetime army were slow, and by the age of thirty-nine, Lee was still a captain after seventeen years on active duty.

Married since 1831 to Mary Anna Randolph Custis, a very wealthy cousin (following in the Lee tradition of marrying well), the Lees had seven children in fifteen years. Because of his military duties, he was unable to spend much time with them. Lee's wife, spoiled by her father and in frail health, chose to reside at her parents' home in Arlington, Virginia. The Custis Mansion and its many acres, which would one day become Arlington National Cemetery, sat nobly on top of a hill on the southern side of the Potomac River, overlooking the city of Washington.

As Lee approached the age of forty and realized that his children were growing up without him, he expressed increasing sadness, irritability, restlessness, and boredom. "I am conscious of having lost a great deal," he wrote to his wife, "the society of you and my children." He considered resigning his army commission but could not bring himself to do so, and by 1846, his country needed him. The United States was at war with Mexico.

Lee was eager to go to war. After almost two decades in uniform, this would be his first chance to test himself in battle. As he had been the model cadet at West Point, so he became the model wartime soldier, working on the staff of General of the Army Winfield Scott, engaged in daring and dangerous reconnaissance missions behind enemy lines.

On one such mission Lee was nearly captured and, in order to evade detection, he was forced to lie motionless beneath a log for several hours while Mexican soldiers camped all around him. Lee had a unique ability to search out routes no one else could find, thus enabling the American troops to outflank the enemy and avoid costly frontal attacks. As the army approached Mexico City, newly promoted Major Lee found a way for artillery to cross a lava bed that the Mexicans considered impassable. Once American guns opened fire from a direction that caught the Mexican troops by surprise, the enemy fled.

In the final attack at Chapultepec, the heavily defended gateway to Mexico City, Lee worked for forty-eight hours without sleep to construct supports for heavy artillery in a location where the Mexicans believed no artillery could ever be placed.

Robert E. Lee became a celebrity and a national hero, his name and exploits lauded in newspapers throughout the country. General Scott called him the best soldier he had ever known and said he would not have been able to defeat Santa Anna's army without Lee's brilliance and dedication. Lee's actions erased the stain from the family name.

Returning to Washington was a major disappointment, beginning the day of Lee's arrival. His wife had sent a carriage to bring him across the river to Arlington, but he missed it and rode up the long hill to the Custis house alone on horseback. When he arrived, no one recognized him at first but his dog. After hugging the children who greeted him, he picked up a three-year-old boy, assuming it was the child named for him, only to be told it was a playmate. The older children who had grown up in his absence were distant and reserved, and his wife was again in poor health. She had grown old and had been bedridden for months, an invalid just like his mother had been.

Lee's celebrity status did not last once the war was over. He resumed the dull task of building harbor defenses, this time in Baltimore. Following that, he was appointed superintendent of the military academy at West Point, where, for a rare change, his wife and children accompanied him. Her health seemed to improve. She entertained the officers and their wives and held open house every Sunday for the cadets. Although Lee enjoyed the presence of his family and the opportunity to train the next generation of officers, he found the demanding schedule and constant paper-work to be exhausting. He suffered a variety of medical complaints, including digestive disorders and eyestrain. In addition, he was growing irritable and short-tempered again. After only three years, he needed a change.

His next assignment sent him two thousand miles west to take command of troops in the field for the first time in his twenty-six-year career. The secretary of war, West Point graduate Jefferson Davis, was forming two new regiments of cavalry to combat the Indian insurrections. The 1st Cavalry Regiment was commanded by Bull Sumner, with Joe Johnston as his second-in-command. The 2nd Cavalry Regiment was led by Albert Sidney Johnston, with Lee as his second-in-command.

In point of fact, Lee had an independent command, which consisted of twelve officers and 226 enlisted men, posted to an isolated fort near what would later become Abilene, Texas. Colonel Johnston and the rest of the regiment were stationed in San Antonio. Lee had not seen such primitive and demanding conditions since the Mexican War. He and his men lived in tents through a freezing winter and a brutally hot summer, and under-took long, grueling missions across the desert searching for hostile Indians. On one mission, Lee led his troops more than one thousand miles in two months.

To his surprise, he found that he liked commanding troops in those austere conditions. The wealthy Virginia gentleman, long used to comfort and luxurious surroundings, adjusted well to the sand, sun, and sky. He made pets of a snake and a chicken, training the latter to jump up on his camp desk, where it invariably knocked over his inkwell.

Lee also enjoyed the camaraderie of the cloistered camp life, bantering with his junior officers, most of whom would later fight for the Confederacy. The time out west may have been the happiest, most carefree period of Lee's entire military service, but it ended abruptly when his father-in-law, George Custis, died. Lee arranged a two-month leave and hurried back to Arlington to manage the family affairs. He found that his father-in-law's estate and properties were in such dismal condition that he ended up staying there not for two months but for two years to put everything in order.

Lee might never have returned to active duty if the abolitionist John Brown and his followers had not taken over the federal arsenal at Harpers Ferry, Virginia, on October 17, 1859. A courier rushed from the War Department to Arlington that afternoon with orders for Lee to report immediately to Secretary of War John Floyd. Lee met with Floyd and President James Buchanan and was ordered to leave at once for Harpers Ferry to quash the uprising.

Dressed in civilian clothes, because there had been no time to change into uniform, Lee commandeered a Baltimore & Ohio Railroad locomotive. The courier who had brought him the message begged to tag along; it was the young lieutenant Jeb Stuart. Lee had only ninety US Marines at his disposal, but they were all he needed. He stopped the insurrection the next day by sending in the Marines under orders not to fire, so as not to endanger the hostages Brown had taken. Within three minutes, one Marine and two abolitionists were dead, and Brown and the rest of his band were under arrest.

Six weeks later, at Brown's hanging, Lee was given command of several thousand troops to keep Brown's supporters from disrupting the proceedings. All was quiet, but among the motley collection of militia units and regular army troops under Lee's command that day were two men who would play important roles in the coming war.

Leading the corps of cadets from the Virginia Military Institute and charged with guarding the gallows was one of the teachers— a pale, thin, ungainly West Point graduate named Thomas Jackson. Another group guarding the site was the Richmond Grays, comprised of the city's socially elite young men. With them was a visitor from the north who had borrowed a uniform because he wanted to know what it was like to be a soldier. When he saw

Colonel Robert E. Lee led the contingent of Marines that quelled John Brown and his band at the federal arsenal at Harpers Ferry on October 17, 1859. (*Library of Congress*)

John Brown's body drop and dangle at the end of the noose, the man—John Wilkes Booth—turned pale. He never again wanted to wear an army uniform.

By the winter of 1860 Lee had returned to Texas on active duty, but he was no longer a happy man. He was experiencing another period of discontent, fearing that he was a failure. He was fifty-three years old and once again living away from his family. He began to question what he had to show for the thirty-four years he had given to the army. He wrote that he was increasingly dissatisfied with his life, "rent by a thousand anxieties," his mind and body "worn and racked to pieces." He believed he had failed as a husband and father and saw no way out of his depression.

His letters to friends and family became self-critical. He mentioned frequently that he felt inadequate and that he needed to repent for his sins, which he did not specify, and seek forgiveness. When a grandson was born that year, Lee wrote to the boy's father that he wished he could give the new arrival a worthier name and a better example to follow. He said he hoped the child would not make the same mistakes he had.

Lee's despair was deeper than at any previous time and might well have worsened had his attention not been diverted by current events. Talk about the secession of the southern states disturbed him; he opposed any division of the United States. He told friends that the only flag he wished to serve under was the Star-Spangled Banner.

When his home state of Virginia elected to join the rebellion, however, Lee's resolve changed. He was concerned about the influence Virginia's secession might have on his family's financial security. It could be ruinous not only for the state, but also for the investments he had made in property over the last few years. On a deeper level, Lee was also driven by the deep loyalty he felt to the people of his native state.

The War Department summoned Lee to Washington with an offer of the rank of major general and command of a new Union army expected to be 100,000 strong—the largest military force ever assembled in the United States. Lee refused. He would not fight against his own people, however greatly he opposed secession.

When Lee told Gen. Winfield Scott, his mentor and friend, of his decision, the old soldier replied sadly, "Lee, you have made the greatest mistake of your life; but I feared it would be so."

On November 20, 1862, the man who could do no wrong led his troops to Fredericksburg, to gather by the river and to meet the enemy once again. In town, at her spacious home at 307 Lewis Street, forty-seven-year-old widow Jane Howison Beale wrote in her diary: "The army of General Lee [is] collecting around us and here a battle must take place ere long."

SIX

WE ARE IN THE HANDS
OF THE PHILISTINES

Helen Struan Bernard had lived a privileged life of luxury and ease at the family plantation, Gay Mont, for all of her twenty-five years. The house was sixteen miles downriver from Fredericksburg, on the south side of the Rappahannock, but even there, in her relative safety, she worried about the coming of war.

On January 20, 1861, three months before the first shot was fired on Fort Sumter, she wrote in her diary:

> We hear of stormy conflicts that threaten to bring war, pestilence and famine, desolation and ruin upon our now prosperous land. Human efforts to avert the plague seem futile. God alone can order the unruly passions of man.

But the unruly passions of man defied order. On April 14, the day after the Union garrison at Fort Sumter surrendered, Bernard noted: "I cannot believe that our glorious land is to be a field of carnage and woe. Who shall make peace when brothers are at war?"

No one made peace, and all across the land, in north and south, in Fredericksburg and Utica, Atlanta and Philadelphia, old men made stirring speeches and young men eagerly signed up to fight.

At Gay Mont, Helen Bernard was more fearful than optimistic about "the great excitement prevailing throughout the whole length and breadth of the land. We talk of war, but we know not what it is." War fever spread quickly. On May 8 she wrote:

> Now there is but one topic of thought and conversation: War! A universal spirit of defiance seems to animate the whole South, every man is under arms. It is said that there are 80,000 volunteers in Virginia alone. Defeat is not so much as spoken of.

Fredericksburg was soon stripped of her young men, as they enthusiastically and optimistically marched off to make quick work of the Yankees. Within a few months, the population of the town of four thousand consisted only of older men, women, children and, of course, the slaves. The as-yet-distant war was a pageant of glorious letters, visits from the town's soldiers on leave, and newspaper stories of stirring battles, heroic deeds, and victory celebrations.

In time there came the grim reminders of the realities of war: the death notices in the newspapers; boys with missing arms, legs, and eyes coming home. But that was to be expected as the price of victory, and in Fredericksburg, as elsewhere, support for the war remained undiminished. The town was imbued with a sense of history, patriotism, and martial ardor, a spirit undimmed—or so everyone believed in those early days.

Fredericksburg had an illustrious heritage. George Washington himself spent eight years of his childhood on the Ferry Plantation across the river. His mother lived out her final years and was buried in Fredericksburg. James Monroe built his law practice in town, and not far from Monroe's office, a thirteen-year-old Scots immigrant and one-day naval hero, John Paul Jones, lived with his brother. Dr. Hugh Mercer opened an apothecary shop in Fredericksburg and later served as a brigadier general in the

Revolutionary War, killed while fighting under the command of his good friend, Washington.

The site for the town was first settled in 1622. A fort was constructed on the river, along with a plantation and a trading station. Fredericksburg was formally incorporated a century later, in 1727, and named for Frederick, Prince of Wales, son of England's King George II. To demonstrate further their fealty to the throne of England, the town fathers named several streets after members of the royal family—Sophia, Caroline, Princess Anne, and Prince Edward.

The town grew into a center for trade in grain, flour, tobacco, and maize. By 1840 Fredericksburg was a thriving community with more than seventy stores, four newspapers, seven schools, two banks, men's and women's seminaries, and several churches. The town even had underground pipes for delivering water from two springs to the homes and businesses—advanced city planning for the time. The population of approximately 4,000 included 2,500 whites, 1,124 slaves, and 370 free Blacks.

The first year of the war did not directly intrude on Fredericksburg, but that changed on April 18, 1862, a year after Fort Sumter fell. Union soldiers were spotted across the river, in Falmouth. McClellan's Peninsular campaign was under way, and a corps led by Gen. Irvin McDowell arrived in Falmouth to protect Washington, DC, from a sudden rebel advance from the south.

Helen Struan Bernard at Gay Mont had an older married sister, Mary Eliza Bernard Guest, who lived at Beaumont, five miles upriver from Fredericksburg. She recorded the day's events in her diary.

> April 18, 1862. Good Friday. I write while the smoke of the burning bridges, depot, and boats is resting like a heavy cloud all around the horizons toward Fredericksburg. The enemy are in possession of Falmouth; our force on this side too weak to resist them, are retiring, and what is to follow, who can say? We are not at all frightened but stunned and bewildered waiting for the end. Will they shell

Fredericksburg? Will our homes on the river all be destroyed?

On the following day, the forces of Union general John Gibbon lobbed a few shells across the river at the Confederate forces. Fredericksburg's mayor, Montgomery Slaughter, and a committee of leading citizens arranged a meeting with a Yankee brigade commander, Col. Christopher Auger, near Falmouth, to assure him that there were no more Confederate troops in town and to request a cease-fire. The Union officer agreed, but that did not assuage the anger of Thomas Barton, an attorney and the oldest member of the group. "We are in the hands of the Philistines," Barton proclaimed.

General McDowell maintained his headquarters at Chatham, a stately home in Falmouth. He ordered his troops to construct a bridge to Fredericksburg, to replace the railroad bridge the Confederates had destroyed when the Yankees first showed up. The bridge gave the "Philistines" easy access to Fredericksburg but they did not turn out to be quite the marauders some Southerners had feared. Still, their presence was clearly unwelcome, a point underscored by the behavior of the residents.

Gen. Marsena Rudolph Patrick had been appointed military governor of Fredericksburg. He did his best to administer the town in a proper, even-handed fashion. A local historian wrote that even the most ardent secessionists agreed that Patrick was "a generous man and a kind, humane officer. Under his government military rule in Fredericksburg was kindly exercised and the people were not oppressed and not a few of them conceived a sincere respect for his character."

General Patrick posted armed guards at homes where women and children lived alone and was quick to punish Union soldiers who stole food or looted houses. Nevertheless, the widow Jane Howison Beale noted in her diary on April 27, "Fredericksburg is a captured town."

Abraham Lincoln visited Fredericksburg on May 23, accompanied by Secretary of War Edwin Stanton, French ambassador to Washington Henri Mercier, and Commodore John Dahlgren, one of the president's close friends. They called on General Patrick at his headquarters at the Farmer's Bank, then toured the town in a carriage drawn by four horses. Later, at McDowell's headquarters, Union officers gathered, eager to meet the president.

When General Gibbon was presented to Lincoln, the president asked, facetiously, if he were the man who had written *The Decline and Fall of the Roman Empire*. Gibbon, perplexed and apparently unaware of the literary allusion, replied seriously that he had written an artillery manual.

"Never mind, General," Lincoln said, "if you will write the decline and fall of this rebellion, I will let you off."

Despite General Patrick's fairness in overseeing the town, friction, distrust, and outright hatred were inevitable. Patrick was aware of these feelings, of course, but tried not to let them influence him. He wrote

> The Secesh people were very indignant at the profanation of the Sacred Soil by Yankees. It was amusing to see the manner in which the Secesh women showed us their Backs. They were all looking until about the time the Cavalcade would get opposite their doors then, with a grand air they would throw back their Crinoline, as Stage Ladies do.

A man from Wisconsin, a soldier in the Iron Brigade, watched other Union soldiers hang an American flag above the sidewalk of the main commercial street. When a group of ladies spied the flag they stepped off the wooden sidewalk into the muddy street so they would not have to walk beneath the hated banner. The Wisconsin soldier wrote to his family, "The boys looked on and enjoyed the scene [and] soon strung seven flags, which covered the whole width of the street. After that the ladies did not walk on that street at all."

Even at Beaumont, five miles away, Mary Eliza Bernard Guest was offended by the presence of the Yankees. On May 12 she wrote:

The enemy are in full possession of the country all around us. Their pickets are stationed on the road just opposite the front door, and a guard [is] in the yard, to protect us from the marauding parties of their own soldiers. Only to think of being under Yankee protection is distraction and to crown all, this afternoon General Patrick drove out to see Mr. Guest and was actually under the same roof with us. May God in mercy forgive the bitter feelings, the hatred, that have filled my heart this day and every day lately.

I am weary and sick with indignation and excitement. We see Yankee soldiers, read Yankee papers, hear Yankee music, and have their detested flag waving proudly over our country. These are indeed dark days.

The days were darker still for the widow Jane Howison Beale. Yankee occupation was bad enough, but on May 13, she received worse news. "Since my last entry," she wrote in her diary, "my heart has been crushed with sorrow, for I have seen the death of my [twenty-year-old] son Charley mentioned in the Richmond papers. He fell in the battle near Williamsburg on Monday the 5th. Sorrow has rolled in on my soul in heavy waves."

She wrote a long entry that day, recording the sense of isolation felt so keenly by the residents of Fredericksburg.

We can hear nothing from our army or our friends. We are shut in by the enemy on all sides and even the comforts of life are many of them cut off. No one is allowed to bring wood to town and we know not how we are to be supplied with the means of cooking the small amounts of food we can procure.

The Yankees even dared to interfere in the traditional master-slave relationship by actively encouraging the slaves to leave town. Some Northerners urged the black servants to stay but to demand payment for their labor. That was too much for the citizens of Fredericksburg to bear. As Jane Beale put it,

It strikes at the root of those principles and rights for which our Southern people are contending and cannot be submitted to. It fixes upon us their incubus of supporting a race who were ordained of high Heaven to serve the white man, and it is only in that capacity they can be happy useful and respected. I love my servants, they are part of my family, and their happiness has been my care as well as that of my own children. I can but hope that no evil influences will be brought to bear upon their minds inducing them to place themselves and me in a more unhappy position than that which we now occupy.

The Yankees were bent on destroying the root and fabric of Southern society, and to protect that precious way of life, many more sons would have to die.

In August 1862, four months after General McDowell's Union forces occupied Fredericksburg, they were replaced by soldiers of the 9th Corps, commanded by Ambrose Burnside. The outfit was fresh from its string of victories along the North Carolina coast. A fair, upstanding, even genial occupier, Burnside promptly issued orders to his men forbidding any and all plundering of civilian property in the town. Unfortunately, the War Department was not as considerate of civilians as were the Union's generals in the field.

In retribution for the arrest in Richmond of several northern-born men suspected of having pro-Union sympathies, the federal government ordered the arrest of nineteen prominent Fredericksburg citizens, including Mayor Slaughter. After they were rounded up, however, Burnside greeted them cordially, dismissed their guards, and offered them a drink of whiskey before they were taken away to Washington's Old Capitol Prison. Although they were released six weeks later, their arrest served no purpose but to fuel the already strong hatred the townspeople felt toward the occupying army.

That four-month occupation ended abruptly in late August when Robert E. Lee defeated yet another new Union commander,

John Pope, at the second battle of Bull Run. The Army of the Potomac retreated to Washington to protect the capital from the Confederates, and Burnside's 9th Corps was also ordered to fall back.

The Philistines left in a wild orgy of fire and smoke as they destroyed tons of supplies they could easily have carried with them. The timetable for rapid departure, as dictated by the War Department, left Burnside no time to pack his wagons full. He could only set the materiel on fire or blow it up.

The retreat was so disorderly and chaotic that hundreds of slaves deserted their masters and swarmed across the river to the Union side. They expected to find freedom there, but they too were left behind with everything else the Union troops abandoned.

On Sunday morning, when Jane Beale came out of the Presbyterian Church, she was overjoyed to see the Union soldiers packing up the equipment at their headquarters at the Farmer's Bank and streaming across the bridges to Falmouth. She and other women looked on, beaming, believing that this hasty departure could only mean that the Yankees had been beaten again. Jane Beale, as though in celebration, wrote:

> [A] thundering sound shook the house, and we knew it was the blowing up of the bridges. Several explosions followed, and soon the bright flames leaped along the sides and floors of the bridges and illuminated the whole scene. The burning continued all night and our slumbers were disturbed with frequent explosions of gunpowder, placed under the two bridges.

The Yankees were gone, and the slaves who had tried to leave with them had no place to go except the only homes they had ever known. Two of Jane Beale's servants knocked on the back door the next morning, begging to be allowed to resume their duties. She wrote:

> I went out feeling a good deal of indignation against them, but they seemed so humble and professed such pen-

itence for having ever thought of going that I could only tell them that if they were willing to go to work again and content themselves in the condition in which God had placed them, I would say nothing more to them about ever having gone.

On September 3, a troop of Confederate cavalry rode into Fredericksburg in triumph. Women lined the streets, cheering and waving their handkerchiefs. The town was safe, life could return to normal, and all was right once again with the world, just as God intended.

But on November 19, fewer than three months later, the Yankees had returned to Falmouth, to assemble across the river from Fredericksburg, in greater and greater numbers. "[We] watched with trembling hearts the long lines of Yankees pouring over the Chatham hills to take the same station they occupied last summer," Jane Beale recorded in her diary. "They come in count-less numbers."

At the same time, rebel troops were gathering by the thousands in the hills just beyond the town. Some people reported that they had even seen Robert E. Lee himself. William Bernard, brother of Helen Bernard and Mary Guest, was a private in the 9th Virginia Cavalry. He was visiting Beaumont on November 20 when he spotted Lee and General Longstreet riding past with their staff officers in attendance. Rumors flew that Jackson, the mighty Stonewall himself, was on his way from the Shenandoah to Fredericksburg.

Lee, Longstreet, Jackson; they were already legendary figures, the flower of the Confederacy. If they were coming to town, the Yankees across the river did not stand a chance.

Maj. Gen. James "Pete" Longstreet had quickly become a favorite of Lee's shortly after Joe Johnston received his disabling wound and Lee took command of the army. Only four days after meeting Longstreet, Lee wrote to Jefferson Davis: "Longstreet is a capital soldier. His recommendations hitherto have been good, and I have confidence in him."

Lee's trust in Longstreet deepened; he referred to him as "the staff in my right hand," and "my old war horse." The two men were almost always together, and Lee's dependence on Longstreet grew. Longstreet was forty-one in 1862, a big, burly man over six feet tall and weighing 190 pounds. The opposite of Lee in bearing and manner, Longstreet was rough, blunt, and often aloof.

With people he liked, however, he could be personable and fun-loving, like the hell-raising cadet he had been at West Point. He enjoyed good whiskey and kept an ample supply for visitors. His officers and men liked and admired him. He was especially helpful to junior officers, such as Jeb Stuart and George Pickett. Some people said that Pickett would never have risen so far and so fast in rank had he not been one of Longstreet's favorites.

Longstreet loved being a soldier. It was what he had wanted to do since his childhood on a farm in Georgia. His father nicknamed him "Pete" for reasons unclear, and as a boy he spent much time reading biographies of military heroes. By age nine, he had decided to attend West Point, and he never changed his mind.

He received an appointment to the military academy where, like Burnside, he came perilously close to being expelled. Not a particularly good student, Longstreet never rose above the lower third of his class academically. He earned numerous demerits for disobeying orders, needing a haircut, failing to clean his room, and missing roll call, among other offenses. He was also absent from the post many evenings, drinking and carousing at Benny Havens, where so many cadets—including Burnside, a few years later—escaped from the demands of their regimented life. One cadet who never frequented the tavern and who thoroughly disapproved of it was Lee.

But Pete Longstreet had no need to be perfect. He was no model cadet, but he was popular, had a quick sense of humor, and was voted the handsomest in his class. He graduated in 1842—fifty-fourth in a class of fifty-six.

Despite his outgoing, independent nature, his best friend during his cadet years was a serious, reserved young man who did not even want to be a soldier. Longstreet and Ulysses S. Grant would remain friends for life; Longstreet even stood as best man at Grant's wedding.

Longstreet learned that he was an excellent combat officer in the war against Mexico. A natural leader, he was promoted to brevet captain in his first battle, for "gallant and meritorious conduct" in leading a charge against a heavily fortified position.

He led another valiant charge five days later against the strongly defended fortress at Chapultepec. He was out in front of his men, waving the regimental

Major General James Longstreet won widespread praise as the finest corps commander in the Army of Northern Virginia. (*Library of Congress*)

colors, when he sustained a serious wound in the leg. He held the flag up for as long as he could before handing it to Pickett, who carried it over the wall of the fort.

The war was over for Longstreet. The wound took a long time to heal and it was not until six months later that he was able to walk properly. He married Louise Garland, the daughter of his first regimental commander, and they eventually had ten children. Longstreet initially approached fatherhood by taking an active role in raising the children, believing he could order them about like soldiers under his command and that they would respond appropriately and obey. When he realized that his home did not function like an army post, he turned over the duties of parenthood to his wife and focused on his career.

Longstreet served at a succession of posts in Texas, Kansas, and New Mexico, and by the time the Civil War began he had been promoted to major. There was no question which side he would fight for, and when he joined the new Confederate army he received the single star of a brigadier general. Six months later he

was a major general, and a year after that a lieutenant general—
one of the Confederacy's highest-ranking officers.

Although he was enjoying great success in his military career,
tragedy struck his personal life. In January 1862, a scarlet fever
epidemic raged through Richmond, claiming three of the
Longstreet children within a week; two other children had died
earlier. Longstreet's grief was so deep he could not even comfort
his stricken wife. He returned to his post a changed man. He gave
up his longstanding passion for gambling and turned to religion
for solace. Ten months later, he was steeling himself to serve again
as Lee's old "war horse."

Thomas Jackson, thirty-nine years old on the eve of the battle of
Fredericksburg, was about to become a father, but he told no one.
The man known to his troops as "Old Jack" and to both North and
South as "Stonewall" since the battle at Bull Run, did not want
even the closest members of his staff to know. He had warned his
wife not to telegraph the news when their first child was born but
to write a letter instead, so that no one else would find out until he
was ready to announce the birth.

It was November 21, the day after Lee and Longstreet arrived
in Fredericksburg. Jackson and his troops were still at their headquarters in Winchester, Virginia. The town had special significance for Jackson. The previous February, in a house not one hundred yards from his headquarters tent, the child his wife was carrying had been conceived. "Wouldn't it be nice for you to be here
again?" he had written to her.

Jackson called on the owners of the house in which he and his
wife had lived the previous winter, then prepared to move his men
out, heading southeast toward Fredericksburg, seventy miles away.
Lee had not yet sent for him; it would be two more days before
Lee decided that Jackson should come. Jackson made the decision
on his own, anticipating Lee's needs before Lee himself knew. He
was certain that the battle would be joined at Fredericksburg, and
he was determined to be there in time.

Jackson was known for certain idio-
syncrasies, although precognition was
never deemed one of them. He believed,
for example, that one side of his body
was withering away. To forestall that
disaster, he avoided contact with pepper
in any form and frequently sucked on
lemons. At one point he tried a diet of
stale bread and meat without seasoning.
When he sat in a chair, his posture was
rigid, as though at attention, both feet
flat on the floor and his back not touching the chair. This position, he said,
assured that his alimentary canal was
kept straight.

General Thomas
"Stonewall" Jackson's corps
held off the Union assault
against the right flank of
the Confederate line at
Fredericksburg. (*Library of
Congress*)

For a time he thought one leg was
bigger than the other, and one arm
heavier than the other. He would raise
the heavy arm high above his head so that the blood would run
down into his body, thus lightening the arm.

Jackson's eccentricities were always on parade—the lack of
grace, the ramrod backbone that kept him stiff in the parlor as he
sat on the edge of his chair and did his social duty, the sometimes
awkward and exaggerated manners and mannerisms, the extreme
conscientiousness that sent him walking miles in the rain to apol-
ogize for a mistaken remark that had been forgotten, the peculiar-
ities in eating habits, and the propensity for falling asleep in the
most conspicuous places.

Even his horse was strange: a fat, round, compact animal named
Fancy, though it was anything but. His men called the horse "Old
Sorrel." On the many forced marches for which Jackson was
known, the horse would lie on the ground like a dog whenever
Jackson gave the command to rest.

For all of Jackson's odd ways and his religious fervor—he would
not even read a letter if it arrived on a Sunday—he was also
intensely ambitious. And this trait disturbed him. "I have written

that he was ambitious," a friend noted, "and his ambition was vast, all-absorbing. Like the unhappy wretch from whose shoulders sprang the foul serpent, he loathed it, perhaps feared it; but he could not escape it; it was himself." In a letter to his sister Jackson wrote, "You say that I must live on [fame] for the present. I say not only during the present, but during life."

By November 21, 1862, the day Jackson's army started for Fredericksburg, he had already gained fame in abundance. Indeed, many of his admirers placed greater stock in Jackson than in Lee as their ultimate savior. Jackson was described as the brightest star in the entire South at that stage of the war. "The revolution has at last found a great Captain," proclaimed a letter to the *Macon Telegraph*. "He is Stonewall Jackson." George Pickett later wrote to his wife, "If General Lee had Grant's resources he would soon end the war; but Old Jack can do it without resources."

Old Jack did not look like a savior, a hero, or an inspiring leader of men. He was not an imposing figure, standing about five feet nine and weighing 170 pounds, and usually seen wearing a ragged uniform and mangy cadet cap dating from his days as a teacher at the Virginia Military Institute.

Overall he looked like a harsh, stern, patriarchal Old Testament figure, but there was also a lighthearted, even merry, side to him, although not many people saw it. Among the few who did were the young officers on his staff who liked to joke and play pranks on Old Jack when they judged the time was right.

Jackson especially enjoyed the company of Jeb Stuart, who was nine years younger. Stuart greatly admired the strange, taciturn Jackson, and Stonewall liked the dashing cavalryman better than anyone else in the army. It would have been hard to find two more different temperaments, yet Jackson permitted Stuart a degree of easy familiarity he never tolerated from others. The two men developed a deep, genuine mutual affection.

Jackson once even allowed Stuart to dress him up like a dandy, accepting the gift of a magnificent coat two months before the march to Fredericksburg. A Richmond tailor had fashioned it with gleaming brass buttons and gold lace and insignia. Jackson had never seen such a garment and at first hardly dared touch it. He told Stuart, "The coat is much too handsome for me, but I shall take the best care of it, and shall prize it highly as a souvenir."

Jackson startled everyone when he emerged from his tent the morning of November 21, prepared to lead the way to Fredericksburg wearing his new coat. He also wore new trousers, a cap with a half-inch gilded band, shiny boots, and a new saber— all gifts from admirers.

His staff stared in amazement. They had ever seen him so resplendent, so dazzling. Neither had his men, and they were free with their comments when they spotted their beloved Old Jack "dressed up as fine as a Lieutenant or a Quartermaster." A colonel summoned the men: "Come here, boys. Stonewall has drawed his bounty and has bought himself some new clothes."*

Jackson's appearance captured everyone's attention, as he had hoped. He wanted to make the point dramatically that they were no longer on the sidelines, off in the Shenandoah fighting on their own. They were on their way to join forces with Robert E. Lee himself.

"Young gentlemen," Jackson announced to his wide-eyed staff, "this is no longer the headquarters of the Army of the Valley, but the Second Corps of the Army of Northern Virginia."

Thomas Jonathan Jackson had come a long way from his days as an orphan living in the far western part of Virginia. Shunted off to an uncle's house at the age of eleven, he showed his independent nature early on by running away the next day. When another family member suggested that he return to his uncle's care, he shook his head. "Maybe I ought to, ma'am, but I am not going to. No; Uncle Brak and I can't agree. I have quit, and shall not go back any more."

---

*The bounty to which the colonel referred was the amount of fifty dollars, which the boys had just received for reenlisting.

He moved in with more agreeable relatives and soon proved himself to be hardworking and determined to make something of himself. Although shy and somewhat awkward, by age sixteen he was teaching school. At seventeen he was sworn in as a town constable, charged with serving notices of lawsuits and tracking down debtors. He had hoped to attend college, but there was no money for that.

A year later he got the unexpected chance to go to West Point—as a replacement. The young man from his district who had won the appointment fled the academy after a few days, finding military life too grim and restricting. Jackson applied to take his slot.

"I am very ignorant," he wrote to an influential friend who was trying to arrange the substitute appointment, "but I can make it up in study."

And he did. Despite being woefully ill prepared for the academic rigors of West Point, and judged to be the least promising member of his class, he succeeded through dedication and persistence. Fellow plebe Dabney Maury, an aristocratic Virginian, commented about Jackson: "That fellow looks as if he had come to stay." By the time he graduated in 1846 he ranked seventeenth in a class of fifty-nine cadets, with few demerits on his record. There were no nightly visits to Benny Havens's tavern for him.

He graduated in time for the Mexican War, in which he demonstrated such bravery—especially during the attack on the Chapultepec fortress—that he received three brevet promotions to the rank of major. An ambitious West Point graduate could not ask for a brighter beginning to his military career.

But in peacetime there were routine assignments to Fort Hamilton on Long Island, and the desolate Fort Meade, sixty-five miles from Tampa, Florida. In 1851, Jackson's life took a dramatic turn when he accepted an invitation from the Virginia Military Institute in Lexington, Virginia, to join the faculty as professor of physics (then called natural and experimental philosophy) and artillery tactics. Jackson was twenty-seven years old.

He was a terrible teacher. His ineptitude in the classroom combined with his stiff, introverted manner made him the target of crude practical jokes and open disrespect. The students "talked back to him, contradicted him, derided him." One cadet refused to answer when Jackson called on him in class. Jackson persisted, and the student replied that Jackson was not competent to judge his performance. Another student refused to stop talking in class. These cadets were expelled, but many others received no punishment for their insolent behavior toward Jackson.

In general, Jackson seemed unmoved by the behavior of unruly students; he usually continued to lecture as though nothing disturbing had occurred. Some taunted him outside the classroom. Once he answered a knock at the door to find a boy tied to a chair that had been tilted against the doorknob. When Jackson opened the door, the student fell backward into Jackson's room.

One day as Jackson walked past the cadet barracks, a brick was dropped from a third-floor window. It came so close that it brushed his hat. "If the culprits expected a reaction, they were disappointed. Jackson walked straight on his course, never looking up or around." But he found the boys responsible and had them expelled.

He was much more successful outside the classroom. In 1853 he married twenty-eight-year-old Elinor Junkins, daughter of the president of nearby Washington College.

None of the cadets at the Institute would have recognized the cold, stern major could they have seen him at home. Relaxed, happy, and thoroughly in love with Ellie, Jackson's naturally warm personality permeated the household. Ellie was responsible for this transformation. She drew him out of his shell of shyness, played with him, joked with him, and took him places.

He had never been so happy, but it did not last. Ellie died in childbirth a year after they were married, and so did the baby she was carrying. Jackson's grief was absolute, but he forced himself to continue with his duties. He invested his energies in his faith and established a Sunday school for slaves and free Blacks, which was considered a scandalous action by many townspeople. He did not oppose slavery, and would eventually own slaves himself, but he provided opportunities for slaves to earn their freedom and was devoted to the care of those who remained with him.

Jackson embarked on a grand tour of Europe in the summer of 1856, visiting every major country to admire the art and architecture, astounding his French hosts with his detailed knowledge of the battle of Waterloo. When he returned to Virginia, he courted an old acquaintance, Anna Morrison; they married in 1857. A baby girl born to them a year later died at the age of three months. Jackson continued as before, teaching his classes, not permitting personal grief to interfere. Duty was not to be neglected, no matter the circumstances.

When the Civil War began, Jackson made a name for himself in the first major battle. As a newly promoted brigadier general, he led his 1st Virginia Brigade to Bull Run and valiantly stood firm against a massive Yankee assault. As he marched his men to the battle line, an old friend from West Point, Gen. Bernard Bee, informed him that the Union troops were beating back the Confederates.

"Then, sir," Jackson said, "we will give them the bayonet!"

Bee rode back to his troops, who had been hit hard and were barely holding on. He pointed up the hill at the stiff, straight-backed figure of Jackson astride his horse.

"Look!" Bee famously shouted to his men. "There is Jackson standing like a stone wall. Rally behind the Virginians!"

However, in late November, the beloved hero of the Confederacy packed away the fancy clothes and saber that so startled his men and led them toward Fredericksburg. On November 28 he reached Gordonsville and there found what he had been waiting for. It was a letter from Anna, writing as if she were their newly born daughter.

My Own Dear Father—
    As my mother's letter has been cut short by my arrival, I think it but justice that I should continue it. I know that

you are rejoiced to hear of my coming, and I hope that God has sent me to radiate your pathway through life. I am a very tiny little thing. I weigh only eight and a half pounds, and Aunt Harriet says I am the express image of my darling papa.

Your dear little wee Daughter.

Jackson told no one about the birth and betrayed no evidence of his great joy. First there was a battle to be fought. Fredericksburg was only forty miles away.

Colonel Robert Ogden Tyler's battery along the Stafford Heights overlooking Fredericksburg to the west. The guns of Tyler's outfit, part of the Center Grand Division, provided artillery support for the Union assault. (*Library of Congress*)

SEVEN

LET THE YANKEES COME

Headquarters of the Army of the Potomac, November 21st, 1862

To the Mayor and Common Council of Fredericksburg: Gentlemen:

Under the cover of the houses of your city, shots have been fired upon the troops of my command. Your mills and manufactories are furnishing provisions and the material for clothing for armed bodies in rebellion against the Government of the United States. Your railroads and other means of transportation are removing supplies to the depots of such troops. This condition of things must terminate, and by direction of General Burnside I accordingly demand the surrender of your city into my hands at or before 5 o'clock this afternoon. Failing in an affirmative reply to this demand by the hour indicated, sixteen hours will be permitted to elapse for the removal from the city of women and children, the sick and wounded and aged, etc., which period having expired I shall proceed to shell the town.

I am, very respectfully, your obedient servant,
E. V. Sumner
Brevet Major-General, U. S. Army
Commanding Right Grand Division

The message demanding the surrender of Fredericksburg was delivered by Brig. Gen. Marsena Patrick who had been the military governor of the town during the Union occupation the previous summer. Now he was the Provost Marshal General of the Army of the Potomac, and he did not like to be kept waiting. But wait he did that day. He went down to the riverbank early in the morning waving a white towel over his head so rebel snipers would not take potshots at him.

No one did, but he stood there a long time until a small boat put out from Fredericksburg bearing Col. William A. Ball of the 9th Virginia. Once on the rebel side of the river, Patrick was told that he would not be allowed to deliver his message in person to the mayor. Instead, it would be delivered by a courier; but none arrived for more than three hours. The courier finally returned more than two hours later to tell Patrick that the ultimatum was being considered; he would have to wait yet longer for a reply.

General Patrick sat in a log cabin guardhouse on the wharf from ten a.m., when he had been ferried across the river, until nine p.m., when he returned to the Union side with the Confederate reply. The mayor of Fredericksburg, after consulting with General Longstreet, assured Sumner that the Confederate forces had no intention of occupying the town for use as a base of military operations. Therefore, Mayor Slaughter concluded, the Union forces had no reason or justification for shelling the town.

Sumner made no reply that night, but many of the townspeople grew anxious when word spread of the Yankee threat to shell the town. Their fears were considerably heightened when Lee, unsure of what Sumner would do, advised residents to evacuate the town as quickly as possible.

The result was pandemonium, aggravated by an overly zealous Union gunner. People started fleeing Fredericksburg on the morning of November 22. Some flocked aboard a train that was ready to pull out of the station bound for Richmond. As it started forward, one of Sumner's guns opened fire on it from across the river.

The shell missed the train and the gunner did not fire again, but the explosion added to the terror. Longstreet and Lee watched the people leave. "The evacuation of the place by the distressed women and helpless men was a painful sight," Longstreet later wrote. "Many were almost destitute and had nowhere to go, but, yielding to the cruel necessities of war, they collected their portable effects and turned their backs on the town. Many were forced to seek shelter in the woods and brave the icy November nights to escape the approaching assault."

"It was a pitious sight," Lee wrote to his wife. "But they have brave hearts. What is to become of them God only knows. Pray he may have mercy on them."

The more fortunate refugees left in wagons and carriages piled high with food, blankets, and clothing. But many others—the poor, the elderly, mothers carrying one child on their hip and leading others by their hands—trudged through the freezing rain and mud with nothing but the clothes they wore. Rebel soldiers were so moved by the sight that they gave away what little food they had to keep the children from starving.

The civilians took refuge wherever they could—in abandoned cabins, barns and pigsties, makeshift shelters, and, if they were very lucky, in the homes of generous farmers and plantation owners who took some of them in. After the exodus had begun, the rebel soldiers were so overcome with pity that Lee ordered army wagons and ambulances to pick up as many of the civilians as possible and take them a few miles out of town.

During the course of that awful day, Mayor Slaughter asked Lee if the residents of Fredericksburg really had to fear the destruction of their homes.

"Yes," Lee replied, "they must fear the worst."

"But," Longstreet added, "let them hope for the best."

Fredericksburg was not destroyed that day. On the afternoon of November 22, Sumner sent a letter across the river promising that he would not shell the town so long as Confederate troops did not fire on his men from there. The Yankee cannon, while clearly visible from town, remained silent, and gradually people began coming back from whatever refuge they had been able to find.

Lee was pleased that the threatened destruction of Fredericksburg had not occurred, but he was also confused and uncertain about Burnside's intentions. Why did he not attack the town while he had such a strong numerical advantage, while he had so many more troops than Lee did? What was he waiting for?

Lee became even more puzzled later that afternoon when the Yankee troops began pulling back from the river. By dawn of the next day, they were almost all gone from view, leaving only a small covering force visible from Fredericksburg. Why did they move away from the river, Lee wondered. Was Burnside preparing to shift his massive army elsewhere and attack from another direction? Might he move his troops by water to Fortress Monroe and attempt another march to Richmond from there, the way McClellan had tried to do?

"I am as yet unable to discover what may be the plan of the enemy," he wrote to Stonewall Jackson on November 23. "He is certainly making no forward movement, though he may be preparing to do so. I am apprehensive that while keeping a force in our front, he may be transferring his troops to some other quarter." Jackson, meanwhile, was already beginning his march from Winchester to Fredericksburg.

Lee continued to wonder about the pullback of the Union troops. He read Northern newspapers, always a valuable source of intelligence, and studied reports from his scouts who rode fearlessly behind enemy lines to gather information. They reported considerable activity at the wharves at Aquia Creek as more supplies arrived by water for the Army of the Potomac. There was, however, no sign that the Union troops who had been pulled back from the banks of the Rappahannock were boarding ships to be transported somewhere else. It became increasingly clear to Lee that

Burnside must be staying in place, which meant that Fredericksburg, or somewhere else along the river not far from there, was still where he planned to cross.

By November 25, only two days after the Yankee pullback, Lee was convinced that he knew Burnside's intentions, as he wrote in a letter to Jefferson Davis.

> I think from the tone of the Northern papers it is intended that General Burnside shall advance from Fredericksburg to Richmond. All their movements which I have been able to discover look to a concentration at this point, and it appears to me that should General Burnside change his base of operations the effect produced in the United States would be almost equivalent to a defeat. I think therefore he will persevere in his present course.

Robert E. Lee may have felt sure of Burnside's plans, but Abraham Lincoln did not. The president was growing increasingly alarmed at the lack of progress by his new choice of commander. He knew that Bull Sumner's corps had reached Fredericksburg on November 17, and that the rest of the Army of the Potomac was in place along the Rappahannock by the twentieth. But there had been no forward movement since. What was Burnside waiting for? Lincoln complained privately to one of his generals "that his new Army commander seemed no faster than his old one."

On the evening of November 26, Lincoln wired Burnside to rather timidly request a meeting at Aquia Creek: "Could you, without inconvenience, meet me and pass an hour or two with me?" There were no witnesses to the conversation between Burnside and the president, but it is known that Burnside complained about the delayed arrival of the pontoons and that Lincoln proposed a new plan to defeat the rebels, which he presented to General-in-Chief Halleck in writing.

Lincoln suggested that Burnside should keep his main force at Falmouth while gathering, from other fronts, two additional units of some 25,000 men each to strike elsewhere. One force would be transported by boat to Port Royal, seventeen miles downriver from Fredericksburg. The other would be shipped to the north bank of the Pamunkey River, more than one hundred miles southeast of Fredericksburg. When both forces were in place, they would then converge at a point south of Fredericksburg, while Burnside's main army attacked the town. Lee would then have to retreat to avoid being cut off from Richmond.

The plan had merit, but both Burnside and Halleck promptly rejected it as being impracticable for that time of year. It would simply take too long to gather that many extra troops from elsewhere and get them into position before the full force of winter hit and stopped all military movement.

Halleck told the president that Burnside must attack Lee immediately, but Lincoln, despite longing for any movement on the part of any of his generals, told Burnside he was prepared to wait until he was ready. Of course, everyone assumed that Burnside *was* ready and that he had been ever since he had reached Falmouth six days earlier. If only the pontoons would arrive, they said. Then he would move.

Burnside returned to Falmouth the next day from his meeting with the president, walking alone through thick mud to reach his headquarters. For once, good news awaited him. While the pontoons had still not arrived, his wife had. She had made a surprise visit to help him celebrate Thanksgiving.

Thanksgiving Day—November 27, 1862—turned out to be the day the pontoons finally reached Falmouth. They were eight days late, and it had taken a superhuman effort on the part of Maj. Ira Spaulding and his 50th New York Engineers to get them there. After finally securing all the teamsters, horses, harnesses, and forage needed to move the two huge wagon trains out of Washington, Spaulding and his men became mired in the mud. The wagons, far heavier than any ordinary army wagon, sank axle-deep. The horses strained and the men sank to their knees as they pushed and pulled the wagons along by hand.

On their best days, they advanced no farther than five miles, leaving horses and men totally exhausted as they tried to sleep in the rain-soaked fields without adequate cover. Spaulding was so discouraged by their slow progress that he ordered a steamboat down from Washington to the mouth of Occoquan Creek, twenty-five miles north of Fredericksburg. When it arrived, he told his men to make rafts out of the pontoons and then had the steamboat tow them fifteen miles down the Potomac River to the supply depot at Aquia Creek. He also sent the horses, unencumbered by wagons, overland to the same destination.

The rafts reached the depot on the night of November 24, but the horses were nowhere in sight. Spaulding, determined not to be stymied by anything, requisitioned more horses from the quartermaster at Aquia Creek. By the time all the horses and equipment were in place, another day had passed, but Spaulding urged his men on and finally got to Falmouth in time for Thanksgiving.

Few people were pleased or grateful to see the pontoons, however, or had any reason to give thanks for their arrival. By then, "everybody concerned would have been much better off if the engineers and their boats had remained stuck in the mud all winter." The men had only to glance across the river at the entrenched Army of Northern Virginia waiting for them to appreciate the folly of using the pontoons by then.

Yet some were still eager to cross immediately, none more so than Bull Sumner. No sooner had the pontoons arrived than Old Bull rode up to Major Spaulding and Capt. Wesley Brainerd to ask "if we could throw a bridge across the river that night, to which we replied that we could throw two bridges across in three hours if he would give us the order to do so." Having taken so much effort to get the bridges there, the engineers were eager to use them, and the sooner the better.

Sumner hesitated, then told them that he would like to give them the order to bridge the river then and there, but could not for fear that it would conflict with Burnside's plans. Not that he knew what Burnside's plans were. Not even Burnside knew yet what he was going to do, but Old Bull had been too long a soldier to give such an order on his own. He told Spaulding and Brainerd how much he had wanted to ford the river ten days earlier, when he had reached Falmouth, but had been told not to do it. Then Sumner fell silent and rode away.

"We were ordered back to camp," Brainerd wrote, "and the 'golden opportunity' passed—a blunder for which we were in no way responsible, but for which we were destined to suffer." They would all suffer for not crossing the river as soon as it could be done, but Burnside issued no order that Thanksgiving Day. Nor did he plan to send his men across in the immediate future, or consider any other strategy but the one that had led him to Falmouth in the first place. He would spend "two more weeks looking down on the town from the left-bank heights, with something of the intentness and singularity of purpose which he had displayed, back in September at Antietam, looking down at the little triple-arched bridge that ever afterwards bore his name."

On Thanksgiving, most of the men of Burnside's army wrote about food or the lack of it in their diaries and letters home. Few, if any, mentioned the arrival of the bridges. They dwelled, instead, on what they had to eat. "We had a dinner of hard tack and salt pork," Capt. John Adams of the 19th Massachusetts wrote.

Sgt. Edward Wightman of the 9th New York decided to go into Falmouth to get a real dinner at a hotel as his way of celebrating Thanksgiving. "I began my search for a hotel," he wrote to his brother. "There was none. Then for a dining saloon. There was none." He finally found two bakeries set up in dirty shanties, turning out tiny loaves of bread and doughy biscuits that were snapped up instantly by hundreds of hungry Union troops.

Wightman finally managed to buy some flat, sour, heavy biscuits. "Now for the butter," he wrote. "There was none in town. No cheese. Nothing but a few small red apples which I purchased at three cents each." He bought some root beer to complete his Thanksgiving dinner of biscuits and apples. "Thousands of people standing round me would have paid triple the amount for the treat; for a good dinner was a thing not to be sneezed at."

High-ranking officers, as usual, dined somewhat better. Col. Charles Wainwright, a thirty-five-year-old artillery officer in Franklin's wing, described his dinner in detail. While noting that the wine list was, unfortunately, limited to champagne, he was otherwise quite impressed with his holiday meal.

> The canvasback ducks were the piece de resistance, and they were equal to what could be got anywhere, cooked to a turn and served up hot. The soup, too, was quite a success; and boiled mutton is always our cook's strong point. I was fortunate enough to have in my private stores a bottle of sherry for the soup, and currant jelly for the duck.

The meal ended with mince and pumpkin pies, fruit cake, whiskey, and real coffee.

For most others, however, life in the Union camp was grim. The men resigned themselves to a long, hard winter and tried to make themselves as comfortable as circumstances allowed. "We settled down in earnest," Fr. William Corby, a chaplain in the Irish Brigade wrote, "built log huts, roofed them with tents, and built chimneys of sticks and mud—for there was plenty of mud." They made huts from felled trees stacked about four feet high, with their canvas tents stretched from wall to wall. The lucky ones managed to find lumber for floors, but most lived in the mud with only rubber blankets to keep out the cold and water, for it was still raining heavily.

Sgt. John Carter of the 1st Massachusetts described his life in a letter home.

> We have been here two nights and last night I was a perfectly soaked man. Here's the way of it. Yesterday our tent blew down in a squall of rain and wind. Blankets and all got wet through and our tent ground filled with water; we did the best possible, and all day long it poured, so that our personal bodies were wet when we retired to a wet bed. I spread my rubber blanket, and then put my woolen on that (I could wring the water from it in sufficient quantities to

fill a water pail), and until midnight I lay awake suffering from the cold, our tents filling every minute with puddles.

Sergeant Carter's brother, Robert, a private in the 22nd Massachusetts, also complained to his family about the cold, wet conditions.

> You have no idea what it is, this winter campaign, with nothing for shelter but thin, open cotton tents, in these extremely rainy, frosty, cold nights. I think it is almost suicidal keeping men out this winter, in water and rain, mud and snow. I have got the rheumatism and a cold which has hung over me for six weeks, owing to getting wet, sleeping in water and snow with wet feet. A great many of the boys have it.

And the full force of winter had not yet even struck.

Each day was a struggle to stay warm and dry and find enough food to survive on. A soldier in the Iron Brigade wrote about his typical menu. "Breakfast—Coffee, Hardtack, Pork. Dinner—Hardtack, Pork, Coffee. Supper—Pork, Coffee, Hardtack."

Some men were not so fortunate as to be able to count on being fed anything regularly. Robert Carter wrote:

> I thought we should all starve. We were hungry enough to eat a nail. I picked up pieces of cracker in the mud under the mules' feet; some picked up bones, and ate the marrow; this with cold frosty weather, and diarrhoea from eating raw pork, took us down a peg. Yesterday we got three days' rations of cracker and pork, and the boys set up a howl; I thought there would be a mutiny.

The Union troops also did not think much of the only town they could get to for diversions—Falmouth. As Sergeant Wightman of the 9th New York learned when he went there for Thanksgiving dinner, it had little to offer the men. Colonel Wainwright, the artillery officer who dined so well on Thanksgiving, wrote, "The village of Falmouth is a wretched

"War Views—Army of the Potomac—The way they cook dinner in camp." One side of a stereograph showing a group of soldiers, including an African American mess attendant with coffee kettle. (*Library of Congress*)

straggling old place, very dirty and now deserted almost entirely." There had been prosperous mills there at one time, and a broad dam once used to supply power to the mills, but now it was like a ghost town, save for the many Union soldiers who wandered through it, looking for any chance to escape their dreary camps.

Charley Goddard of the 1st Minnesota volunteered to fight the year before when the regiment was formed, even though he was only fifteen. He managed to pass for eighteen, and by the end of 1862, he was a hardened veteran. He called Falmouth "one of the most Godforsaken places I ever saw in my life. The inhabitants that are around in the street standing or leaning up against the corners look as if they had not a friend in the world. The greater part of them do not know how to read and write."

Those men who were still stationed close to the river got along better with the rebel soldiers on the other side than they did with the people of Falmouth. The pickets of both armies patrolling the riverbanks were so close to each other that it was easy to carry on a lively conversation to break the monotony of guard duty. They could just as easily have shot at one another, but they were more interested in talking than fighting.

"Here was a good opportunity for target practice between the pickets," said Pvt. Bill McCarter of the Irish Brigade. "But not a trigger was pulled on either side." When not yelling back and forth, the men of both sides sometimes simply watched their enemies going about their daily business. McCarter wrote:

> I frequently stood near the bank of the river and watched whole companies of Rebel infantry drilling. I witnessed hundreds of Rebel cavalrymen leading and riding their horses down the streets of the city. The cavalrymen brought their horses into the Rappahannock to drink, not 200 yards from my post. I watched the Rebs playing ball, running races and jumping. They always presented not only a gay and happy appearance but also a most defiant one.

Charles Coffin, a thirty-nine-year-old reporter for the *Boston Journal* wrote an article about how well Union and rebel pickets got along. "There is constant badinage. The Rebel picket asks the Yankee when he is going to Richmond. The Yankee asks the rebel if he don't want a pair of shoes." Coffin's only complaint was that the men on both sides used a lot of profanity in their conversations. Those on picket duty were enjoying themselves. They had something to take their minds off the constant cold and rain. For the rest of the Union troops, life was gloomy.

Thomas Meagher, the flamboyant leader of the Irish Brigade, vowed to give his men something to look forward to and to remember in the years to come. A group of wealthy businessmen in New York had announced their intention to present new battle flags to the Brigade, to replace the old ones that had been tattered and torn by enemy shot and shell in previous battles. Meagher never did anything on a small scale. He sent an officer to Washington with enough money to bring back a huge supply of whiskey and champagne and put his men to work building a large hall and decorating it with evergreens.

The Irish Brigade was going to have a grand party—a lavish banquet at which the new colors would be formally presented. Meagher set the date for December 13. His adjutant, Bill McCarter, who had saved Meagher from falling into a campfire while drunk, wrote, "The men anticipated spending what many of them termed 'a gay and happy winter in Dixie's land.' But alas, poor fellows, hundreds never left the place. Such is the fate of war." The fate of war would strike them on the very day Meagher had planned for his gala celebration.

Days passed, and still the pontoon bridges remained in camp and Burnside's army did not move. The weather turned more forbidding; squalls of snow mixed with freezing rain. The mud froze over and still the army did not move. Food, blankets, and tents became even scarcer; the men grumbled because they had not been paid for months, and yet the army did not move.

Those who had been there the longest—the ones who came with Bull Sumner on November 17—remembered how few rebel soldiers they had seen across the river back then. Now there were thousands of them. Everywhere a man looked on the hills beyond Fredericksburg, he saw the Southerners' positions getting stronger every day. And still Burnside's army did not move. Sgt. Maj. Walter Carter of the 22nd Massachusetts expressed his concern in a letter to his family: "I am at a loss to understand why we are here at a standstill, idle, and allowing the Rebs to fortify and gain strength."

No one knew what Burnside was planning to do—least of all, it seemed, the general himself. His officers talked among themselves about what might happen—when the army might move, and most important, *where* it might move. No one believed Burnside would dare to carry out his original plan to span the river at Fredericksburg and drive south from there. That was a fine idea when there were only a few rebels on the other side of the river. But surely not now when Lee's whole Army of Northern Virginia had gathered to face them. That would be tantamount to suicide, some said, and could only lead to a senseless slaughter. Others remembered Antietam and shook their heads at the thought of Burnside's bridge and his fixation on crossing only at that point.

Burnside looked terrible. He was utterly exhausted under the strain of still attending personally to every detail of the routine operations of his army. He slept little and his face and body appeared to sag under the awesome weight of his responsibility, and the decision he had to make about where to attack Lee. He was not optimistic about it, as he revealed in a message to the War Department in early December. "I deem it my duty to say that I cannot make the promise of probable success with the faith that I did when I supposed that all the parts of the plan would be carried out."

Soon the stress of so much waiting and wondering, along with the meager diet and awful weather, took its toll on Burnside's men. They started to lose confidence not only in their leaders but in themselves and the cause for which they had already endured so much. Capt. Oliver Wendell Holmes Jr. of the 20th Massachusetts was one among many to express his despair in letters home.

> I've pretty much made up my mind that the South have achieved their independence and I am almost ready to hope spring will see an end. The Army is tired with its hard and its terrible experience and still more with its mismanagement and I think before long the majority will say that we are vainly working to effect what never happens— the subjugation (for that is it) of a great civilized nation. We shan't do it—at least the army can't.

Lt. Col. William Draper of the 36th Massachusetts expressed the same pessimism in a letter to his wife. "The men in the old regiments here are not very sanguine of success. The general opinion is that if we don't take Richmond by spring the Southern Confederacy is a fixed fact."

Defeatism was in the air and it spread through all the ranks. "I don't think we can ever conquer them," Pvt. Miles Peabody of the 5th New Hampshire wrote, "and if this war is carried on to the end of three years we shall have to acknowledge their independence after all."

Along with a general air of pessimism was the gnawing fear of attempting to take the rebel positions so clearly visible in the hills overlooking Fredericksburg by a frontal assault. The men were too dispirited. They knew it could not be done, at least not by them. Capt. Francis Adams Donaldson of the 118th Pennsylvania wrote of it to his brother. "I am no prophet, nor the son of a prophet, but I can predict certain defeat should Burnside attempt to attack Lee in his present entrenched position."

A soldier from Pennsylvania wrote, "It looks to me as if we were going over there to be murdered." "I am sure we cannot take those hills," another Union soldier wrote, "and I think those in high authority if they run us up against such works will be guilty of the blood of every man slain."

Father Corby of the Irish Brigade never forgot his conversation with a frightened young soldier.

"Father, they are going to lead us over in front of those guns which we have seen them placing, unhindered, for the past three weeks."

"Do not trouble yourself," Father Corby told the boy, "your generals know better than that."

Robert E. Lee was also certain that Burnside would not attack him at Fredericksburg; not now that it was so strongly held. The only sensible way for Burnside to proceed, as far as Lee was concerned, was to try to outflank Fredericksburg by crossing the Rappahannock at some point above or below town. But where? "General Burnside's whole army is apparently opposite Fredericksburg," he wrote to his daughter Mary, three days before Thanksgiving. "What his intentions are he has not yet disclosed."

Lee thought the Yankees would most likely try to cross below town. If Burnside had wanted to cross upriver, he could have done so easily on his march down from Warrenton, which was made along the river. Lee focused instead on Port Royal, the little town seventeen miles downriver that President Lincoln had suggested to Burnside as a strategic point. It was southeast of Fredericksburg, which meant it was closer to Richmond. If Burnside succeeded in moving his army across at Port Royal, he could get between Fredericksburg and Richmond and force Lee to retreat rapidly from his present positions to avoid being cut off.

When Stonewall Jackson arrived in Fredericksburg on the evening of November 29 in the middle of a snowstorm, Lee gave him dinner and told him to cover a fourteen-mile front from Longstreet's right flank, which extended three miles downriver from Fredericksburg, all the way to Port Royal. Jackson's corps was spread thin over a very wide front, but his troops could be quickly concentrated once Burnside's intended point of crossing became known.

Jackson's men, many of whom had marched 175 miles in the previous twelve days, were in high spirits and confident of victory even though few of them had uniforms and many had no shoes. While his troops were optimistic of success, Jackson was unhappy with the defensive position Lee had given him.

"I am opposed to fighting here," he told his brother-in-law, Gen. D. H. Hill, "we will whip the enemy, but gain no fruits of victory." He wanted to set up a defensive line farther south along the banks of the North Anna River, where he could catch the Union army out in the open and try to annihilate them when they were far from their base of supplies. But that idea had been overruled days before, so Jackson had no choice but to make the best of his long line of defense behind the Rappahannock.

Longstreet's portion of the Confederate line was along a series of hills, some forty to fifty feet high, beyond the western edge of Fredericksburg. The hills were covered by thick growths of trees and rose abruptly from a flat, open field marked by a thirty-foot-wide canal. At the base of Marye's Hill, the most formidable rise, was Telegraph Road, which was a sunken road running five hundred yards with a stone wall along one side that bordered the field. Longstreet had placed riflemen there, resting the muzzles of their weapons atop the stone wall. Their field of fire covered the half mile of open space any Yankees foolish enough to attack would have to cross.

"The road was filled with rebel troops perfectly protected," wrote Union general Herman Haupt, "they could stoop to load, then rise and fire without exposure. An assaulting column had no chance." Brig. Gen. Thomas Cobb, commanding a brigade of Georgians along the sunken road put the matter more bluntly: "Well! If they wait for me to fall back, they will wait a long time."

Lee also ordered the town of Fredericksburg itself to be occupied. Maj. Gen. Lafayette McLaws sent Brig. Gen. William Barksdale's Mississippi brigade of 1,600 men to construct a defensive line in the houses along the river. They dug rifle pits with zigzag trenches connecting them and chopped holes in the cellar walls so they could move from one house to the next without being seen. They did all their work at night and dug so quietly that the Union troops across the river had no idea they were even there. If Yankee engineers tried to put their bridges across at that point, they would come under very heavy and well-directed fire.

One evening after Barksdale's men had completed their defenses, they watched several Union bands gather on the Yankee side of the river, where they began playing patriotic songs. They rang out "Hail Columbia" and, of course, "The Star Spangled Banner." The rebel troops listened to the music, which was, as General McLaws put it, "once so dear to us all," but made no response. Then the Union bands blared out "Dixie" and men on both sides suddenly started laughing and cheering boisterously. The troops had a high old time, but the playing of the Southern song aroused General McLaws's suspicions that the Yankees were up to no good. He took it as an indication that they were going to attack at Fredericksburg, and so he ordered Barksdale's men to dig even more rifle pits along the riverbank.

Robert E. Lee heard the music too. With him was Maj. James H. Lacy, whose home, Chatham, had become Bull Sumner's headquarters. Through his field glasses Lacy saw his broad front porch and once pristine front lawn filled with Yankees. The sight of his once lovely home and the sound of the hated Yankee music filled Lacy with anger, and he asked Lee for permission to fire their long-range cannon and destroy Chatham, to blow it to dust.

Lee smiled sadly and shook his head as he continued staring across the river at the large plantation. The house had special meaning for him and he could not bear the thought of seeing it destroyed. One of the happiest times of his life had been spent there.

"Major," he said to Lacy, "I never permit the unnecessary effusion of blood. War is terrible enough at best to a Christian man; I hope yet to see you and your dear family happy in your old home. Do you know I love Chatham better than any place in the world except Arlington! I courted and won my dear wife under the shade of those trees."

Johann Heros von Borcke was a giant of a man, 240 pounds and well over six feet tall. A Prussian soldier-of-fortune, who had sailed on a rebel blockade runner so he could fight for the Confederates, he was serving on Jeb Stuart's staff. As flamboyant, dashing, and colorful as Stuart himself, von Borcke quickly became a favorite of the cavalry leader. Stuart had chosen von Borcke to present Stonewall Jackson with his elegant new coat because he knew the German could charm Jackson into accepting it. Constance Cary, a Richmond belle, described him as follows:

> A giant in stature, blond and virile, with great curling golden mustaches, and the expression in his wide-open eyes of a singularly modest boy. It was said that he rode on

the biggest horse and wielded the heaviest sabre in the army. Von Borcke, whom the troopers styled "Major Bandbox," won brilliant renown in the service, and was equally popular in society in Richmond. To dance with him in the swift-circling, never-reversing German fashion was a breathless experience.

Von Borcke had an amazing array of talents, which he displayed in the theatrical productions that Stuart loved to put on. He could do everything from painting scenery to singing and dancing. He once played a woman wearing a greatly enlarged white ball gown and was "sweetly ornamented with a half-a-bushel of artificial flowers in [his] hair."

Johann Heros von Borcke was conspicuous on the battlefield because of his great height and weight and the unusually large sword he carried. (*Library of Congress*)

But what von Borcke loved to do more than anything else, even more than consuming gargantuan meals washed down with great quantities of whiskey, champagne, and fine wines, was to fight. On December 4, he found himself caught in the middle of a heated battle between two of Lee's divisions when General McLaws's men attacked the troops of Gen. John Bell Hood—with snowballs.

Hood's men counterattacked in a formal battle line with colors flying and officers leading them on. The battle raged back and forth, with spirited charges and countercharges, and kept getting close to Jeb Stuart's headquarters tent. Stuart and von Borcke raised a white flag and yelled that they were neutral, but to no avail. Soon they were caught up in the excitement and found themselves standing on boxes, cheering both sides on and getting hit with snowballs themselves.

Suddenly, soldiers from another division reinforced McLaws's men, and Hood's troops fell back, leaving a trail of wounded on both sides. One man had a broken leg and another lost an eye, but such were the fortunes of war, and the men thought it had been a fine adventure that they talked and laughed about for days.

Von Borcke saw the snowball fight as "ample proof of the excellent spirits of our troops who, in the wet, wintry weather, many of them without blankets, and some without shoes, regardless of their exposure and of the scarcity of provisions, still maintained their good-humour, and were ever ready for any sort of sport or fun that offered itself to them."

The men of the Army of Northern Virginia were more than ready for those Yankees across the river. They may not have had shoes or enough food to eat, but they were eager to fight and confident of success. They believed in themselves, in their generals, and in the strong positions they held. Let the Yankees come.

EIGHT

Bring the Guns to Bear

At five o'clock on the morning of December 9, General Burnside wrote the order. He had finally decided to move. As usual, he had been awake much of the night, considering when and where to attack Lee, and attending to the everyday operations of his army. His initial order did not give his commanders much information, only to prepare to cross the Rappahannock River soon. They were advised to bring their divisions to a state of readiness and to issue each man sixty rounds of ammunition and cooked rations sufficient for three days. They were also told to report to Burnside's headquarters, at Phillips House, at noon on December 10.

Although Burnside released no more details of his attack plan during the course of the day, rumors began to circulate, which gained credence with repetition, that he was planning to attack Lee at the Confederates' strongest point—the hills behind Fredericksburg. The rumors and the inevitable opposition were particularly virulent in that wing of the army commanded by Bull Sumner. After all, it would be Sumner's troops, the gossip held, who would spearhead the assault. Worried whispers spread through the ranks. Would the men fail to obey orders when they learned of the attack on those hills, which could only lead to sense-less slaughter?

When news of the dissension reached Burnside, he summoned the generals and colonels of the army's Right Grand Division to Sumner's headquarters at Lacy House that evening. He described enough of his plan to show them that the rumors were true. Sumner's wing would attack Lee's forces at their most heavily defended point. Burnside explained that he was ordering the assault there precisely because it *was* the rebels' strong point. Burnside had reasoned that Lee would not be expecting an attack there and so would be taken by surprise. The officers present offered no protest or criticism. They seemed unwilling to express publicly any reservations they held.

Brig. Gen. William French, unlike most of the other officers, was highly enthusiastic about the plan. He proclaimed that they could win the battle in forty-eight hours; so certain was he that he called for three cheers for General Burnside. They were obediently voiced by most of the men.

After the meeting adjourned, Burnside strolled down the wide center hall of Lacy House and stopped to talk to Col. Rush Hawkins, a brigade commander in Burnside's old 9th Corps, and Col. J. H. Taylor, who served on Sumner's staff.

"What do you think of [my plan]?" Burnside asked Hawkins.

Without hesitation, Hawkins answered, "If you make the attack as contemplated, it will be the greatest slaughter of the war. There isn't infantry enough in our whole army to carry those heights if they are well defended."

Burnside seemed surprised. He addressed Colonel Taylor.

"Colonel, what do you say about it?"

"I quite agree with Colonel Hawkins," Taylor said. "The carry-ing out of your plan will be murder, not warfare."

Hawkins later wrote that Burnside was irritated by their candid responses. Burnside, Hawkins said, "made a remark about my readiness to throw cold water upon his 'plans.' He repeated the assertion of [General] French about victory within forty-eight hours, and passed on."

At eleven thirty that night, Burnside telegraphed the War Department to inform General Halleck of the forthcoming attack.

> All the orders have been issued to the several commanders of the grand divisions and heads of departments for an attempt to cross the river on Thursday [December 11]. I think now that the enemy will be more surprised by a crossing immediately in our front than in any other part of the river. The commanders of grand divisions coincide with me in this opinion, and I have accordingly ordered the movement.

Burnside closed the telegraph message with an offer to send Halleck the details of the plan, and he requested Halleck's approval.

> If the General-in-Chief desires it, I will send a minute statement by telegraph in cipher tomorrow morning. The movement is so important that I feel anxious to be fortified by his approval. Please answer.

Halleck replied the next day but did not address the plan directly, nor did he give any indication of approval or disapproval. His only concern was the security of the telegraph line for future communications: "I beg of you not to telegraph details of your plans, nor the times of your intended movements," he wrote. "No secret can be kept which passes through so many hands."

Halleck was correct in suspecting that the telegraph line between the War Department and Aquia Creek was not secure, but he apparently did not know the source of the leaks. Lee had a spy working in the Union army's telegraph office at the Aquia Creek depot, who passed on to Lee every message of military importance. In addition, on the night of December 10, a woman living on the northern side of the Rappahannock would walk down to the water's edge and wave to get the attention of the rebel pickets on the far shore. She would inform them that the Yankee troops had been issued a large supply of cooked rations, always a prelude to an impending attack.

Burnside held his official meeting at Phillips House with his grand division commanders and their subordinates at noon on December 10 as planned to confirm what they already knew: The next day they would cross the river and attack the Army of Northern Virginia. Sumner would cross at Fredericksburg while Franklin launched his attack near the mouth of Deep Run Creek, a mile below the town. Hooker's wing would be kept in reserve. Burnside believed that Longstreet's corps and Jackson's corps were more widely separated than they actually were. He expected that Franklin's crossing at Deep Run would put his men between the two bodies of Southern troops, thus forming a wedge and cutting them off from each other.

To keep Jackson's men concentrated some distance from Fredericksburg, Burnside ordered a unit dispatched to Skinkers Neck, twelve miles south of town. Their mission was to feign a crossing at that point. They would chop down trees, making no effort to conceal the sound from the rebels, and lay a corduroy road of the felled trees to the river's edge. The Confederates would assume that these actions were the preliminary stage to building a bridge and thus would be forced to keep troops there to deal with the Union threat.

After describing his plans, Burnside asked for comments. Sumner, as expected of a loyal subordinate, pledged to do everything in his power to carry out his part of the operation. He raised no objections and asked no questions. Franklin said that he foresaw no problem crossing his men at Deep Run. Once across, Franklin added, he expected to receive detailed plans on how to proceed. Burnside assured him that all the commanders would receive specific orders from him sometime that night.

The only one who raised an objection to Burnside's plan was Hooker, who had no active role to play; his troops would stand in reserve. That decision rankled an ambitious man like Hooker and may have fueled his opposition. Maj. Gen. William "Baldy" Smith, a corps commander in Franklin's wing, recalled that Hooker said that it was "preposterous to talk about our crossing the river in the face of Lee's army; that he would like to be in command of 50,000 men on the other side of the river and have an enemy make the attempt."

General Smith went on to note that "General Burnside closed the conference by stating that his mind was made up; that we must prepare our commands for the work before them; and that we should receive the proper orders in due time."

Due time turned out to be much later, long after each commander had expected to receive his orders for the following day. Burnside spent another sleepless night, and finally prepared the orders for Sumner at 4:20 in the morning, those for Hooker at 4:45, and the ones for Franklin at 5:15. Perhaps because of Burnside's exhaustion, his orders to his commanders were vague and imprecise, lacking the kind of detail that subordinate commanders—particularly cautious ones like Franklin—required. The orders failed to specify exactly what the generals were expected to do.

Almost every soldier from private to general spent an awful night of waiting, uncertainty, and dread. Colonel Hawkins, of Burnside's old 9th Corps, wrote to his mother:

> Tomorrow, if our present plans are carried out, the great battle of the war will commence. I have little hope of the plans succeeding. I do not think them good. There will be a great loss of life and nothing accomplished. I am sure we are to fight against all chances of success.

Clara Barton could not sleep. At two o'clock that morning she left her room at Lacy House and went outside to wander over the grounds. She stopped to gaze at the hundreds of campfires spreading eerie flickering light over the huts and tents the men had built for themselves. She wondered how many of those men she would have to nurse back to health over the next few days—and how many she would lose. It seemed as though she could remember no personal life that did not involve the screams of the wounded, of suffering and death.

She was forty years old but looked to be in her late twenties. Described by her biographer as "small, slender, and striking: only five feet tall, with silky brown hair parted in the middle and combed into a bun in the back of her head. She had a round face, a wide, expressive mouth, and exquisite dark brown eyes." Even in the early hours of morning she was dressed in her traditional battlefield uniform: a bonnet, a plain blouse, a dark skirt, and a red bow tied around her neck.

She had never married, by her own choice, and possessed a fiercely independent and forceful nature. Before the war she had been one of the few women employed by the federal government, working as a copyist in the US Patent Office, making handwritten reproductions of civil documents. She was so fast and accurate on the job that she earned $1,400 a year, an unusually high salary for a woman. By contrast, the average annual salary for a female schoolteacher was $250.

Barton paid a price, however, for her competence and her gender. The men at the Patent Office felt threatened and subjected her to various forms of harassment. They glared at her and shouted crude remarks, calling her a slut, spreading tales that she had given birth to illegitimate black children. Thanks to a supportive boss, she kept her job until 1856, when President Buchanan's new Democratic administration fired all Republican employees.

Tired and unhappy, she returned home to North Oxford, Massachusetts, unable to find work. She suffered a nervous breakdown and was preoccupied with thoughts of death. She was saved by Lincoln's election in 1860, which gave her the opportunity to return to the Patent Office, albeit at a greatly reduced salary. But at least it was employment, something to do every day, even if it was no longer satisfying or fulfilling.

When the war began, Clara Barton found her true calling—or at least as close to it as any woman was allowed to get in those times. She wanted to be a soldier, like her beloved father had been in the Revolutionary War. She worshipped him, and he had treated her like a son destined to follow in his martial footsteps. He liked to say that she was more like a boy than a girl, and he had taught her to shoot and to ride. She could drive a wagon team and use tools as well as any man. She had never played with dolls, never even had one, and certainly never wanted one.

Clara Barton brought here own medical supplies to Civil War battlefields and nursed wounded soldiers back to health. (*Library of Congress*)

"Where other little girls listened to fairy tales and Mother Goose wonders," Clara recalled, "I sat on my father's knee and asked him for 'more stories about the war' and how the soldiers lived. The patriot blood of my father was warm in my veins." Clara never got along with her mother, whom she felt neglected her, and who had a violent temper that she frequently displayed in quarrels with Clara's father. Their troubled marriage deeply disturbed the young Clara.

She grew up to be attractive, lively, and intelligent, and had several suitors, each of whom she turned away when he proposed marriage. Who, after all, could compare to her father? No one else stood a chance.

With the coming of war Clara saw the opportunity to emulate her father. "I don't know how long it has been since my ear has been free from the roll of a drum. It is the music I sleep by, and I love it." Now she would follow the drum. And she would do it her own way, not, as many women were doing, by joining the army nursing corps being organized by Dorothea Dix. Clara Barton was too independent for the authoritarian Miss Dix.

With the help of Senator Henry Wilson from Clara's home state of Massachusetts, she began her war effort by becoming a "one-woman relief agency, cooking food and buying stores out of her own salary and distributing them to the military hospitals and the hilltop encampments" around Washington. But her greater goal was to help wounded soldiers on the battlefield, a sentiment heightened when she learned of the hundreds who had died at Bull Run for lack of the most basic medical care.

By the time of the battle of Fredericksburg, Clara Barton had become known throughout the Union as a ministering angel. She brought food, blankets, medicines, and other supplies donated by the people of the North directly to the fields of battle, and set about nursing the wounded. She arrived in Fredericksburg on December 7 with a huge store of supplies for the Army of the Potomac. After settling in at Lacy House, she distributed them to the soldiers, undeterred by rain, mud, and snow, and waited, like everyone else, for the battle to begin.

In the early hours of December 10, after watching the campfires in the cold early morning hours, and wondering who would live and who would die, Clara returned to her room and wrote to her cousin Elvira.

> It is the night before a battle. The enemy, Fredericksburg, and its mighty entrenchments lie before us, the river between. At tomorrow's dawn our troops will essay to cross, and the guns of the enemy will sweep those frail bridges at every breath.
>
> The moon is shining, through the soft haze with brightness almost prophetic. For the last half hour I have stood alone in the awful stillness of its glimmering light gazing upon the strange sad scene around me striving to say, "Thy will, Oh God, be done."

At that same early hour, rebel pickets along the riverfront in town detected noise in the darkness from the Union side of the river. It sounded like large wagons and heavy equipment being brought down to the bank. To Brig. Gen. William Barksdale, that could only mean one thing: the Yankees were getting ready to put their pontoon bridges across the river. Barksdale ordered his Mississippians on full alert and sent word to his superior, General McLaws.

Barksdale's men continued to listen. They peered into the darkness but could see little, though the sounds seemed to be getting closer. The Union engineers, under the direction of Major Spaulding, were working as fast as they could before daybreak made them targets. Once light formed in the east, they could be cut down at will. They had no cover and no weapons; their hands were full with hammers, planks, and heavy beams. Their only hope was speed. Get it done fast or die.

Six bridges were under construction. The one Spaulding's men were building was the most dangerous because it would cross the water at the point where Barksdale's men were well dug in. The plan called for a second bridge to be built alongside it. A third bridge would span the river a mile downstream, where only a few defending Confederate troops waited on the far shore.

The other three bridges were being put across at Deep Run. The engineers there were working in twenty-four-degree weather and half-inch-thick ice, but at least no one was taking aim at them. There was some desultory fire at Deep Run when dazed rebel pickets awoke to find that the bridges were almost completed, but Union artillery scattered them. The bridges would be finished and ready for use by nine o'clock that morning, as would be the bridge at the lower end of town. The bridges in town would take a lot longer.

By six a.m., the sky was bright enough to see across the river, although thick morning fog shrouded the water itself. The fog magnified the sounds of hammering as the heavy planks were set in place. Barksdale and his Mississippians were certain that the work was coming steadily closer. He sent word to McLaws that it was time to sound the alarm: the Yankees were coming over the river. Two rebel cannon fired in quick succession, putting the Confederate soldiers up and down the line on alert.

Barksdale then ordered his men to fire into the fog, using sound rather than sight to guide their aim.

> Every time a sound was answered with a minié ball, silence followed. At last, as wintry dawn slowly dissipated the darkness and thinned the fog, the boys strained their eyes for a glimpse of the end of the closest pontoon. When

finally they could distinguish it from the liquid gray, they calculated the distance as eighty feet from the west bank where they were hiding.

It was easy for the rebel marksmen now, and they hit Spaulding's engineers one after another. Some of the men toppled into the freezing water. Clara Barton, watching from the second-story verandah of Lacy House, saw bodies float downstream and disappear. After the first volley of shots, the engineers raced back to the Union shore. Gen. Darius Couch sent a long line of infantry to the river's edge to return the Southerners' fire and give cover to the engineers, but they could not pick off the Confederates hidden in the cellars and rifle pits. Couch's men fired often but hit very few of the Mississippians.

The engineers were ordered back out onto the open bridge, only to lose a few more men each time and make hurried retreats. Nine times they returned to the bridge, but every attempt failed. The bridge could not be completed as long as Barksdale's riflemen remained in place. It was nothing less than suicide to run onto the open bridge in full view of the Confederates, carrying tools, heavy beams, and stringers.

Some rebel bullets ranged far beyond the pontoon bridge, striking Union soldiers as far behind the lines as Lacy House. Clara Barton saw wounded men collapsing on the lawn beneath her window. Other shots whizzed past, striking the mansion's windows and walls.

Some high-ranking officers asked one another—though none asked Burnside—why the bridges at Deep Run, already finished, were not being used to cross troops. Franklin's wing of the army was still on the Union side. Why didn't Burnside order Franklin to cross? He knew there was little opposition on the rebel side; Franklin could cross easily, march on Fredericksburg and clear out the deadly Mississippians who were menacing Spaulding's engineers.

But Burnside did not want to advance across any bridge until all of his forces were ready. Yet the one opposite Barksdale's posi-

Alfred R. Waud's sketch showing Union engineers building a pontoon bridge while under fire from Confederate forces on the other side of the Rappahannock. (*Library of Congress*)

tion was not likely to be ready for a long time. The engineers could not survive out in the open that close to the rebel position. Something else would have to be done to get the Union forces across.

Shortly before ten o'clock, General Burnside sent an order to Brig. Gen. Henry Hunt, chief of artillery for the Army of the Potomac. Clara Barton, on the balcony at Lacy House, watched a courier hand Hunt the message while he waited on the lawn below where she stood. He promptly turned around and loudly repeated the news to a subordinate: "Bring the guns to bear and shell them out."

For the first time in the War Between the States, one side would deliberately launch an artillery barrage against a large town occupied by the enemy. General Hunt had spent more than a week diligently spotting his artillery on high ground along Stafford Heights overlooking Fredericksburg. He had more than 140 cannon in place, and when he ordered them to open fire, the immense roar and thick smoke enveloped the heights.

Each Union gun was ordered to fire fifty rounds. Clara Barton watched spellbound and saw "roofs collapse, walls and chimneys cave in, buildings blow apart, timbers and bricks explode through the air, and houses burst into flame, sending up geysers of black smoke against the sun."

Confederate general Pete Longstreet wrote:

> The town caught fire in several places, shells crashed and burst, and solid shot rained like hail. In the midst of successive crashes could be heard the shouts and yells of those engaged in the struggle, while smoke rose from the burning city, and the flames leaped about, making a scene which can never be effaced from the memory of those who saw it.

The firing continued for more than two hours. Tons of solid shot, shell, shrapnel, and cannister inundated the town. Columns of flame rose from the streets like pillars reaching for the sky. Most of the civilians had fled as soon as Barksdale's men started firing on the Yankee engineers earlier that morning, but some remained in their homes. Jane Beale was at home with her children, servants, and Beverly Lacy, the Presbyterian minister. They gathered in the kitchen to recite the Twenty-seventh Psalm. When the shelling came near, they ran for a closet by the wood cellar. Jane Beale remembered, "my youngest son, a boy of ten years, fell against me with the cry, 'Oh Ma, I'm struck,' and by the aid of the candle light as I looked down, I saw that his sweet face was as white as the wall."

The boy had suffered a glancing blow from a twelve-pound cannonball, which left him stunned but otherwise unhurt. The group huddled in the closet while shells fell all around the house. Nevertheless, the servants brought them blankets and prepared coffee, sausage, and biscuits for breakfast.

In another part of town, a little girl, Frances Bernard, ventured into the backyard of her house to see what all the excitement was about. The rest of her family, meanwhile, headed for the cellar. Years later she wrote:

> I beheld, it seemed to me, the most brilliant light that I had ever seen; as I looked, my aunt reached out her arms and pulled me, quivering with terror, into the cellar. A shell had exploded in the back of the garden, in reality at some distance, but to me it was as if it had been at my very feet.

The family cowered in the cellar as shells exploded overhead. Brick walls crashed down, stout timbers cracked and splintered, and smoke and dust threatened to choke them. When it appeared that the cellar would hold and not collapse on them, hunger began to overtake fear. One of Frances's aunts ordered Aunt Sally, the longtime family cook, to go upstairs—even though the firing continued—to brew coffee. Aunt Sally refused and was promptly called a coward. Aunt Sally replied that she was no more a coward than the rest of them, and that as far as she was concerned, General Lee himself would not go upstairs and make coffee in that tornado. The matter was dropped.

On impulse, Frances's mother raced upstairs to retrieve a portrait of her beloved husband, who had died before the war. She climbed onto the sofa, hoisted the painting off the wall, and stepped down. Frances remembered:

> [Mother] had just reached the door opposite when a shell came crashing through the wall, demolishing the sofa on which she had so recently stood, as well as many other articles of furniture. She reached the cellar, white and trembling, but with the portrait unhurt in her arms.

The target of the Union bombardment, General Barksdale's riflemen in the houses along the waterfront, stayed in their positions throughout the worst of it. Houses exploded and collapsed above them but the cellars, rifle pits, and trenches remained relatively untouched. Few lives were lost in the shelling.

Barksdale was troubled, however, by the number of houses in his sector that had been set afire. He sent a message to Longstreet, asking if he should send soldiers out to douse the flames.

"You have enough to do to watch the Yankees," Longstreet replied.

At the height of the shelling, a formally dressed and dignified elderly lady walked calmly down the street toward the general's headquarters. She appeared unperturbed by the destruction all around her. "She apparently found the projectiles very interesting," one officer reported, "stepping a little aside to inspect a great, gaping hole one had just gouged out in the sidewalk, then turning her head to note a fearful explosion in the air."

When she reached Barksdale's headquarters, she demanded to see the general. An aide suggested that she take shelter until the bombardment ended, and besides, the general could not possibly see her now. She said that no true Southern gentleman would refuse to receive a lady paying a call, no matter the circumstances, and she refused to budge. The aide reported the situation to the general. Barksdale cursed the interruption but went to the door to find her waiting for him calmly, as if standing in church on a quiet Sunday morning.

"For God's sake, Madam," Barksdale pleaded, "go and seek some place of safety; I'll send a member of my staff to help you find one."

"General Barksdale," the woman replied, with an indulgent smile, "my cow has just been killed in my stable by a shell. She is very fat, and I don't want the Yankees to get her. If you will send someone to butcher her, you are welcome to the meat."

Barksdale thanked her for the offer but did not mention that his soldiers had no time to deal with her cow.

A courier arrived from General Lee, asking about the well-being of Barksdale's men.

"Tell General Lee," Barksdale answered, "that if he wants a bridge of dead Yankees, I can furnish him with one."

Atop Telegraph Hill, Lee had been watching the bombardment with mounting anger. "Those people," he said, meaning the Yankees, "delight to destroy the weak and those who can make no defense; it just suits them!"

The bombardment stopped abruptly at one o'clock, leaving a startling silence to settle over Fredericksburg. The Union engineers sauntered out onto the bridges, confident that the Confederate riflemen who had menaced them before were now dead or driven from their hiding places along the river. But that was not the case, and several engineers were shot, sending the rest scurrying for cover. This time no persuasion, threat, or order could make them return to finish the bridge. If the Union troops were ever to cross the Rappahannock River, they would have to do so some other way.

Gen. Henry Hunt, whose artillery bombardment had failed to rout the entrenched Confederates, decided that the only way to get them out was to send infantry in a house-to-house search. Hunt mentioned this to Col. Norman Hall, a brigade commander in Sumner's wing. Acting on Hunt's idea, Hall planned to send some of his men across the river by having the engineers row their pontoons over as if they were assault boats.

The 7th Michigan volunteered to spearhead the attack, supported by the 19th and 20th Massachusetts regiments. While Union sharpshooters along the riverbank kept up a steady covering fire, Hunt's artillery opened up again on the waterfront. The men of the 7th Michigan climbed into their boats, but the engineers fled at the first sign of enemy fire. The infantry would have to row themselves over, even though they had no experience in handling small boats.

As the boats were being pushed away from shore, Robert Henry Hendershot, a twelve-year-old drummer boy, jumped aboard.

"Get out," an officer yelled. "You can't go."

"I want to go," the boy said.

"No, you will get shot. Out with you."

Hendershot, an obedient soldier, climbed out of the boat, but he remained in the freezing water to help shove the pontoons away from shore. Although he had been ordered out of the boat, no one had said anything about hanging on to it. When the boat reached the rebel shore, he hauled himself and his drum up onto the river-bank. A piece of shrapnel from a Union shell tore through the fabric of the drum. He quickly threw it away, grabbed the musket of a dead Union soldier who had fallen nearby, and joined the fight.

The 7th Michigan attacked Barksdale's Mississippians in a vicious firefight while the 19th and 20th Massachusetts regiments rowed across to join them. The 19th came ashore and assembled at the first street parallel to the river, bypassing some enemy troops who then opened fire on them from behind. One company lost ten men out of thirty in their first five minutes ashore. The regiment fell back to the river and began to fight from house to house. Barksdale's men held their positions tenaciously, fighting for every cellar, every pile of bricks, every street.

Capt. John Adams led his men through one yard and stopped at the gate, hesitant to cross the wide street in front of them. The temporary regimental commander, Capt. H. G. O. Weymouth, demanded to know why Adams had halted the advance.

"Can't you go forward, Adams?"

"It is mighty hot, Captain."

Weymouth looked out through the gate and thought the situation appeared not all that bad.

"I guess you can proceed," he told Adams. He opened the gate and started through, only to be met by a terrific hail of fire.

"It is quite warm," Weymouth agreed. "Go up through the house."

Adams directed his men through the rear door of the wrecked house, which backed up to the river, and up a flight of steps to the front door. Pvt. Gilman Nichols was in the lead. "He found the door locked," Adams wrote later, "and burst it open with the butt of his musket. The moment it opened he fell dead, shot from a house on the other side of the street."

The acting regimental commander of the 20th Massachusetts, Captain Macy, led his men a short distance from the shoreline up a street until they were confronted by heavy fire. He calmly issued an order to his second-in-command, Capt. Henry Abbott.

"Mr. Abbott, you will take the first platoon forward."

Abbott drew his sword and turned to his men.

"First platoon. Forward, march!"

They moved smartly up the street. At the first intersection they were caught in a deadly crossfire. In no more than a few seconds, a third of Abbott's platoon had been hit, and the rest ran away. Abbott, seemingly undisturbed, walked back to his company.

"Second platoon. Forward!" he ordered, and he led them back to the same intersection.

An observer later remarked, "The end was distant only a few seconds, but if you had seen [Abbott] with his indifferent carriage, and sword swinging from his fingers like a cane, you would never have suspected that he was doing more than conducting a company drill on the camp parade ground."

Abbott survived another round of rebel bullets at the same intersection. He rallied the survivors of his company and sent them right and left to outflank the rebels. His outfit, and other Union troops, slowly began to push the Confederates back away from the waterfront.

The battle raged all that afternoon—a desperate, bloody affair, a footnote in the history of the war but a defining moment in the lives of those who were there. It took until four thirty to push the rebels one block back from the water's edge. General McLaws decided it was time to order Barksdale to retreat—and to evacuate the town. While the fighting was taking place, the Union engineers had completed work on the bridge, opening the way for more Union troops to join the fight for Fredericksburg. If Barksdale waited much longer to leave, his men would be surrounded.

But Barksdale was not yet ready to give up the fight. He refused to withdraw, preferring to kill as many Yankees as possible. If left to his own devices, he would likely have chosen to fight to the last man rather than retreat in the face of the enemy, but McLaws gave

him no choice. He sent another order to fall back, and this time Barksdale reluctantly obeyed rather than risk a court-martial. Barksdale sent men through the rubble and wrecked houses to make sure everyone got the word to withdraw, and by seven o'clock that night, most of his men had evacuated the area.

Everyone, that is, except for one unit. Barksdale had ordered the 21st Mississippi to cover the withdrawal by serving as rear guard. The unit moved slowly, forcing the Union troops to remain under cover until the rest of the Confederate troops reached safety. At the rear of the 21st Mississippi was a unit commanded by Lt. Lane Brandon, who learned from captured Union soldiers that the commander of the company pursuing him was a former friend and classmate from Harvard Law School—Captain Abbott.

"That was enough for Brandon," wrote one of Lee's biographers, "Cost what it might, he would whip Abbott then and there! Brandon halted his rearguard, turned about, attacked the Twentieth Massachusetts and momentarily pressed it back."

Brandon was ready to fight to the water's edge if need be rather than be beaten by an old friend-turned-enemy.

Union soldiers cross the Rappahannock River on December 11, 1862 to occupy Fredericksburg. Confederate forces fell back to the heights west of the city during the Union's massed artillery bombardment of the city which caused extensive fires and damage. (*Alfred R. Waud, Library of Congress*)

Barksdale saw the incident and ordered Brandon to stop the fight and withdraw. Brandon refused to fall back, so determined was he to outdo his classmate. The only way Barksdale could stop the headstrong lieutenant was to order his arrest.

The battle ended at nightfall, but to Burnside's disappointment, the bulk of the Union army was still on the north side of the Rappahannock. That was not what he had intended. The army was supposed to have crossed in the morning, attacked Lee's men in the hills, and been on their way to Richmond by then. But the valiant stand by Barksdale's 1,600 Mississippians along the riverbank had ruined Burnside's plan.

Jane Beale and her family and servants survived the bombardment. After it was over, her brother John knocked on the cellar door; he urged them to leave town. Then the Union guns opened fire again in support of the troops rowing the pontoons across the river. Jane wrote that the explosions "echoed in our ears, the shrieking of those shells, like a host of angry fiends rushing through the air, the crashing of the balls through the roof and upper stories of the house, I shall never forget to the day of my death."

The family huddled in the cellar until four thirty that afternoon when John returned to tell them that the Yankees were on the Fredericksburg side of the river. The Beales would have to leave immediately. John had secured an army ambulance for Jane and the children, but there was no room for the servants. The servants assured Jane that they were not afraid. And if it became too dangerous to stay, they would ford the river to the Yankee side, where they expected to find their freedom.

As the family passed through the wreckage of their house and yard, rebel soldiers hurried them along, shouting warnings that the enemy was only two blocks away. Their ambulance raced through the streets, occasionally struck by bullets, past crowds of refugees trying to get out of town on foot—whole families dragging children and possessions behind them.

The Beales were among the fortunate few who found a warm, safe place to sleep. Friends on a farm outside of town took them in. Seated in a comfortable chair by the fireplace at the end of that horrible day, Jane Beale wrote in her diary that she "truly felt that praise for our deliverance was and ought to be the burthen of our song that night."

Frances Bernard, whose mother had saved her husband's portrait, left the cellar with her family when the bombardment stopped.

> What a scene met our eyes. Our pretty garden was strewn with cannon balls and pieces of broken shells, limbs knocked off the trees and the grape arbor a perfect wreck. The house had been damaged considerably, several large holes torn through it, both in front and back.

As the Bernards gaped at their house, a Confederate officer they knew rushed up to tell them to leave at once. He passed on the rumor that General Lee might shell the town rather than see it fall into Yankee hands. The family grabbed what they could carry and fled on foot as the Union shelling resumed. They stumbled across fields and hiked over roads that had been torn up by the bombardment and turned to thick mud by marching soldiers and heavy wagons. They walked for two miles to the home of friends, already overflowing with other evacuees from Fredericksburg. But they were taken in and offered care and solace. Frances remembered:

> And so great was our relief to feel that we had escaped from the horrors of that day, that such small matters as having to sleep in the room with a dozen people, having no milk and no coffee, our principal diet consisting of corn bread, bacon, and sorghum, seemed only slight troubles.

Clara Barton, unlike the town's refugees, was heading into Fredericksburg. After watching the battle unfold across the river from the second-story verandah of Lacy House, Clara rushed downstairs as soon as the first wounded Union soldiers were brought back. A dressing station was hurriedly being set up while the battle was still raging for control of the streets. A courier raced in with a message from Dr. J. Cutter, a surgeon and old friend of Clara's who had established an aid station in town.

"Come to me," Cutter said. "Your place is here."

Clara walked down to the water's edge and crossed the swaying pontoon bridge on foot, "the water hissing with shot on either side," as she later described it. She was still under enemy fire when she reached the far side. A Union officer chivalrously offered his hand to help her climb over the debris. As he did so, a shell fragment ripped through her skirt. A moment later, a cannonball whizzed overhead, killing a Union soldier riding by on horseback.

Clara thanked the officer who had assisted her and made her way through the burning city streets to find Dr. Cutter's aid station. She worked throughout the day as more and more wounded soldiers were brought in. "Oh what a day's work was that," she wrote later, but it was what she thrived on. When the officer who had so kindly helped her at the end of the bridge was brought to the aid station, she was greatly saddened. It was too late to help him; he was already dead.

By nightfall, Barksdale's Mississippians were gone and Union soldiers occupied Fredericksburg. At his headquarters at Phillips House, General Burnside changed his plan of operations. He never revealed why, but he revised his orders to General Franklin and to General Sumner, telling them to keep most of their troops on the Union side of the river. Thus a whole day was lost, thanks to Barksdale's courageous stand and Burnside's failure to move all of his army across the bridges that night so that it would be in position to attack Lee at daybreak.

Burnside's biographer suggested that the decision was a clever ruse on the general's part to keep Lee guessing about the Yankees' intentions. According to this viewpoint, Burnside was trying to create the impression that all the bridge-building, as well as the battle to capture the town, were merely diversions; the real attack would come elsewhere. "Still," Burnside's biographer admitted, "it would have been better had Burnside crossed all his troops during the night and made a vigorous attack in the morning." But it was too late for that now.

On the Southerners' side of the Rappahannock River, Lee had not been deceived. He had not been fooled into thinking that Burnside had launched a diversion while intending to attack elsewhere. Accordingly, Lee ordered Stonewall Jackson to recall the two divisions that had been sent to Port Royal and Skinkers Neck. Lee also ordered Jackson to shift two additional divisions closer to Longstreet's position. Lee was certain the Yankees would attack precisely at his strongest position, in the hills behind Fredericksburg where he had been massing infantry and artillery for weeks.

This was exactly where Lee wanted Burnside to attack. His hope was about to be fulfilled.

NINE

A City Given
Up to Pillage

The Army of the Potomac crossed over the river on December 12, in all its majesty and splendor. There were so many troops, wagons, and supplies that it took the better part of the day to bring everything over to the rebel side. The spectacle was magnificent and awe-inspiring to behold.

Long columns of blue-uniformed soldiers, thousands upon thousands of them, marched down the sloping riverbank and across the swaying bridges. Scores upon scores of bright, multicolored regimental flags fluttered in the morning breeze. Thousands of muskets—diagonal brown slashes across the blue jackets—added to the power and might of the sunlit scene. The northern troops looked invincible—and they were in plain view of the Confederates.

The Yankees could have been decimated easily by rebel artillery, if only their cannon had been able to reach that far. A few rounds were fired near Deep Run, where General Franklin's men were crossing, but the only damage was a cannonball through the paymaster's tent on the Union side of the river.

The ball struck as the paymaster was laying out large piles of paper money on a table fabricated from crude planks resting atop some barrels. The greenbacks were tossed in the air and scattered around the countryside. For a time, it was literally raining money. All discipline was lost among the nearby troops.

That was about the only excitement for the Yankees that day. Most of the men were quiet, thinking about what lay ahead. It was easy enough to see what the enemy had prepared for them, and it was a truly sobering sight. Capt. Francis Adams Donaldson of the 118th Pennsylvania, part of Sumner's wing, wrote to his aunt:

> We could distinctly see the enemy's earthworks on the hills back of Fredericksburg. What under the sun could have induced General Burnside to attempt storming them is beyond my comprehension. Why, even to one who knew scarcely nothing about the art of war the thing looked simply preposterous. The men were anything but enthusiastic over it. They could tell at a glance how impossible it would be to take the works. My God! what fearful blundering, what an infernal want of military skill the change of commanders [from McClellan] had brought us.

As the men tramped across the bridges over the Rappahannock River and gazed at the fortified hills, they wondered why the rebels weren't making any attempt to stop them. Why was Lee permitting them to reach the southern side of the river at the edge of town with barely a shot fired? It almost seemed like Lee was inviting them; or was it a trap?

As usual, the new troops—those not yet bloodied in battle—were more confident. They believed Lee did not have enough artillery ammunition to spare, or that he was too afraid of massive retaliation from Union artillery if he were to open fire on the Yankees on the bridges. And a few thought that once the Confederates realized the size of the oncoming Union army, they would not dare to attack—and were probably already preparing to fall back.

The grizzled veterans who had fought Lee before knew better. When a newspaper reporter asked one old-timer why the rebels were letting them march into town unopposed, he replied, "Shit.

They want us to get in. Getting out won't be quite so smart and easy. You'll see."

General Longstreet watched the seemingly endless columns of Union troops march into Fredericksburg. There seemed to be so many that he indeed worried whether he had sufficient artillery to stop them. When he expressed his concern to his artillery chief, Col. Porter Alexander, the colonel eased his doubts.

"We cover the ground now so well," Alexander said, "that we will comb it as with a fine-tooth comb. A chicken could not live on that field when we open on it."

Robert E. Lee also watched the Yankees pouring over the bridges. Around noon, he rode down to Stonewall Jackson's portion of the line. Jackson had prepared the defenses with his usual attention to detail, but he was concerned because it seemed to him that some of his men had been holding back at Sharpsburg and he would not tolerate that sort of behavior in the coming battle. He sent a note to his provost marshal, instructing him to take harsh measures to prevent straggling.

Jackson's orders were explicit and direct. The provost marshal guard was authorized to shoot any soldier who refused to go to the front line. Any soldier in Jackson's command who was seen by two witnesses to be straggling a second time was to be shot: "If the straggler would not go back into the fight, give him a bullet and end the matter."

Lee and Jackson rode together along the Confederate line until they met Jeb Stuart's aide, the irrepressible Heros von Borcke, who was bearing a message from Stuart. He had learned that the Union troops in General Franklin's command were converting a road into a formidable defensive position and massing a large force of infantry and artillery. Von Borcke told Lee that he had counted thirty-two Yankee guns in one battery alone. Lee said that he wanted to see the buildup for himself.

They left their cavalry escorts behind, so they would not present such a large target, and rode off with von Borcke and a lone orderly. Von Borcke led them to a barn, where they left the horses with the orderly and proceeded on foot. Cautioning Lee and Jackson to remain quiet and stay low, he directed them to a ditch. The men crept along the ditch until they reached a hill where two old gateposts formed the entryway to a large plantation.

Lee and Jackson raised their heads cautiously and looked around. Only a few hundred yards away they spotted the bulk of the Union troops. They were so close that any halfway decent Northern sharpshooter could have picked them off easily. Von Borcke wrote later:

> I must confess I felt extremely nervous as regards their safety, so close to the enemy, who surely little suspected that the two greatest heroes of the war were so nearby in their clutches. One well-directed shot, or a rapid dash of resolute horsemen, might have destroyed the hopes and confidence of our whole army.

Lee had seen enough to be convinced that the enemy troops crossing at Deep Run were preparing for a major advance. This was not a feint or diversion but had the potential to be as danger-ous as the large force gathered at the town. Jackson's wing of the army would soon face a major test, and so would Lee as he attempted to counter two Union assaults at two places along his line. As always, however, he remained confident of success. "I shall try to do them all the damage in our power when they move for-ward," he said.

Sumner's men filed over the bridges to Fredericksburg and quickly occupied the town. Back at Lacy House, Clara Barton made her way to the hospital hurriedly set up for the 2nd Corps. She spent the day nursing the wounded from the previous day's fighting. She also took meticulous care to record the essential details of the dead, to make sure no soldier's fate remained unknown to his fam-ily. No one would end up in an unmarked grave if she could help it.

The extensive damage to Fredericksburg was recorded by a photographer soon after the Union occupation. (*Library of Congress*)

One of the young soldiers she tended was Wiley Faulkner of the 7th Michigan, the first outfit to cross the river the day before. He was dying, shot through both lungs. He sat propped in a corner because it was too painful for him to lie down. He could not swallow food or water, and every breath was agony. Stretcher-bearers tried to move him out of the way to make room for the wounded who had a better chance of surviving, but Faulkner refused to be shunted aside. He clung to his bit of wall, with no one to care for him but Clara Barton.

Clara heard General Sumner's booming voice from downstairs, bellowing orders in mounting anger and frustration as the day passed. Old Bull was irate because Burnside had ordered him to remain at Lacy House during the coming battle. Burnside knew that this was the only way to prevent Sumner from leading the troops himself in the assault on Marye's Heights. The old soldier would have liked nothing better. He believed that the only proper place for a general in battle was at the head of his troops. As fate would have it, Old Bull would never have another chance to lead his men in combat.

"When I went into town, a horrible sight presented itself." So wrote the provost marshal of the Army of the Potomac, Brig. Gen. Marsena Patrick, in describing the sights of Fredericksburg. He continued:

> All the buildings more or less battered with shells, roofs and walls all full of holes, and the churches with their broken windows and shattered walls looking desolate enough, but this was not the worst. The soldiery were sacking the town! Every house and store was being gutted! Men with all sorts of utensils and furniture, all sorts of eatables and drinkables and wearables, were carried off, and as I found one fellow loading up a horse with an enormous load of carpeting and bedding I ordered him to unload it, which failing to do I gave him a cut or two with my riding whip.

It was chaos. The men of Sumner's wing, and some officers, too, were wrecking the town, engaging in an orgy of looting, vandalism, and destruction on a scale not seen before in the war. They had reached their assigned places in the town, stacked their arms and cartridge boxes in neat, orderly rows, and collected more ammunition. Then they began breaking into houses and stores, stealing whatever they could carry and destroying everything else. Many of the men were drunk, but some were sober enough to search for jewelry and other expensive luxuries, and to blow up bank safes and steal piles of Confederate money along with the Union greenbacks many banks had been prudent enough to keep. One man boasted of stealing thirty-seven watches.

A half dozen men from the 4th Rhode Island entered a house and stopped to listen to a young private playing the piano. When he stopped, another soldier raised his musket and used the butt to crush the keyboard to pieces. Other troops carried grand pianos

Soldiers from many different Union regiments looted and pillaged shops and houses in Fredericksburg. (*Library of Congress*)

into the yards and streets, smashed them to kindling, and made bonfires of them to keep themselves warm.

Books, furniture, glassware, and paintings were tossed through windows; barrels of molasses and flour dumped on fine carpets; family portraits slashed with bayonets. Rifle butts smashed mirrors into thousands of tiny shards, and women's clothing was scattered about or put on over uniforms as trophies.

The men of the 15th Massachusetts decided to sleep on featherbeds for the first time in the year and a half since they left home. They carried more than one hundred beds into the streets, arranged them in a line with military precision, and made themselves comfortable under the blankets, boots and all.

Charles Coffin, a *Boston Journal* reporter, described the time as "a carnival night. One fellow appropriated a heavy volume of Congressional documents, which he carried about several days.

Another found a stuffed monkey in one of the houses, which he shouldered and bore away. One soldier had a dozen custard cups on a string around his neck." The men were having a high old time.

"Boys came into our place loaded with silver pitchers, silver spoons, silver lamps and castors," wrote Maj. Francis Pierce of the 108th New York. He added:

> Great three-story houses furnished magnificently were broken into and their contents scattered over the floors and trampled on by the muddy feet of the soldiers. Splendid alabaster vases and pieces of statuary were thrown at six and seven hundred dollar mirrors. Closets of the very finest china were broken into and their contents smashed onto the floor and stomped to pieces. Finest cut glass ware goblets were hurled at nice plate glass windows. Beautifully embroidered window curtains torn down, rosewood pianos piled in the street and burned or soldiers would get on top of them and kick the keyboard and internal machinery all to pieces. Little table ornaments kicking in every direction, wine cellars broken into and the soldiers drinking all they could and then opening the faucets and let the rest run out. Boys go to a barrel of flour and take a pailful and use enough to make one batch of pancakes and then pour the rest in the street; everything turned upside down. The soldiers seemed to delight in destroying everything.

Meagher's Irish Brigade was in the thick of the vandalism. One man lugged around a featherbed, refusing either to put it down or rest on it. Another soldier toted a ten-gallon coffeepot, cradling it as if it were worth its weight in gold, or at least silver. Some tried on ladies' bonnets and men's tall beaver hats. They retrieved huge stores of tobacco from warehouses and from the river where the rebels had tossed it.

They had no trouble finding whiskey, wine, and ale to help them through the night. "With tobacco for their clay pipes and a drink or two at hand, in the sure knowledge that the odds were against their seeing another sunset, the men passed the uneasy night. The more thoughtful wrote their names on bits of paper and pinned them to their coats so they would not end up in an unmarked grave."

Some Union soldiers regretted their own thoughtless actions and those of their fellow soldiers. David Beem, an attorney serving with the 14th Indiana, expressed the hope that "whatever I may witness in the future, I pray I may never be called upon to behold another ruined city." Others, like Captain Donaldson of the 118th Pennsylvania, justified their behavior—in his case, stealing a book—by saying that the town would probably have been destroyed anyway in the coming battle.

Brig. Gen. Alfred Sully, commander of the 1st Minnesota, acknowledged that he acted out of personal spite. He took over a large house as his headquarters. It belonged to his brother-in-law, whom he characterized as "a blamed rebel." The house contained many fine portraits by Thomas Sully, the general's father, the most highly regarded American portraitist of his time. Among the paintings was one of Alfred, done when he was a child.

When soldiers from the 1st Minnesota barged in, General Sully told them whose home it was and invited them to take whatever they wanted. However, on learning that it was owned by their commander's brother-in-law, the soldiers perversely left the house and its contents alone and even posted a guard to keep marauders out.

Capt. Henry Livermore Abbott, a Harvard College graduate from a wealthy Massachusetts family and a member of the Harvard Regiment, 20th Massachusetts, described his search for souvenirs in a letter to his wife.

> I tried to get you some memento of Fredericksburg, but got nothing better than a commonplace edition of Byron. I did get a most beautiful writing desk but it was taken away from my servant. I have two children's books for Frank and Arthur. I went into nearly every house to get some nice little silver thing for mamma but it was too late.

Although no one was able to stop the looting and destruction, Gen. Darius Couch and Gen. Marsena Patrick did try to keep stolen property from being carried back across the river. They placed guards at the bridges; piles of confiscated property accumulated as disappointed soldiers were turned back and forced to give up their loot.

The men of the Army of the Potomac had behaved shamelessly. A historian of the 14th Indiana suggested that

> the men were motivated by a bitterness that went beyond their desire to retaliate against the enemy. [They were] in a surly mood, "demoralized." They had lost too much, too often; their energies had turned sour, passing from cider to vinegar in about three months' time. They were lawless and on the rampage—like a gang of tough boys who find the soda shop closed and go to smashing windows. Their bitterness was also increased by one final realization—the knowledge, gradually dawning, that the Northern position in the battle tomorrow was probably hopeless.

While Sumner's troops were sacking Fredericksburg, Franklin's wing had crossed the river at Deep Run, a mile downriver from town, and made camp while they waited for orders. They were surrounded by open farmland and stands of timber that led from the river to gently rising hills. The men dug trenches in case the rebels attacked.

General Franklin commandeered a plantation house, Old Mansfield, for his headquarters, over the vehement objections of the owner, William Bernard. When Bernard continued to protest, he was forcibly escorted to the Union lines under armed guard.

That afternoon, Franklin met with his corps commanders, John Reynolds and Baldy Smith, to discuss the plan of action. They agreed that the only sensible course was to attack the Confederates who were positioned along the range of hills, using two columns totaling forty thousand men. Once the rebels retreated and the

The pontoon bridges south of Fredericksburg that were used by General William Franklin's forces to cross the Rappahannock were still in place when the Union army returned to the city in the spring of 1863 during the second battle of Fredericksburg. (*Library of Congress*)

Union soldiers got behind the hills, they would head toward Fredericksburg to roll up the right flank of Lee's position, leaving the way clear for Sumner to assault the rebels dug in on Marye's Heights. Under attack from two directions, Lee would have to retreat toward Richmond.

Burnside visited Franklin's headquarters around five o'clock that afternoon. He took a brief tour of the army's position to see the hills occupied by the Confederates. At Franklin's headquarters, the officers explained their plan to Burnside, who gave the clear impression (according to accounts left by Franklin, Reynolds, and Smith) that he agreed with the plan.

"Yes! Yes!" Burnside replied eagerly, according to Smith.

When Burnside left, the officers worked out the details of the operation and set in motion what was required to mount the attack in the morning. All that remained was for Burnside to issue formal orders for the assault.

Franklin waited several hours for his orders, longer than necessary for Burnside to return to his headquarters at Phillips House, and he continued waiting long after darkness fell. Surely, he thought, the orders would arrive momentarily, but his doubts grew with each hour. General Smith later wrote,

> Would Burnside adopt our plan, and if so, why this delay which was costing us so much valuable time? We had all known Burnside socially, long and intimately, but in his new position of grave responsibility, he was to us entirely unknown.
>
> Where were the orders? Why did Burnside delay? Had he changed his mind or devised a new plan?

Francis Palfrey, a historian of that time, wrote,

> It is a pitiful picture, but is probably a true one, that Burnside passed the evening of the 12th riding about, not quite at his wit's end, but very near it. As far as can be made out, he finally came to the conclusion that he would attempt to do something, he did not quite know what, with his left [Franklin's wing], and if he succeeded, to do something with his right [Sumner's wing].*

At three o'clock in the morning on December 13, Franklin, Reynolds, and Smith still had received no orders. Sunrise was only a few hours away.

At nine o'clock that evening, in Washington, Abraham Lincoln received a visitor who brought alarming news. Brig. Gen. Herman Haupt, the chief of military railroads for the Army of the Potomac, had earned the respect of nearly everyone of whom he had run afoul in doing his job so superbly. When Haupt spoke, sensible people paid attention. The president did so that night.

Haupt had just returned from Fredericksburg. He bluntly informed Lincoln that Burnside would cripple the Army of the Potomac if he stuck to his plan of assaulting Marye's Heights in

---

*Palfrey published a book on Fredericksburg in 1882, and it is likely that he interviewed the officers who had contact with Burnside that night.

the morning. Haupt was a West Point graduate, and an engineer who knew something about fortifications. And he knew that the rebel positions in the hills beyond Fredericksburg were all but impregnable.

The president reacted immediately. If Burnside was going to be stopped, the order would have to be issued quickly. Lincoln and Haupt went to see Henry Halleck, General-in-Chief of all the Union armies. After Haupt repeated his warning, Lincoln asked Halleck to telegraph an order to Burnside summoning him and his army back from the Confederate side of the Rappahannock.

Halleck said nothing for several minutes. He paced the room, puffing furiously on his cigar and vigorously scratching his elbow, sure signs of deep concentration. Finally, he came to a halt in front of the president.

"I will do no such thing," Halleck announced. "If we were personally present and knew the exact situation, we might assume such responsibility. If such orders are issued, you must issue them yourself. I hold that a general in command of any army in the field is the best judge of existing conditions."

Silence filled the room. Lincoln contemplated the likelihood of another defeat for the Union at the hands of yet another general he had selected. Finally, in an effort to end the increasingly embarrassing silence, Haupt said that perhaps the situation at Fredericksburg might not be quite as perilous as he had suggested. It is unlikely that Haupt believed what he was saying, but Lincoln said that Haupt's words gave him some comfort. Lincoln said no more to Halleck, nor did he overrule him and send an order to Burnside himself. The moment that might have prevented the disastrous battle had passed.

Burnside slept no more than four hours that night. By six o'clock the following morning, he was dictating the orders for the coming battle that were to be dispatched to Sumner and Franklin. The orders, the ones for which Franklin had been waiting since the previous afternoon, were "composed by a man with an enormous sleep deficit [and] were not models of technical clarity." That proved to be an understatement.

Burnside's orders to Sumner appeared reasonably straightforward. He was told to push on with a division or two to seize the hills behind Fredericksburg, including the heavily defended position known as Marye's Heights. At the base of these heights was the stone wall along the sunken road lined with eager Confederate soldiers. Sumner's orders may have been impossible to carry out successfully, but they did not seem confusing or contradictory to what Sumner had been led to expect.

That was not the case with the orders to Franklin, however. They were delivered in person by Burnside's chief of staff, Brig. Gen. James Hardie, who left Burnside's headquarters a little past six o'clock that morning. The distance from Phillips House to Deep Run was only about two miles by road, and could be covered in fifteen minutes riding at a gallop. But it was still dark and the roads were treacherous, glazed with ice. Also, Hardie took time to have a hearty breakfast first, and he did not arrive at Franklin's headquarters until well after seven.

It was already too late by then for Franklin to attack at dawn in the two-pronged, forty-thousand-man assault Franklin, Reynolds, and Smith had discussed with Burnside the previous evening. As Franklin finally read Burnside's formal orders, he was shocked to see how they differed from the agreed-upon plan.

Instead of moving ahead with a massive assault, Franklin was directed to keep his whole command "in position" for a rapid movement toward Lee's right flank in Fredericksburg. Despite waiting for word to send his entire command forward, he was told he would send a division or two, a force considerably smaller than the expected forty-thousand-man assault. He was "to seize, if possible" a certain hill, "taking care," the orders added, "to keep his attacking force well supported and its line of retreat open." This was no bold, aggressive maneuver; it was a timid, tentative movement by a small force to take a single hill—if possible!

In addition, Burnside's use of the word "seize" had special significance in military parlance. The word was traditionally used when a weak or unguarded position was to be occupied or taken by a sudden, surprise assault by a small force. It was used in situations where not much resistance or opposition was anticipated, which was certainly not the case with the rebel fortifications in the hills facing Franklin's wing.

In situations where heavier resistance was expected, the word "carry" was traditionally used, a word that also implied the use of an assaulting force considerably larger than one or two divisions. Also, the admonition to keep a line of retreat open did not engender confidence or foster an aggressive spirit in a commander, particularly someone like Franklin, who was not all that aggressive or bold to begin with.

And so, the defining and limiting parameters of the battle were set before it began.

> Franklin believed there was no time to ask Burnside for clarification of his orders. Sending word to General Headquarters and waiting for a reply would waste what morning still remained. Franklin and his officers were obligated to Burnside's quizzical orders and bound to execute them as swiftly as possible. That decided upon, Franklin determined to follow the orders to the letter of the law.

That would leave Bull Sumner's men to take Marye's Heights on their own. They could expect no help from Franklin's wing of the army. Or from anyone else.

Union troops hunkered down behind an embankment waiting to assault Fredericksburg during the second attack on the city in May 1863. Six months earlier, soldiers at the first battle of Fredericksburg similarly had huddled in the cold following their unsuccessful attempt to dislodge the Confederates from their defensive positions. (*Library of Congress*)

TEN

There Was
No Cheering

"There was something eerie about the morning of the battle," wrote a noted Civil War historian. "Heavy cold mist filled the air. In the air, too, palpable as the December fog itself, was the chill suspicion that cruel disaster lay just out of town to the west." And an officer wrote more bluntly to his friend: "I expect to be sacrificed."

Every street, alley, front lawn, porch, and rear yard was crammed with Union troops trying to stay warm in the brutal cold. Men who had slept on the ground awoke to find their clothes stuck to the frozen mud. A glaze of white frost covered their blankets. No fires had been allowed during the night, in a misguided effort to keep the Yankees' presence in town a secret from the rebels, as if there were any way to hide that many troops from the Confederates who had watched them stride across the bridges all day.

The Union soldiers were so tightly packed together that they could not move around enough to get warm. Many men were still missing from their commands, busy looting and vandalizing Fredericksburg's houses. To heighten the confusion and chaos, as well as the growing sense of dread, enterprising representatives of undertakers walked through the crowds passing out their business cards, offering to have bodies shipped home. Officers quickly drove the salesmen away, but the damage to morale had been done.

Gen. Oliver Otis Howard, commanding the 2nd Division in General Couch's 2nd Corps, had been awake since three o'clock in the morning, writing a letter to his children.

> We are in a house abandoned by Mr. Knox, and near the front line. One or two shells have passed clear through the house, but my room is in pretty good shape. I am sitting on this floor near a fireplace, writing on my lap, having an inkstand, candlestick, and paper on a large portfolio.

A few hours later, a Southern woman who had chosen to remain in town watched General Howard and his staff at breakfast. The officers were listening attentively to a Bible reading, which was followed by a prayer. General Howard commented to the woman that the Union would win the war. She shook her head. "You will have a stone wall to encounter, hills to climb, and a long street to tread before you can succeed."

But when she saw the Yankee officers' cheerful attitude as they prepared for the fight, she sounded less certain.

"Now I fear you more than ever," she told General Howard, "for I had understood that all of Lincoln's men were bad. What! So cheerful when going straight into battle?"

In the hills beyond town the Confederate troops were also preparing for battle. Lt. William Miller Owen of the Washington Artillery of New Orleans stepped upon the gallery that overlooked the heights behind the picturesque colonial town of Fredericksburg.*

> Heavy fog and mist hid the whole plain between the heights and the Rappahannock, but under the cover of the fog and within easy cannon-shot lay Burnside's army. The

*The gallery being the upper balcony at Brompton, the grand house on Marye's Heights.

buglers and the drum corps of the respective armies were now sounding reveille and the troops were preparing for their early meal. All knew we should have a battle today, and a great one. Last night we had spread out blankets upon the bare floor in the parlor of Marye's house, and now our breakfast was being prepared in its fireplace, and we were impatient to have it over. After hastily dispatching this light meal of bacon and cornbread, the colonel, chief bugler and I mounted our horses and rode out to inspect our lines.

The sun rose at 7:17, not strong enough yet to burn off the morning fog but bright enough for other rebel officers to inspect their lines. Longstreet—hearty, alert, and calm—rode slowly along his front, stopping to talk with Gen. John B. Hood on the right flank. Hood said he believed the main Yankee assault would be launched against his portion of the line, or so he hoped. Longstreet disagreed. He predicted that the enemy's main attack would come farther south, against Jackson's part of the line. Longstreet also expected an attack near the center of his own line but felt he could beat back any Union assault there without having to call on Hood for assistance, or on George Pickett, whose division was also at the end of the right flank.

Longstreet rode ahead to the top of Telegraph Hill—forevermore known as Lee's Hill, for that was where Lee would remain throughout the day to survey the fighting.

Stonewall Jackson was also out early that morning. To the amazement of all, and the amusement of most, he was wearing the fancy uniform Jeb Stuart had given him. "Thus glorified, 'Old Jack' was dazzling to the eye if manifestly embarrassed. The remarks of his men did not lessen his discomfort. Said one soldier, with a shake of his head, 'Old Jack will be afraid of his clothes and will not get down to work.'"

Wherever he rode that morning, his outfit met with the same astonished reaction. At Telegraph Hill, Lee and Longstreet were also surprised at Jackson's sartorial splendor but chose not to comment about it. Jeb Stuart was delighted that Jackson was dressed so magnificently but he, too, wisely kept silent. He knew Jackson would not appreciate any teasing about his clothes that morning. Despite his choice of attire for the day, Jackson had only one thing on his mind: how to beat the enemy. He urged Lee to let him attack the Yankees immediately, while the fog prevented them from using their superior numbers of artillery. Jackson wanted to swoop down from the hills onto the open plain, take the Union forces by surprise, and send them scampering back across the bridges. Jeb Stuart supported the idea, and pressed Lee for permission to proceed. But Lee argued that the risk was too great. They would kill more Union soldiers by letting them initiate the attack. Wear them down, Lee insisted, reduce their numbers, and then we can attack.

By ten o'clock the fog had begun to dissipate, revealing church steeples, the upper floors of houses and stores, and, at last, the broad band of the river and the thousands of troops in blue. As far as one could see from Lee's Hill, Union soldiers stretched in orderly lines along with clusters of artillery and long columns of supply wagons. The plains by Deep Run were almost covered in blue, as was virtually every open space in the town. Longstreet gestured toward Deep Run, Jackson's section of the Confederate line, and tried to joke with him about the great number of Yankees his men were facing.

"Are you scared by that file of Yankees you have before you down there?"

Jackson, not noted for his humor, replied soberly, "Wait till they come a little nearer, and they shall either scare me or I'll scare them."

As Jackson turned away to mount his horse, Longstreet asked another question.

"What are you going to do with all those people over there?"

"Sir," Jackson said, echoing the words he spoke to General Bee at Bull Run, "we will give them the bayonet."

Shortly after the fog cleared, the Union artillery located well behind Sumner's headquarters at Lacy House opened fire. Almost instantly the Confederates returned fire. Some of the shells struck the house, endangering Clara Barton, several army doctors, and the wounded soldiers in their care. As the house rocked under the impact, Clara discovered a box of fruit a girl had sent for the soldiers. "I opened little Mary's box of delicious fruit," Clara recalled, "and cut the apples in quarters and divided them among the poor suffering men."

When she finished, she went to the door to look outside. A shell exploded on the lawn, severing the artery in a soldier's ankle. His buddies carried him to Clara, who twisted her handkerchief into a tourniquet and tied it around the man's leg. When she saw him later that morning, he clutched her skirt. "You saved my life," he said, and he repeated that every time he saw her.

Stonewall Jackson observed the Union shelling, as well as what he assumed to be preparations for an infantry assault. He sited his guns in the best position to repulse it. Heros von Borcke expressed his concern over the enemy threat.

"Major," Jackson replied, "my men have sometimes failed to take a position, but to defend one, never! I am glad the Yankees are coming."

By eleven o'clock that morning, Burnside gave up waiting for word that General Franklin had broken through Lee's line at Deep Run. He ordered Sumner to begin the assault on Marye's Heights. Sumner dispatched orders for Darius Couch to attack with his 2nd Corps.

Marye's Heights rose 130 feet, giving the Confederates a commanding position for their artillery fire. Once the Union troops left the relative safety of the town's buildings, there were few places for them to find cover. The open plain they would have to cross was a half-mile wide. When the troops left town, their line of march would take them down a slight hill under fire from rebel cannon until they reached a ditch thirty feet wide and six feet deep. The ditch, in which only a little water flowed, was the spillway from a canal. The sides were too steep to climb.

Three bridges spanned the canal, which meant that the attacking troops would have to bunch up to form three lines to cross.

The Confederates had pulled up all the planks from one bridge, leaving only the stringers, which were several feet apart. The men would have to jump from one to the other while under heavy artillery fire.

Once across the bridges, the soldiers were to fan out to the right and left to form two long lines of attack, one positioned behind the other. At this point the ground rose steeply, providing some cover.

Then the land leveled out to only a slight incline all the way to the stone wall along the sunken road at the base of Marye's Heights. The distance from the spillway to the wall was approximately four hundred yards. A rise that began about one hundred yards from the wall gave just enough shelter to protect a man from rebel fire if he lay prone and did not raise his head. If he decided to push on toward that monumental pile of stones, he stood no chance of seeing the sunset. There were no more places to hide.

Brig. Gen. William H. French's 3rd Division was selected by General Couch to spearhead the assault. French's three brigades would charge the heights in three successive waves. Brig. Gen. Nathan Kimball's brigade would go first. As French marched his division down Caroline Street toward the edge of town, Clara Barton watched them move out. She had rushed across the bridge from Lacy House as soon as the battle order was given.

As she made her way through the streets, she was stopped by Marsena Patrick, the provost marshal, who mistook her for a local resident.

"You are alone," he said, "and in great danger, Madam. Do you want protection?"

Clara gestured to the soldiers marching by. She told Patrick that she was the best-protected woman in the country.

"That's so, that's so," shouted the passing troops, who cheered as they recognized her.

General Patrick took off his hat and bowed to her.

"I believe you are right, Madam," he said.

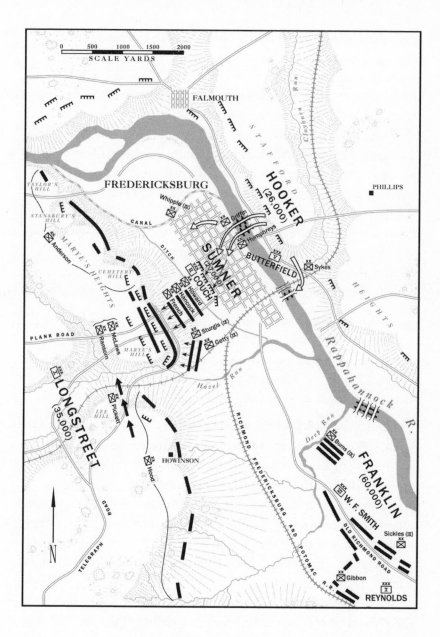

General Kimball led his troops to the edge of town. He turned in his saddle to address them.

"Cheer up, my hearties!" he shouted. "This is something we must all get used to. Remember, this brigade has never been whipped, and don't let it be whipped today."

With that admonition, he led them out onto the open field. The men marched forward in two columns. Rebel artillery opened up immediately and mercilessly. Kimball recalled "several shells bursting in the ranks and destroying a company at a time. Yet all the regiments moved steadily forward without confusion, those in the rear quickly closing up the gaps left by their fallen comrades."

What Kimball and many other officers would leave out of their official reports of the day's action was that not all men acted bravely. An enlisted man wrote

> It is not every man that can face danger like this. I saw a few so overcome by fear that they fell prostrate upon the ground as if dead. I have seen men drop on their knees and pray loudly for deliverance, when courage and bravery, not supplication, was the duty of the moment.

But the majority of the Union soldiers marched stolidly forward, closing up the increasingly large gaps in the lines, heading up the incline toward the stone wall thick with rifles aimed down at them. Behind the wall the Georgians of Brig. Gen. Thomas R. R. Cobb's brigade were well stocked with ammunition, water, and a cussed determination to shoot down every man in blue. Their mascot was a rooster that never missed a battle. The men had trained it to crow at the sound of gunfire and it crowed then, adding a raucous cry to the din.

As the Union troops closed to within musket range, they fired their single shots and rushed forward yelling "Hi! Hi! Hi!" The Georgians fired; the survivors described the scene as a wall of flame. Yankees fell by the hundreds, as if a great wind were sweeping them off their feet. The line stopped for an instant in shock, and then some men ran toward the wall. No one even came close.

A late nineteenth-century illustration of Confederate general Thomas R. R. Cobb's brigade firing from behind a stone wall at advancing Union soldiers. (*Library of Congress*)

The rest turned and fled. Many were cut down in their tracks. Some dropped behind the swale that was the only place to hide. In less than half an hour, a thousand of Kimball's soldiers were dead, wounded, or hugging the ground, unable to risk raising their arms to reload their muskets for fear of being hit.

All they could do was lie there and watch the second and third brigades of French's division start courageously up the slope. The solid blue lines, just like the first brigade, ended up dead or maimed or cowering in the dirt. One of every three men in the division had been hit. It was a slaughter, a killing field. "It was magnificent," one Confederate soldier said, "but it was not war."

The rooster crowed again behind the stone wall not long after the Georgians stopped General French's 3rd Division. Three more brigades were ready to follow in their footsteps, to march over their bodies, to try to accomplish what their fellow soldiers had not been able to do—to break through the rebel line at the stone wall.

It fell to Gen. Winfield S. Hancock's 1st Division, but it would be even more difficult for them than for French's assault force because General Cobb's Georgians along the sunken road had been reinforced. When Hancock's 3rd Brigade, led by Col. Samuel Zook, crossed the canal and started up the incline, feeble cheers rose from French's survivors as they huddled in the dirt.

Some of the men staggered to their feet to join the new wave in their assault, but none of them lasted long. It was over in minutes. More bodies littered the field, many dead or dying, the rest struggling to stay alive behind that blessed slight rise in the ground. In short order, a fourth Union brigade had been destroyed while the fifth prepared itself to follow over the same bloody path.

Next in line was Brig. Gen. Thomas Meagher's Irish Brigade. Meagher was resplendent in a well-tailored dark green coat, the silver stars of his rank embroidered on black epaulets, and a bright yellow silk scarf draped diagonally across his chest. All 1,700 men of his brigade wore green sprigs of boxwood in their caps. There would be no mistaking the soldiers of the Irish Brigade.

As they marched to the edge of town, a breeze rippled the brigade's green flag, which bore the ancient Gaelic battle cry, *Riamh Nar drhuid O sbairn Lan.* "Never retreat from the clash of spears."

Meagher spoke to each regiment. The eyes of the world would be on them today, he told the men; they must uphold the proud fighting tradition of the Irish. They were Americans now, he said, and they had a duty to defend their country, whatever the cost. "I know this day you will strike a deadly blow to those wicked traitors who are now but a few hundred yards from you, and bring back to this distracted country its former prestige and glory."

Meagher's adjutant, Pvt. Bill McCarter, heard the order to fix bayonets. He joined the rest in attaching the long, sharp steel blade to the socket of his musket. He remembered how "the clink, clink, clink of the cold steel sounding along the line made one's blood run cold."

Then it was time to move out: "Shoulder arms. Left face. Forward, march."

They had taken only a few steps when they passed an unnerving preview of their fate: the wounded survivors of French's failed assault being carried back from the field.

"They presented to us, who were just about to go into it, fearful pictures of the horrors of war," Private McCarter wrote. "One poor fellow was carried past us on a window shutter by two soldiers. His uniform indicated the rank of captain. His face was young and deathly white. He had been hit in the leg above the knee by a cannonball, which had almost torn the limb from his body, a small thready sinew only apparently holding both together." The lower half of his leg dangled from the makeshift stretcher, swinging painfully back and forth with every step of the bearers.

"Lay him down and cut the leg off at once," shouted someone near McCarter. "That will ease him."

The men carrying the wounded captain paid no attention. Suddenly, one of the Irishmen darted out of line and sliced through the sinew with his penknife. The dead limb dropped to the ground. The officer smiled and nodded his head in gratitude to the man who had relieved his pain.

The Irish Brigade crossed the bridges over the canal and spread out to form two long lines of attack.

"Irish Brigade, advance! Forward, double-quick, guide center!"

The stone wall lay directly before them. Behind it, the Confederate troops caught sight of the colors and recognized who was coming at them this time.

"There are those damned green flags again," yelled Gen. D. H. Hill, who had fought the Irish Brigade before.

Many of the soldiers of General Cobb's Georgia brigade were also Irish immigrants, and they, too, had met the Irish Brigade in the past. It bothered them greatly to fire on their own.

"Oh God, what a pity!" one cried. "Here comes Meagher's fellows!"

The Irish Brigade troops were the bravest of the brave, but even they, for all their magnificent form and determination, could not stand up to the withering fire from the stone wall and the rebel artillery.

Lt. William Miller Owen, of the Washington Artillery of New Orleans, watched them approach.

> On they came in beautiful array, and seemingly more determined to hold the plain than before; but our fire was murderous, and no troops on earth could stand [what] we were giving them.

Pvt. Alexander Hunter of the 17th Virginia was on Marye's Heights when the Irish Brigade met its fate. He and others around him were "filled with wonder and a pitying admiration for men who could rush with such unflinching valor, such mad recklessness into the jaws of destruction."

Protected by the rise in front of the stone wall, Pvt. Thomas Galwey, of French's division, who had survived the first charge, watched the assaults that followed. Later he wrote in his diary.

> Line after line of our men advance in magnificent order out from the city towards us. But none of them pass the position which we took at our first dash. There is one exception, the Irish Brigade, which comes out from the city in glorious style, their green sunbursts waving. Every man has a sprig of green in his cap, and a half-laughing, half-murderous look in his eye. They pass just to our left, poor fellows, poor glorious fellows, shaking goodbye to us with their hats! They reach a point within a stone's throw of the stone wall. No farther. They try to go beyond, but are slaughtered.

The Irish Brigade's chaplain, William Corby, watched as the men "simply melted away before the grape and cannister." The field in front of the stone wall was "a slaughter pen," he wrote, in which the brigade was "cut to pieces." Those who survived the fire from Cobb's Georgians took shelter back of the rise, joining the survivors of earlier assault waves.

One of every three men had been hit; almost every officer was down, with the curious exception of General Meagher, who was no longer leading his men. In fact, he was no longer even with them. Claiming a painful ulcerated knee joint, which he said he had "concealed and bore up against for days," Meagher had returned to town. He insisted that he could not walk because of the pain, yet he walked back to town—to get his horse, he said.

Henry Villard, a reporter for the *New York Tribune* (who had a low opinion of the Irish in general) saw Meagher astride his horse in town with a few hundred of his men—some wounded and some not—who had made their way to safety from the front. Meagher led them across the Rappahannock River to the Union side, out of range of rebel artillery fire, claiming that General Hancock had given him permission to do so.

That was untrue, as Meagher said he learned later, "much to his embarrassment." He quickly brought his men back into town when he found out he had not been authorized to leave, but Villard was unforgiving in his treatment of Meagher. "His retreat across the river without orders was nothing but a piece of arrant cowardice," the reporter wrote. Regardless of the interpretation of Meagher's actions, there is no denying that most of the men of the Irish Brigade covered themselves with far more honor and glory than did their commander.

While Meagher and his group were seeking safety, the rest of the brigade was pinned down below the rise at the stone wall, along with the casualties from earlier assaults. Meagher's adjutant, Bill McCarter, had been hit in the shoulder and was bleeding heavily.

> I laid disabled, disheartened, hope a mere shadow. I might be torn to pieces by a cannonball or shell at any moment or sent into eternity by the lesser, but just as fatal, rifle ball or musket bullet. To rise up and run was impossible. Had I done so, I would undoubtedly have been shot down again, and perhaps instantly killed. It became evident that the enemy was picking off our wounded men on

the battlefield, firing at them and killing them outright. To get aid or even to expect it from any of our men was out of the question.

One man did try to help McCarter. His company commander, Lt. Samuel Foltz, knelt beside him and asked how badly he had been wounded. He said he wished he could get McCarter out. Suddenly the lieutenant grabbed McCarter's rifle and moved a few yards away, making no effort to dodge the rebel bullets.

"Bill," he yelled. "I see the bastard that laid you there. I'll fetch him."

McCarter watched Foltz take aim at a rebel soldier behind the wall, wondering how his friend could pick out the one who had shot him. But before Foltz could fire, he dropped the rifle, raised a hand to his forehead, and fell backward, with a gaping hole above his left eye.

McCarter was overcome with sorrow at the loss of this brave young officer and feared he had little time left himself. Fortunately, he had sufficient presence of mind to take the thick blanket roll from his backpack and put it on the ground in front of his head facing the stone wall. It seemed like little protection, but it would save his life.

> The prospect of death now seemed to increase. My clothing was being literally torn from my back by the constant and furious musketry fire of the enemy from three points. A ball struck me on the left wrist inflicting another painful but not serious wound. Another one which would undoubtedly have proved instantly fatal but for my blankets pierced through six plies of the blankets. It left me the possessor of a very sore head for six weeks after. With such force did this bullet come that for some time I really thought it had embedded itself in the skull.

When McCarter reached the safety of the Union lines in Fredericksburg the next day, he found thirty-two bullets in his blanket roll.

A dramatic lithograph of a wave of Union soldiers marching against the Confederate stronghold along the high ground outside of Fredericksburg. The Union advance incurred some of the highest casualty rates of the war. (*Library of Congress*)

Another wave of Union troops was preparing to head up the slope toward the unreachable sunken road. Brig. Gen. John Caldwell, commanding Hancock's 1st Brigade, led this fifth attempt. Caldwell's men, particularly the 5th New Hampshire, were the ones who had finally broken the rebel line at Antietam. Now they were facing a bloodier challenge. It was around noon when the brigade received its orders to attack.

"Caldwell," General Hancock said, "you will forward your brigade at once. The Irish Brigade is suffering severely."

Col. Edward Cross, the twenty-nine-year-old commander of the 5th New Hampshire—the Fighting Fifth they called themselves—addressed his men.

"Attention!" Cross shouted. "Every man is expected to do his duty today. If I fall, never mind me. Fix bayonets! No man to fire a shot until he is inside the rebel lines. Shoulder arms! Trail arms! Forward, march!"

The Fighting Fifth crossed the canal, formed two lines, and moved up the hill. Rebel shells tore huge gaps in their ranks. A shell exploded directly in front of Colonel Cross. Shrapnel hit his chest, the back of one hand, and his forehead, knocking out two teeth and leaving him flat on the ground. He lay still for a moment, barely aware of what had happened to him, when a larger fragment struck his leg.

He managed to get to his hands and knees. As he spit blood, stones, and sand from his mouth he looked around. What he saw pleased him.

> The tattered colors of my regiment, thank God, were in the van. I tried to get on my feet, but could not stand. I then tried to crawl, but the balls came so thick and tore up the ground so spitefully, that I could not do it, besides a ball struck my sword scabbard, knocking me over. After that warning, I concluded to be still, so placing myself on my back, feet to the foe, awaited death.

In the midst of the battle, with his men charging the stone wall in subsequent attacks, Cross was aware of the soldiers racing past on their way up the hill and the survivors running past as they retreated. He lay there throughout the afternoon and later recorded that he observed "many acts of cowardice and bravery. Many officers and men ran shamefully from the field without a scratch, others counterfeited wounds, other skulked and lay down. It was a sad and shameful sight."

The *New York Tribune* reporter Henry Villard also witnessed cowardice along with much bravery and sacrifice. Villard described "the rapid disintegration of our troops. I passed at least a thousand officers and privates making for the town; perhaps one fourth of them were slightly wounded, many of whom were needlessly helped along by skulkers, a very common trick on battlefields. The remainder simply were tired, hungry, and thirsty, and had no more stomach for fighting."

For a time, however, it appeared that nothing would stop Colonel Cross's Fighting Fifth New Hampshire men. Other regiments of General Caldwell's brigade disintegrated under the persistent Confederate artillery fire, but not the 5th, which held its tight formation as it advanced up the hill. But not even they could withstand the savage rifle fire from the stone wall. Their assault collapsed, as had all the others, leaving the survivors hunkered down behind the rise a hundred yards from the sunken road, from which there was no retreat.

Like the others before them, all the men could do was hug the ground and pile up their blanket rolls and the bodies of their fellow soldiers before them for protection. They prayed and cursed, and watched how slowly the noonday sun moved overhead. They knew they had only a slight chance of surviving as long as there was daylight. Evening was still many hours away.

Not all of the day's casualties at Fredericksburg were Yankees. Although few of Cobb's Georgians were hit—only a fraction of the number of the Union casualties—the general himself was shot in the thigh, apparently during Major Howard's attack. Despite the protests of his men, Cobb had been riding up and down the line in clear sight of the enemy when he was hit by a sharpshooter firing from a window in the second floor of a house at the edge of town.

Cobb, a popular officer who had helped write the Confederate constitution, sustained the wound within sight of his mother's birthplace, the same house where she and Cobb's father had married forty years earlier. "Had not the smoke of a terrific battle screened it, [Cobb] could have clearly seen the windows of the room in which his parents were married." As a child, Cobb had spent summers playing on the spacious lawn.

He never saw the house again. With blood gushing from the severed artery in his leg, he was carried to a bullet-scarred house on a sunken road that belonged to Martha Stevens. Surgeons tried unsuccessfully to staunch the bleeding; there was nothing more they could do. The regimental chaplain, R. K. Porter, bathed Cobb's forehead with wet rags.

"It's very painful," Cobb said.

He was offered whiskey to ease his suffering but died before he could take a sip.

The Stevens house was the only refuge for wounded Confederate troops, the only place Cobb's men could be taken without leaving the cover provided by the wall. Mrs. Stevens remained at home. She refused to leave while wounded men needed her help. She selflessly "stayed all day," despite the constant rifle fire, "giving the wounded drink, and bandaging their wounds until every sheet and piece of clothing in the house had been used to bind a soldier's hurts."

The fighting came so close that there were soldiers in the yard, and sometimes Union soldiers concentrated their fire on her house because they knew rebels were sheltered inside. When General Lee found out that the Stevens house had become a target, he was livid; he was always angry when civilians were put at risk. Standing up on Telegraph Hill, watching the bullets strike her house, he was overheard to say, "I wish those people would let Mrs. Stevens alone."

Gen. Darius Couch, commanding Sumner's 2nd Corps, watched from the courthouse steeple as his troops were slaughtered.

> I remember that the whole plain was covered with men, prostrate and dropping, the live men running here and there, and in front closing upon each other, and the wounded coming back. The commands seemed to be mixed up. I have never before seen fighting like that, nothing approaching it in terrible uproar and destruction. There was no cheering on the part of the men, but a stubborn determination to obey orders, and to do their duty. I don't think there was much feeling of success.

Couch continued to watch in horror as the rebel shelling tore apart each formation. His men closed their much-depleted ranks and forged on until they were stopped a hundred yards short of the

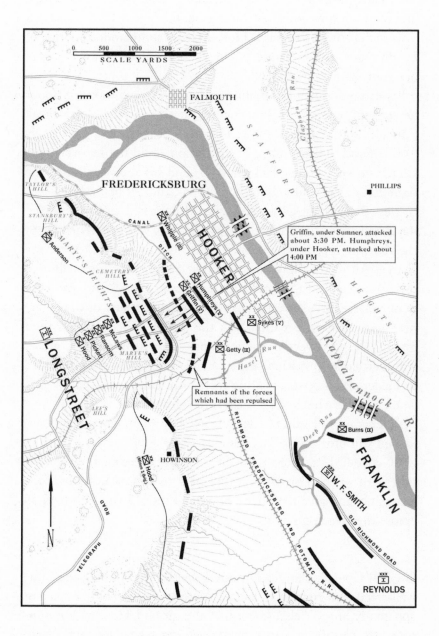

Griffin, under Sumner, attacked
about 3:30 PM. Humphreys,
under Hooker, attacked about
4:00 PM

Remnants of the forces
which had been repulsed

wall. Every brigade—and by now, six brigades had tried to breach the enemy position—"would do its duty," Couch wrote, "and melt like snow coming down on warm ground."

Couch turned to General Howard, who commanded another of his divisions, and exclaimed, "Oh, great God! See how our men, our poor fellows, are falling!"

Couch was convinced that no matter how many waves of troops he sent up against the sunken road, it was impossible to break through the Confederate line. The rebel position was too heavily fortified and the advantage of the terrain could not be overcome. Couch ordered General Howard to send his men farther to the right end of the wall, hoping to outflank and get behind it.

Less than a mile-and-a-half away, Robert E. Lee also observed the slaughter of the Yankee troops. He, too, was concerned about the outcome even though his Georgians had beaten back every charge. Although the plain was littered with Union casualties— more Yankee dead than most Confederate generals had ever seen in one place—Lee was apprehensive, largely because of the eagerness and persistence with which the enemy kept renewing their assaults despite every previous failure. They continued to attack with fierce determination, and so many more Union troops massed in Fredericksburg were waiting their turn. Lee feared that his line would be overwhelmed by sheer force of numbers.

"General," Lee said to Longstreet, "they are massing very heavily and will break your line, I am afraid."

"General," Longstreet replied, "if you put every man now on the other side of the Potomac on that field to approach me over the same line, and give me plenty of ammunition, I will kill them all before they reach my line."

General Couch's plan for Howard's division to outflank the stone wall from the right was sound. Unfortunately, neither he, nor apparently anyone else, knew that the ground Howard was supposed to cross was a marsh that proved impassable for such a large body of troops. As a result, the first two waves of Howard's attack were forced to shift to the left, to the same open ground other Union outfits had crossed. Howard's men passed the dead and wounded of the previous divisions and, like them, were riddled by enemy fire long before they neared the sunken road.

Howard's men did their best, as most of the others had done, but it was not good enough. Capt. John B. Adams of the 19th Massachusetts survived to write about the fate of his outfit.

> Led by our gallant Captain Weymouth we moved up the bank. The two color bearers, Sergeant Creasey and Sergeant Rappell, were the first to fall, but the colors did not touch the ground before they were up and going forward.
>
> Captain Weymouth fell, shot in the leg, which was afterwards amputated. Captain Mahoney took command of the regiment and he was also seen to fall, shot in the arm and side. Down went the color bearers again.
>
> Lieutenant Newcomb grasped one, a color corporal another. Newcomb fell, shot through both legs, and as he went down he handed the color to me. Next fell the color corporal and the flag he held was grasped by Sergeant Merrill, who was soon wounded. Another seized the color but he was shot immediately, and as it fell from his hands the officer who already had one caught it.

Men went down but the colors did not. Captain Adams was awarded the Medal of Honor for his actions that day. Keeping the regimental colors from dropping in the dirt and being dishonored was a soldier's solemn, sacred duty, and many a man died that day trying to save the flag.

Clara Barton was watching as the boys of her beloved 21st Massachusetts started their march, to be decimated almost immediately by rebel artillery fire. It was then that Sgt. Thomas Plunkett lost both arms to an exploding shell.* Plunkett managed

---

*This incident is described in greater detail in the prologue.

to remain upright and raise the bloodstained flag until another man took it from him. The rest of the 21st moved up the incline, leaving Plunkett where he fell, his blood saturating the ground.

Clara Barton made her way to town to help tend the wounded. Hundreds now filled the houses, churches, schools, and shops. Many rested on front lawns and in backyards. Soldiers cried out for water, for a blanket, for chloroform or whiskey—or for God to put an end to their agony.

"This was Clara Barton's war," her biographer wrote, "the war against death in the battlefield dressing stations. Driven as never before, she seemed a ubiquitous presence, now in a church, now a home, now the courthouse, holding some battered boy to her chest, wiping the brow of another." When the maimed body of Sergeant Plunkett was brought back from the field, Clara stayed with him while the surgeons severed the stumps of both arms. Later someone showed her the flag Plunkett had held on to despite his wounds. She wrote that Plunkett's blood "literally obliterated the stripes." But the flag had never touched the ground.

Pvt. Bill McCarter, wounded during the charge of the Irish Brigade, remained sheltered behind the rise at the stone wall, still unable to move. He saw General Howard's division advancing, closing within twenty yards of his position before it was stopped by rebel fire. Howard's first two brigades were shattered under the impact.

The Confederate fire was so intense and steady, wrote McCarter, that "the noise was deafening and caused the ground under and around me to shake to such a degree that at times I actually thought it was sliding away. The dead and wounded now lay very thick all around. The cries of some of the latter were heartrending in the extreme."

McCarter saw a horse dash out from behind the stone wall, dragging a dead rebel soldier whose foot was caught in the stirrup. "The poor animal presented an appearance wild, beautifully wild if

I may term it so. Snorting so loud that I distinctly heard the noise with nostrils extended and like to burst, the horse darted to and fro, its mane standing stiff on end." The horse ran madly back and forth between the opposing lines until it fell dead, riddled with bullets from both sides.

The private was overcome by a terrible thirst. His canteen was empty, and there were none others close enough to reach without exposing himself to gunfire. He spied a group of Union soldiers about twenty yards away and shouted, begging them to toss him a canteen. One man started to crawl toward McCarter, but he was shot. No one else dared to try.

Only one Union officer disobeyed Burnside's order to assault Marye's Heights. He was Brig. Gen. Alfred Sully, commander of General Howard's 1st Brigade. After seeing Howard's first two brigades cut to pieces, Sully refused to send his men to their deaths. "They might court martial me and be damned," he said. "I was not going to murder my men, and it would be nothing less than murder to have sent them there." In the end, no disciplinary action was ever taken against General Sully.

Shortly before three o'clock in the afternoon, following the last assaults of Howard's brigades, a lull settled over the battlefield. General Couch, who had seen three divisions shattered in the futile attempt to take Marye's Heights, received a dispatch from Bull Sumner. At 2:40 p.m., Sumner had written, "Hooker has been ordered to put in everything. You must hold on until he comes in."

Maj. Gen. Hooker was senior in rank to Couch. He was to assume command of the operation and add his fresh troops to the remainder of Couch's force. Couch rode down to the river to greet Hooker as he was coming across the bridge. If there were to be further attacks, Couch wanted to push forward with them immediately. Too long a break in the fighting would allow the Confederates time to reinforce their position and bring up reserves of ammunition. Hooker would need to send in his soldiers right away, even though Couch was not optimistic about their success—

not after so many lives had already been lost for nothing. Eight bloody assault waves had not gained so much as one yard of rebel territory.

"I can't carry that hill by frontal assault," Couch told Hooker. "The only chance we have is to try to get in on the right."

Hooker walked away to speak with Hancock, commander of Couch's 1st Division, before rejoining Couch.

"Well, Couch," Hooker said, "things are in such a state [that] I must go over and tell Burnside it is no use trying to carry this line here."

Hooker believed it was pointless to continue with the assault. Unfortunately, it would be two hours before he returned from his meeting with Burnside. Couch was left in command during that time and he would opt to send another division struggling up the hill. It would fail, as all the others had done.

Hooker and Burnside had a stormy confrontation at Phillips House across the river in Falmouth. Hooker told his commanding general that the stone wall could not be taken, no matter how many troops were sent up against it. But Burnside was adamant: The attack had to continue. According to the accounts of several officers present, Hooker then let loose with "a torrent of vitupera-tion [that] made the air blue with adjectives." The language Hooker used was so strong and profane that those officers left the room to avoid becoming involved in the argument.

Burnside would not be swayed. He was still expecting Franklin to advance down at Deep Run and roll up Lee's right flank, even though Franklin had made no significant progress all day long. Stubbornly, he ordered Hooker to press the attack on Marye's Heights.

While the argument raged in Falmouth, Couch, in Fredericks-burg, ordered Brig. Gen. Andrew Humphreys—commanding the 4,500 men of the 3rd division of Hooker's Center Grand Division—to attack. Humphreys had only two brigades in his

Brigadier General Andrew Humphreys led one of the final assaults on the Confederate positions at Fredericksburg. In the late afternoon of December 13, Humphreys found himself alone at the front of his troops, bravely encouraging his men to rally, but to no avail. (*Library of Congress*)

command, made up mostly of nine-month militia troops, none of whom had seen previous combat. They marched out bravely enough, with Humphreys and his staff officers in the lead.

General Humphreys had long been under suspicion of sympathizing with the enemy because of his close prewar friendship with Jefferson Davis. Those suspicions had delayed his opportunity for promotion, so at Fredericksburg he was out to prove his loyalty to the Union. He was prepared to die in the attempt if need be.

He brought his men across the canal, formed them into two lines, and ordered a bayonet charge. The soldiers were not to stop and fire at the rebels. Humphreys insisted that they keep running up the hill and scale the stone wall with bayonets at the ready. So on they went in the fading light, double-timing up the hill.

On the Confederate side, Col. Edward Porter Alexander, Lee's chief of artillery, watched them come.

That was just what we wanted. Our chests were crammed full of ammunition, and the sun was low; so we set in to improve each shining hour, and get rid of as much as possible of that ammunition before dark. It was for just this sort of chance that we had been saving it up since the beginning. So now we gave them our choicest varieties, cannister and shrapnel, just as fast as we could put it in.

Humphreys's forces came on without pause, despite the loss of hundreds to artillery fire. For green troops, they were making a good showing. It was not until they reached the dead and the wounded survivors of earlier assaults that they faltered. Some of the fallen soldiers reached out and pulled the fresh troops to the ground. They grabbed at their overcoats, shouting for them to give up the fight, that it was suicidal to keep on. "No one lives who goes there," they warned.

General Humphreys remained in the lead, alone on horseback, bullets and shells tearing up the earth around him as he tried to rally his men. But it was no use. They went to ground, the charge disintegrated, and no amount of posturing or cajoling, no inspiring words or threats of court-martial, would rouse them to their feet again.

It was four o'clock, nearing sunset, but there was still enough light for men to die. Couch ordered additional units forward, trying to rush as many troops into battle as he could before dark. Brigadier Generals Charles Griffin and George Sykes were ordered to attack to the left of where Humphreys's men had gone in.

The rebel artillerymen saw Griffin and Sykes coming and tore them apart in their tracks. Couch watched them fall. In anger and frustration he ordered a battery of Union artillery to ride out onto the open plain, unlimber their guns in full view of the rebel artillery, and shell the Confederate gunners. When Capt. C. H. Morgan, Couch's chief of artillery, received the order, he protested to Couch: "General, a battery can't live there."

"Then it must die there," Couch said.

Most of them did die there, and the action changed the outcome of the battle not one bit. And yet, although darkness was finally, mercifully, settling over the battlefield, Couch ordered still more Union troops forward.

"God help us now," said Col. Adelbert Ames of the 20th Maine to his second-in-command, Lt. Col Joshua Chamberlain. The men from Maine reached the rise where all previous assaults had foundered, and there they stayed. "We reached the final crest," Chamberlain later wrote, "before that all-commanding, counter-manding stone wall. Here we exchanged fierce volleys at every dis-advantage until the muzzle flame deepened the sunset red, and all was dark."

But the battle for Marye's Heights was not yet finished. There remained one more grisly scene to be played out. Brig. Gen. George Getty's division included a brigade led by Col. Rush Hawkins. It was Hawkins who, a few nights earlier, had told Burnside that his plan to attack the rebels on Marye's Heights would be the greatest slaughter of the war. Throughout the day, from the roof of a house on the edge of town, Hawkins had watched his prediction come true. Now it was his turn.

He did not go meekly to the slaughter. He protested the order to General Getty, arguing that further attacks would be pointless, a useless waste of lives. Getty had his orders, however, and he was reluctant to protest to his superior or to refuse to carry them out.

Getty led the men forward. They had seen the killing and knew that the outcome was preordained. They realized that they had no chance of reaching the stone wall, but they proceeded nonetheless. When the Confederate soldiers saw them advancing up the hill, they fired their weapons automatically; it was almost dark. Their fire suddenly lighted the field as if a chain of lightning was danc-ing across the top of the wall from one end to the other.

The Union line broke. The men ran for cover, shoving one another, trampling the dead and wounded. The only thing that saved the soldiers behind them was the blackness that descended over the town and the exhaustion of the Confederates, who had been shooting all day. "The attack of our division," Colonel

Hawkins wrote, "closed a battle which was one of the most disastrous defeats to the Union forces during the war."

Fighting Joe Hooker returned to Fredericksburg from his meeting with Burnside, seething over Burnside's refusal to halt the attacks. He quickly grew even angrier when he learned that another of his divisions had been ordered by General Couch to renew the attack. He immediately canceled the order.

"Finding that I had lost as many men as my orders required me to lose," Hooker wrote, "I suspended the attack."

The battle for Marye's Heights was over.

ELEVEN

DEATH HAS BEEN DOING FEARFUL WORK

No one who saw it ever forgot the sight: the entire left wing of the Army of the Potomac—General Franklin's 60,000 troops—arrayed in a magnificent display of military might. It was ten o'clock on the morning of December 13, two miles south of Fredericksburg near the Yankee bridges at Deep Run. The other part of Burnside's plan, which called for Franklin to break through Stonewall Jackson's line with one or two divisions and then head for Lee's right flank at Marye's Heights, was about to commence.

Heros von Borcke, standing with Jackson on Prospect Hill, watched spellbound as the drama unfolded. He wrote:

> And now the thick veil of mist that had concealed the plain from our eyes rolled away, like the drawing up of a drop-scene at the opera, and revealed to us the countless corps, divisions, brigades, and regiments of the Federal army forming their lines of attack extending as far as the eye could see, a military panorama, the grandeur of which I had never seen equaled.
>
> On they came, a beautiful order, as if on parade, a moving forest of steel, their bayonets glistening in the bright sunlight; on they came, waving their hundreds of regimen-

tal flags. I could not rid myself of a feeling of depression and anxiety as I saw this innumerable host steadily moving upon our lines.

Von Borcke need not have worried. This was Franklin the Confederates were facing, not Bull Sumner. The Union force may have looked impressive when the fog burned off, but the majority of the soldiers were not advancing on the Southerners' position. Although this wing of the army appeared to be a massive force, von Borcke overestimated the size of the outfit that was marching toward Jackson's line when he wrote about it years later. It was not all 60,000 Union troops advancing, but less than a tenth that number—Franklin's smallest division, led by Maj. Gen. George G. Meade, which consisted of no more than 4,500 men.

These were the "innumerable" troops expected to pierce the line held by the 39,000 tough, lean veterans of Stonewall Jackson's corps, plus Jeb Stuart's 10,000 cavalrymen waiting in the woods and on high ground. Meade thought he would have support; at least that was the plan. Brig. Gen. John Gibbon would protect the right flank while Brig. Gen. Abner Doubleday would safeguard the left. But even if everything worked properly, Meade simply did not have enough troops to breach Jackson's position.

As soon as the fog dissipated enough to reveal the location of the Union troops, Jackson ordered his artillery to open fire. The Yankee soldiers on the plain quickly sought shelter in dips and swales and behind ridges. Their officers tried to keep the men calm during the intense bombardment by going about their business, setting an example of coolness under fire as though the exploding shells were nothing more than a nuisance.

Capt. James Hall of the 2nd Maine Artillery sat astride his horse, talking to two colonels from the 16th Maine Infantry. Soldiers cowering on the ground watched in admiration as a shell barely missed the officers. It hit an ammunition caisson, setting off a gigantic explosion.

None of the officers seemed disturbed by the uproar, but Captain Hall glanced toward the rebel line with a look of annoyance. He dismounted, walked over to one of the guns in his artillery battery, aimed it at the rebel gun that had fired at him, and signaled his gun crew to fire. The shot blasted the offending rebel artillery piece out of existence. Satisfied, Captain Hall mounted his horse and continued his conversation.

General Meade rode slowly from one regiment to the next, seemingly without concern. He stopped to chat with the men as if it were a casual afternoon in camp. He talked with Col. William McCandless, known as "Old Buck," of the 2nd Pennsylvania Reserves. Meade pointed to the insignia rank on McCandless's shoulder strap and joked about whether Old Buck would get promoted in the coming fight.

"A star this morning, William?" Meade asked.

"More like a wooden overcoat," McCandless said.

No sooner had he spoken than a rebel shell struck and killed his horse, leaving McCandless untouched.

The officers continued their show of outward calm for the good of the men, but privately they agreed on the bleak prospects for success. Being so greatly outnumbered, it was hard to be optimistic about the outcome.

The Union artillery responded to the Confederate shelling. A duel of exploding cannon fire ensued as the Federal guns tried to silence the rebel batteries. As if the noise, chaos, and death were not enough, two horse-drawn Confederate guns moved out from under cover near enough to the Yankee position to expose the gunners to both artillery and rifle fire. It was a foolhardy gesture, but it inspired awe on both sides, along with a fierce determination among the Yankees to obliterate the guns, their crews, and the daring young officer who led them.

That officer was twenty-four-year-old Maj. John Pelham from Alabama, who had quit the military academy at West Point shortly before graduation because he was eager to fight for the Confederacy. Dubbed "Gallant Pelham" during an earlier military action, he served as artillery chief to the equally daring Jeb Stuart. Some Richmond society women declared that Pelham was even handsomer than Stuart, who was known for his good looks.

Lee's artillery chief, Col. Edward Porter Alexander, wrote

[Pelham was] a very young looking, handsome, and attractive fellow, slender, blue eyes, light hair, smooth, red and white complexion, and with such a modest and refined expression that his classmates and friends never spoke of him but as "Sallie" and there never was a Sallie whom a man could love more!

Pelham's gun crews worked rapidly, loading and firing so fast that Union artillerymen thought they were dealing with a battery of at least four guns. However, the Union gunners quickly zeroed in on Pelham's cannon, knocking one out of commission and wounding so many of the men that Pelham himself was helping to fire the remaining weapon. Even though he moved the gun frequently, Union artillery soon found it again and sent cascades of shells exploding all around it.

There was a limit to how long even the gallant Pelham could last in the open against such overwhelming fire. Jeb Stuart ordered von Borcke to ride out and tell Pelham he should retire.

"Tell the General I can hold my ground," Pelham answered.

Stuart sent two more riders to Pelham telling him to leave the field, but Pelham refused. He continued to fire until he was almost out of ammunition and then retreated reluctantly. When he got back to Stuart's headquarters, he removed the red-and-blue striped Grenadier Guards necktie he had wound around his cap and returned it to an English officer who had asked him to wear it into battle.

Robert E. Lee watched Pelham's courageous action from his post atop Telegraph Hill. He asked an aide who the brave officer was. When told it was Pelham, Lee said, "It is glorious to see such courage in one so young."

Meade's infantrymen, meanwhile, remained immobile during the artillery duel, flattened on the ground while the shells from both sides burst all around them. "The air warmed steadily and the ground became disagreeable for the soldiers, who found themselves in three inches of cold, clinging mud. Filth covered the men from head to toe and made them look as 'dingy and muddy as turtles.'" The ground beneath the mud was frozen solid and the men chilled as they sank in the ooze. They were more than ready to move out when the rebel artillery fire finally died down. By then it was eleven o'clock in the morning.

Meade organized his division into three long lines and led them across the barren farmland—fields covered with wheat stubble—toward the woods and a railway embankment where the rebel infantry awaited them. On they went, crossing through three ditches, each five feet deep. By the time they climbed out of the last one, their lines were ragged. They had lost the perfect alignment that made officers glow with such pride.

"Hold your fire, boys, until the command is given," a rebel officer cautioned his men. "Be sure you make every shot count."

Suddenly the Union officers halted their men just before they reached the railroad line. They had spotted the waiting enemy infantry and had stopped the men to dress ranks, to re-form into straight, orderly lines. When once again neatly arrayed, the Union soldiers opened fire with buck and ball—a deadly combination of a musket ball wrapped in a cartridge with three buckshot. Each shot spewed out four missiles, an impressive display of firepower.

By luck, the Union troops struck close to a six-hundred-yard gap in the Confederate line between two brigades. It was a boggy, marshy area thick with trees and undergrowth, but with not a single rebel soldier to stand in the way of Meade's men. The Yankees poured into the gap, scattering the closest elements of the two rebel brigades and taking several hundred of the men prisoner.

Meade's Pennsylvanians raced forward. Some Confederate outfits behind the front lines were caught with their muskets stacked. They ran, leaving the weapons behind.

It was a disastrous rupture of Jackson's defensive line. Meade's men headed for the military road Lee had constructed to link his two corps. If Meade's troops, followed by substantial reinforcements, reached the road and turned right, they would be behind

Jackson's line. They could roll up Lee's right flank at Marye's Heights, leaving Lee no choice but to fall back.

Burnside and his staff waited outdoors in the cold, gathered on the porch roof of his headquarters at Phillips House to observe the battle at Deep Run. Burnside saw Meade's three blue lines advance until the smoke of battle obscured them from sight. At ten thirty, during the artillery duel that preceded Meade's planned advance, Burnside had sent an aide to General Franklin to inquire about the situation.

At eleven, Burnside received a message by telegraph from his chief of staff, Gen. James Hardie, whom he had sent to Franklin's headquarters earlier that morning. The telegram notified Burnside that Franklin had sent in Meade's division, which was advancing on the enemy. "General Meade has just moved out. Doubleday supports him. Meade's skirmishers engaged, however, at once with enemy's skirmishers."

Burnside still had no idea whether his plan that called for Franklin's troops to break through on Lee's right would succeed. Therefore, he did not yet order Sumner to launch his attack on Marye's Heights. But there was a limit to how long he dared wait before doing so. Burnside would have to make this decision on the basis of almost no sound information from Franklin's front. When he ordered the assault on Marye's Heights, it was based more on hope—and desperation—than on conviction.

To Burnside's dismay, while the first charge against the stone wall was barely under way, he received a less-than-encouraging message from Hardie. It said simply that Meade was moving slowly against the Confederate line: "Meade advanced half a mile, and holds on. Infantry of enemy in woods in front of extreme left. No loss [of troops], so far, of great importance."

This did not sound as optimistic or as hopeful as General Hardie's previous message, so Burnside sent an aide, Capt. James Cutts, to tell Franklin to advance the 6th Corps, led by Maj. Gen. William Smith, and the 1st Corps, led by Maj. Gen. John

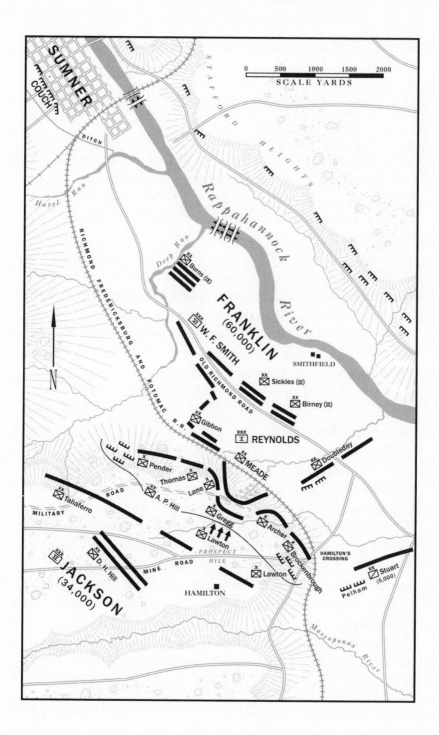

Reynolds. These corps would provide ample support for Meade's small division. Their deployment also would expand the length of the line of attack and provide sufficient troops to exploit any breakthrough Meade's troops might make.

Thus, Burnside's orders broadened the scope of the attack he expected Franklin to make, committing two full corps instead of only a single division. Burnside was counting on a major battle on Lee's right flank to take the pressure off Sumner's men as they proceeded against Marye's Heights. Franklin had some 60,000 soldiers and Burnside expected him to use more of them on his end of the line.

Shortly after noon, Burnside was disappointed to learn that Franklin had agreed to commit—but had not yet ordered forward—only Reynolds's 1st Corps, and was holding back Smith's far larger 6th Corps. Why Franklin was keeping these troops in reserve was not clear. But what was abundantly plain to Burnside was that Franklin was not going to attempt a serious, large-scale assault. Burnside was frustrated. Although he did not have a clear picture of what was happening in Franklin's sector, he did realize that Franklin was not putting forth a maximum effort against Stonewall Jackson's line.

The situation became even more vexing by early afternoon. Burnside's aide, Captain Cutts, returned to Phillips House with word that Franklin had not sent any more troops forward. Worse, Franklin told Cutts specifically that he would be unable to do so.

"But he *must* advance," Burnside told Cutts, and he sent yet another aide to Franklin with orders to commit his entire force to the attack. It was nearly one thirty in the afternoon. Sumner's casualties at the stone wall were numbering in the thousands while Franklin continued to hold back from the battle the majority of his 60,000 men.

Telegraphic messages continued to arrive at Phillips House from General Hardie at Franklin's headquarters.

> 1.25 o'clock P.M. Meade is in the woods in his front, seems to be able to hold on.

1.40 o'clock P.M. Meade having carried a portion of the enemy's position in the woods . . . Meade has suffered severely.

2.15 o'clock P.M. Gibbon and Meade driven back from the woods. Things do not look as well on Reynolds' front.

2.25 o'clock P.M. Dispatch received [Burnside's order to Franklin to attack with his entire force]. Franklin will do his best.

3.40 o'clock P.M. Gibbon's and Meade's divisions are badly used up, and I fear another advance on the enemy on our left cannot be made this afternoon.

Long before Burnside received the last message, Meade's division was in serious trouble. The Union advance had collapsed.

Meade had been left entirely on his own in the deep pocket his troops had created in the enemy line. Neither Gibbon nor Doubleday was able to advance far enough to fully protect Meade's flanks, as they were supposed to have done. That left Meade surrounded on three sides by enemy units that outnumbered him six to one, and which were quickly reorganizing and beginning to exert pressure on him. As heavy fire poured into his position, some of his men started to retreat.

A ball ripped through the crown of Meade's hat, missing his head by a fraction of an inch. Another ball struck his horse in the neck. Worse, Meade was nearly shot by one of his own officers who was running away from the fight. Meade chased the deserter down on horseback and ordered him to return to his regiment. The lieutenant aimed his musket at the general and seemed ready to shoot. Meade raised his sword and with the flat side bashed the man's head so hard that the blade snapped at the hilt. The man then meekly went back to the line.

Meade directed much of his anger at his fellow generals. He desperately needed reinforcements. His advance had been stopped; his troops were retreating, the casualties mounting. With neither Gibbon nor Doubleday able to provide help on the flanks, Meade tried to obtain assistance from Brig. Gen. David Birney, whose division, part of the 3rd Corps, had been held in reserve.

Birney, however, had problems of his own. One of his brigades had gotten lost and the other two were separated from each other by artillery batteries, making communication between them difficult. Birney had been instructed to follow the orders issued by the 1st Corps commander, General Reynolds. However, no one had told Birney that he was required to obey the orders of Reynolds's subordinates as well, and that included Meade. When Birney refused to respond to Meade's request for help, Meade was incensed.

He ordered his aide to return to Birney's headquarters, demanding that he obey the order of a superior officer and rush his men forward. Birney again said no. Meade's aide had to ride back through the gauntlet of rebel gunfire bearing the news of yet another refusal. Outraged, Meade mounted his horse and rode off to confront Birney in person. When Meade found him, he lit into him in language so strong, according to a soldier standing nearby, that it "almost made the stones creep."

"I assume the authority of ordering you to the relief of my men," Meade shouted.

An officer who witnessed the incident recalled that Meade "was almost wild with rage as he saw the golden opportunity slipping away and the slaughter of his men going for naught."

Meade turned to Reynolds, his corps commander: "My God, General Reynolds, did they think my division could whip Lee's whole army?"

Birney hastened to assemble his widely scattered command, but the best he could do was send part of one brigade to Meade's relief. It was too little, too late. Meade's valiant division, which by then had lost 40 percent of its men, was in full retreat. And the Confederates were coming after them.

There was no sound on earth quite like the rebel yell. It sent spasms of fear through the hearts of countless Yankees. It surely did that day when Gen. Jubal Early's men arrived on the scene and began to overrun the remnants of Meade's division. They drove the rearguard units of Union soldiers out of the swampy gap they had occupied for such a short time and back over the open wheat fields. Confederate artillery shelled them every step of the way, and every time they looked back, screaming Confederate soldiers were closing in.

Sgt. Jacob Heffelfinger of the 7th Pennsylvania was shot in both legs. In considerable pain, he lay helpless in the path of the approaching enemy. He took a small diary out of his pocket and jotted down his thoughts while bullets and shells whistled above him. He wrote that the men of his division

General George Meade commanded the smallest division in Franklin's forces at Fredericksburg. (*Library of Congress*)

> were driven back over me in disorder. All that we gained at so fearful a cost is lost. I am still lying where I fell. The rebels have advanced in a line over me, so that I am a prisoner. I am now exposed to the fire of our artillery, which is fearfully destructive. Death has been doing fearful work today.

The artillery of both sides were engaged in another deadly duel. Meade's retreating infantry was caught in the middle. Some of the Confederate gunners concentrated on them, cutting them down by the score.

Stonewall Jackson watched his troops advance. He rode to one end of his line, accompanied by an aide, James Smith, whom Jackson enjoyed teasing. As the men dismounted and walked closer to the front, a bullet whizzed between their heads, missing by inches.

"Mr. Smith," said Jackson playfully, "had you not better go to the rear? They may shoot you!"

Jeb Stuart also had a close call. As usual, he was where the fighting was most fierce. His distinctively garbed figure on horseback was an inviting target for Yankee sharpshooters sheltered behind a hedge. They aimed and fired, tearing his uniform in two places, leaving holes to admire later but no wounds.

General Meade tried to stop the retreat of his men. He and Old Buck McCandless grabbed the colors of two regiments and waved them back and forth to rally the troops, but the men streamed past, ignoring them. All order, all semblance of organization, was lost, along with any hope of survival.

Meade remained in the open for a while, carrying the colors and watching the approaching line of Confederate troops. For a long time he refused to budge, as if he still expected General Birney to send reinforcements so they could stop the rebel advance.

But no help came for Meade's troops that afternoon. Men died or were forced to surrender. Several hundred Union captives were sent under guard to the rear. Few of the rebel soldiers wanted to care for the prisoners, however. They preferred to kill the Yankees and chase them back far enough to raid their camps and forage for food, coffee, and warm clothing.

General Birney finally organized two regiments to send forward, out of the nineteen in his division. His older brother, Col. William Birney, led one. Before they had advanced very far they were overrun by a horde of Meade's troops who were fleeing the rebels. They shouted at Birney's men to turn back. One referred to the fleeing troops as like a herd of buffalo stampeding.

Meade, Birney, and Reynolds galloped out in front of the regiment to try once again to halt their flight. "It was useless," General Birney recalled. "They went right through us."

Robert E. Lee watched with enormous satisfaction as Jackson's men pursued the Yankees at Deep Run. Longstreet was stopping them at the stone wall and now Jackson was delivering another major victory. Lee stared at Meade's fleeing men in blue and remarked to Longstreet, "It is well that war is so terrible. [Otherwise], we should grow too fond of it."

And then the battle turned. It was time for Confederates to die. Generals Franklin and Reynolds had not committed many men to the failed offensive, but they had tens of thousands in reserve to defend against attack, along with hundreds of artillery pieces. The

Union artillerymen waited as the Confederate troops ran toward them across the open field. Their cannon were loaded with cannister and shot. When the rebels got close enough, the Yankees opened fire, spraying tiny lethal balls and chunks of steel into the ranks, mowing them down by the hundreds.

The Confederates turned and raced back to the shelter of the woods. It was all over in minutes. The sudden silence was broken only by the moans of the wounded. At the other end of Lee's line, waves of Bull Sumner's troops were still sacrificing themselves at the stone wall, but down at Deep Run the battle was over, even though most of Franklin's men had not even fired a shot.

Franklin was reported to have "felt he was outnumbered and must keep a large reserve to repel any surprise attack. [He] did nothing more than hold his original position from that moment forward."

Of the eight divisions in Franklin's command, only three saw combat that day. An entire corps, consisting of 24,000 men—the largest corps in the Union army—had not been involved in any fighting at all. Of Franklin's 60,000 troops, only about 18,000 played even a tangential role in the battle, and they had been deployed in piecemeal fashion rather than as a unit, where the weight of numbers would have had a greater effect.

Despite holding back most of his troops and making only a halfhearted attempt to pierce Stonewall Jackson's line, Franklin appealed to Burnside for help, exaggerating the danger facing him.

"All of my troops are in action at that point," Franklin wrote, "and the result is so doubtful that any movement to my front is impossible at present. The truth is, my left is in danger of being turned. What hope is there of getting reinforcements across the river?"

Not only had Franklin refused to attack, he apparently believed his situation was so precarious that his 60,000-man force needed protection from Jackson's smaller force. "I put in all the troops I thought it proper and prudent to put in," Franklin said a week later on December 19, when he testified before the Joint Congressional Committee on the Conduct of the War. "I fought the whole strength of my command as far as I could, and at the same time keep my connection with the river open."

The congressmen did not agree with Franklin's assessment. The committee's reported stated:

> The testimony of all the witnesses before [this] committee proves most conclusively that had the attack been made upon the left with all the force which General Franklin could have used for that purpose, the plan of General Burnside would have been completely successful, and our Army would have achieved a most brilliant victory.

Although Franklin was reluctant to make further attacks that afternoon, Stonewall Jackson was not.

"I want to move forward," he told his staff, "to attack them [and] drive them into the river yonder." A staff officer recalled that Jackson's "countenance glowed as from the glare of a great conflagration." Jeb Stuart rode up, fresh from a reconnaissance of the enemy line. He told Jackson that from what he had seen, the Union troops were demoralized. That clinched it. Jackson would attack.

His plan called for a heavy artillery bombardment toward sundown, which would so shatter the Northerners' morale that even their superior numbers would be unable to stop a Confederate offensive. Jackson ordered the artillery pieces brought forward from under cover in the woods. They began to fire, and to everyone's surprise, the shelling was met with an overwhelming return fire from a far greater number of Union cannon.

Jackson watched the Union shells sweep over the field his infantry would have to cross, and he knew his plan could not succeed. He later wrote that the enemy bombardment "so completely swept our front as to satisfy me that the proposed movement should be abandoned."

Everyone agreed that this was the sensible thing to do. Even Jubal Early, as aggressive as anyone, wrote that "nothing could have lived while passing over that plain. I feel well assured that, while we were all ready to obey the orders of our heroic commander

[Jackson], there was not a man in the force ordered to advance who did not breathe easier when he heard the orders countermanding the movement."

The fighting may have been over on Jackson's front, but the suffering and dying were not. Littering the plain over which both Yankees and rebels had fought, thousands of wounded men begged for help. Hundreds of horses screeched hideously, thrashing in agony on the blood-soaked ground.

The survivors, safe behind their own lines, found the cries of human and animal suffering unnerving. No one dared venture out to help for fear of being shot. Then a new horror arose, too awful for most survivors to describe. The exploding artillery shells had left patches of black powder smoldering in the dry grass. Here and there, pockets of flame erupted in the twilight, quickly causing raging fires to spread out in all directions.

Some of the wounded men tried to drag themselves out of the path of the flames, but soon there were too many fires, cutting off escape even to those who could still crawl. Others flailed at the flames with their bare hands or their coats. A lucky few came away with hands that were dripping shreds of skin, and hair and whiskers burnt off, leaving only blackened flesh.

Many soldiers died in the fires. Confederate army captain John Keely recalled one man who tried to beat back the fire by striking with the steel ramrod from his muzzle-loading rifle. It was all he had. Keely saw the flames approach him. The man's screams grew more shrill as his uniform began to blaze. Finally the fire took hold of the man's cartridge box and he disappeared in a flash of red and gray smoke. Helpless soldiers from both sides watched in horrified silence, shaken, one said, to the core of their "hardened soldiers' hearts."

The sun set at 4:34 on the afternoon of December 13 and soon a merciful darkness blotted out from sight, if not from memory, the color of red—of blood and fire from the battlefield. But shortly

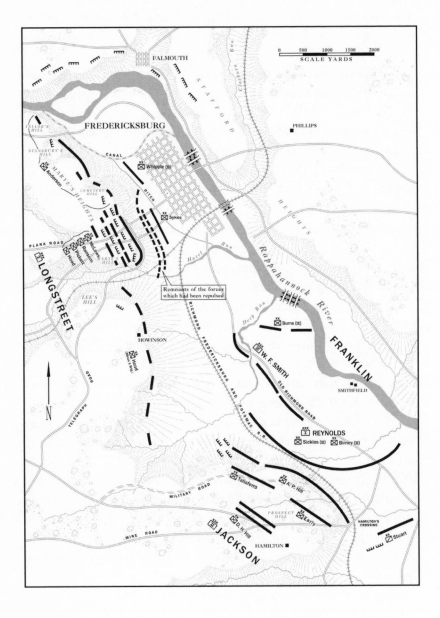

thereafter, at least according to some accounts, the sky turned fiery crimson, as if heaven itself were being consumed by flames.

Men gazed in awe and wonder, and those who had never seen such a display before, rare that far south, whispered about what it might be. Had some ammunition depot beyond the horizon caught fire? Was a forest or a field of wheat stubble burning? Col. Joshua Chamberlain of the 20th Maine described the sight as "fiery lances and banners of blood and flame, columns of pearly light, garlands and wreaths of gold, all pointing and beckoning upward."

> The sky flashed and grew dark again, now shining white, it reddened and dimmed and blazed once more till it lighted the faces of the marveling soldiers. It could be nothing less than [the] "Northern lights," the fantastic sky-painting of the Aurora Borealis.

Some Southerners took it as a sign that God was reveling in their victory and wanted them to know it. "Of course," one Confederate soldier wrote, "we enthusiastic young fellows felt that the heavens were hanging out banners and streamers and setting off fireworks in honor of our victory."

Other, more superstitious Southerners thought the name of the phenomenon, *Northern* lights, was a bad omen.* Coming as it did from the direction of the Union lines, the garish display had to be a sign of foreboding. Those glaring red lights could have only one meaning: The Yankees would come again in the morning, and this time they would be successful.

---

*George Rable, in his book *Fredericksburg, Fredericksburg,* wrote that the Aurora Borealis occurred December 14, not December 13. He based that conclusion on the accounts of survivors who described the event in diaries and letters. Joshua Chamberlain, whose description is included here, also claimed that the lights occurred on December 14. However, the British newspaper correspondent Charles Lawley stated that the lights occurred December 12. Other historians cite survivor accounts that date the occurrence to December 13. These include Douglas Southall Freeman (*Lee's Lieutenants* and *Robert E. Lee: A Biography*), Frank Vandiver (*Mighty Stonewall*) and Lenoir Chambers (*Stonewall Jackson*).

A photograph taken from Marye's Heights soon after the second battle of Fredericksburg. Union forces took control of the area in the spring of 1863. Fredericksburg can be seen in the background. (*Library of Congress*)

TWELVE

Alone with
the Dead

"It's all arranged," General Burnside announced. "We attack at early dawn, the 9th Corps in the center, which I shall lead in person."

He turned to Col. Rush Hawkins, who only four days earlier had told Burnside that the intended assault on Marye's Heights would lead to the greatest slaughter of the war. Although Hawkins had been proven correct, Burnside was intending to do it all over again.

"Hawkins, your brigade shall lead with the 9th New York on the right of the line, and we'll make up for the bad work of today."

It was one o'clock in the morning of December 14 at Burnside's headquarters at Phillips House. The roomful of officers was not surprised by Burnside's decision. They had known it was coming and they dreaded it. No one spoke, and Burnside seemed unnerved by the silence. He had expected enthusiastic support.

Finally, Bull Sumner, who had been obeying orders since the day he joined the army—five years before Burnside was born—spoke up. Old Bull talked more quietly and soberly than anyone could ever remember him doing. Clearly, what he had to say was painful for him.

"General, I hope you will desist from this attack," Sumner said. "I do not know of any general officer who approves of it, and I think it will prove disastrous to the army."

This was Edwin Vose Sumner's finest moment. As Burnside's biographer wrote:

> With this reluctant admission Sumner did the country, and Burnside, the greatest service of his long career. No one else could have convinced the harried commander of the need to concede defeat. From anyone else it would have seemed to be either continued insubordination or the voice of inexperience, but Sumner [had been] his heartiest supporter. Burnside could not ignore the advice.

Burnside questioned his other commanders. Without exception, they all disapproved of renewing the assault. Even Fighting Joe Hooker was opposed to it. He spoke out more emphatically than Sumner, arguing that the fighting at Fredericksburg should stop altogether. Burnside finally realized that he had lost the battle. The possibility that he could redeem himself by winning in the morning—or dying gloriously at the head of his army—was gone.

Burnside left to call on Maj. Gen. Darius Couch at his headquarters. Couch's troops had spearheaded the ill-fated attack against the stone wall. Couch had watched the battle unfold from the cupola of the courthouse and he recounted the events for Burnside. The men talked for about an hour. Couch recalled that Burnside was "cheerful in his tone and did not seem greatly depressed, but it was plain that he felt he had led us to a great disaster, and one knowing him so long and well as myself could see that he wished his body was also lying in front of Marye's Heights. I never felt so badly for a man in my life."

Maj. Gen. William F. Smith also saw Burnside after his commanders had rejected his plan to renew the attack. Smith found Burnside pacing in his tent, looking greatly distressed.

"Oh, those men!" Burnside cried. "Oh, those men!"

When Smith asked what men he was referring to, Burnside pointed across the river toward Marye's Heights where thousands of Union soldiers lay dead or dying in the frigid night air.

"Those men over there," Burnside said. "I am thinking of them all the time."

Robert E. Lee was convinced the Yankees would attack again the next day. He knew that despite heavy losses, Burnside still had a much larger number of troops in reserve. At nine o'clock on the night of December 13, four hours before Sumner persuaded Burnside to abandon the idea of pursuing the attack, Lee sent a telegram to James Seddon, the Confederate secretary of war. After briefly describing the events of the day, Lee wrote, "I expect the battle to be renewed at daylight. Please send this to the president."

Not all of Lee's commanders agreed with him. At a meeting with Longstreet and several division commanders, some expressed doubt that Burnside would press on, given the devastating losses he had already suffered. While they were discussing the matter, one of Longstreet's scouts arrived with a written message taken from a captured Union courier.

The paper contained Burnside's plans for a new assault to begin in the morning. He had drafted it for Franklin before Sumner and the other generals had dissuaded him. To Lee, of course, the dispatch confirmed his belief that the Yankees would assault the heights again, and he issued orders to his generals to strengthen the defenses and bring up more ammunition. If Burnside was coming, Lee would be ready for him.

Several thousand Union soldiers spent the night of December 13 trapped behind the slight rise in the ground in front of the stone wall. "The night was bitter cold," General Couch reported, "and a fearful one for the front line hugging the hollows in the ground, and for the wounded who could not be reached. It was a night of dreadful suffering. Many died of wounds and exposure, and as fast as men died, they stiffened in the wintry air, and on the front line were rolled forward for protection to the living."

Clara Barton's biographer wrote that the Union troops in front of the stone wall lay

> in every conceivable posture, some on their backs with gaping jaws, some with eyes as large as walnuts, protruding with glassy stare, some doubled up like a contortionist, here one without a head, there one without legs, yonder a head and legs without a trunk, everywhere horrible expressions, fear, rage, agony, madness, torture, lying in pools of blood, lying with heads half-buried in mud, with fragments of shell sticking in oozing brain, with bullet holes all over the puffed limbs.

About every ten minutes throughout the night the Confederate soldiers behind the stone wall fired a salvo of shots into the darkness, catching those Northerners who foolishly got up to help a friend, to stretch or answer a call of nature, or to try to escape. The Confederates also lobbed shells onto the open field, killing more of those who had not already frozen to death.

Despite the dangers, some Union soldiers roamed the field, attempting to save the wounded. They tore shutters off the walls of houses to use as stretchers, to carry the wounded back to town. Even in the darkness it was not difficult to locate the wounded; there was no missing their cries for help.

Pvt. Samuel North, of the 126th Pennsylvania, wrote to his brother that his impression of the battlefield "seemed to be burned on my brain, the still pale faces of the dead, and the shrieks and groans of the wounded and dying. Oh! It is awful!" Another Pennsylvania soldier remembered how "the cries of the wounded rose up over that bloody field like the wail of lost spirits all the night; cries for water, blankets, and 'to be borne off the field' in all the paroxysms that terror and suffering can excite, went up from the sad victims of the day's havoc and filled the very air with pain."

Alfred R. Waud's sketch of Union stretcher bearers carrying wounded soldiers from the battle front. (*Library of Congress*)

Pvt. Bill McCarter, General Meagher's adjutant, was determined to drag himself back to town to get medical treatment for his wounds. He waited until eight o'clock that night, just after another volley of rebel fire erupted from the stone wall, and then he stumbled to his feet and headed toward town. He frequently tripped over bodies in his path. His injured right arm, which he was supporting with his left, bled freely.

When he judged that ten minutes had passed, he flattened himself to the ground just as the rebels peppered the field with yet another round of bullets. One hit the heel of his shoe, tearing it off, but it did no damage to his foot. McCarter slowly stood up and made his way out of range of enemy musket fire, then collapsed from exhaustion.

> A burning, raging fever now attacked me, I felt as though I was being consumed. The pain of my wounds increased. My thirst grew to such an agonizing degree that my tongue literally stuck fast to the roof of my mouth. I really prayed to God with all my soul to end my life then and there or send me water.

McCarter lay still for an hour, resigned to death, when suddenly he heard voices and saw the glare of a lantern moving closer. It was a search party looking for wounded men, and they turned out to be troops from his own company of the Irish Brigade.

They gave him two canteens of water and carried him to an ambulance already filled with eleven other wounded men. The vehicle was stuck in mud, but the soldiers managed to get it rolling and it jolted and bumped its way into Fredericksburg. The trip took an hour in the darkness, over rocks and tree stumps, ditches and gullies.

The wounded men begged the driver to slow down—the jarring ride was too painful—but he would not. By the time they reached their destination, two of the men had died. The ambulance pulled up in front of a four-story house, and the driver ordered everyone out. They were left on their own to seek treatment. McCarter crawled up the sidewalk to the house and found every room crammed with wounded soldiers. He was lucky to find space to lie down. The pain was numbing his mind worse than before, and he was hungry and exhausted. He hoped an army surgeon would find him before he died.

While some Union soldiers were combing the freezing field looking for the wounded, others were establishing a defense line in case the Confederates came charging down the hill during the night. Pvt. Robert Carter, of the 22nd Massachusetts, had not been wounded in the assault, but, like so many others, in the heat of battle he had thrown way his cumbersome haversack. Now he was hungry.

Carter and his buddies went foraging in the dark, ready to drop to the ground the instant the enemy fired another salvo from the stone wall. The first full haversack they found contained hard bread, spoons, and a handful of breadcrumbs mixed with what felt like sugar. It was a feast—the first food they had eaten since morning. To their surprise, the mixture also contained fiery red pepper. "We sneezed, coughed, choked, spluttered and spit, until it seemed as though our tongues were on fire and our throats burned out."

He found another haversack beneath the corpse of a Union soldier. He rolled the body over and greedily stuck his hand in the sack feeling around for bread. What he came up with was a pasty mix of flour and clotted blood.

> My hand had plunged in to the wrist. A large wound in the man's side had been over the opening, and the blood pouring in had soon congealed. A chill almost froze the marrow in my bones, my teeth came together with a snap, my hair slowly rose on end. I was all alone with the dead, in utter darkness, upon the battlefield, and my hand dripping with cold, clotted blood. I foraged no more, for I was not hungry again that night.

When the 20th Maine was ordered to move up close to the sunken road during the night to relieve another regiment, Lt. Col. Joshua Chamberlain was without a blanket or an overcoat. He felt overwhelmed by the horrible moans and screams of the wounded, "a wail so far and deep and wide, as if a thousand discords were flowing together into a keynote, weird, unearthly, terrible to hear and bear."

Trying to protect himself from the biting cold and wind, Chamberlain fashioned a shelter between two corpses, with a third body near his head. Even Chamberlain, a sensitive, cultured, highly educated college professor, had become so inured to death and suffering that, on that night in that terrible place, "the living and the dead were alike to me."

The Irish Brigade held a banquet that night in honor of the presentation of the regiment's new colors, which had finally arrived. The elaborate hall the soldiers had constructed for the affair was now out of bounds on the far side of the river. In its place, General Meagher had commandeered a theater, which somehow had been overlooked in the army's quest for hospital space.

The hall was festooned with banners, and the tables creaked under the weight of the food, liquor, and champagne Meagher had arranged to be sent down from Washington. Even with the free flow of spirits and the colorful decorations, however, it was a staid and solemn evening. General Couch attended, as well as General Hancock and a number of distinguished visitors from New York who had brought the new flags.

During the dinner, a Confederate cannon shell shattered the windows and tore off part of the roof. Meagher insisted that the proceedings continue unimpeded, as if the noisy interruption was simply part of the pageantry. He told the visitors how proud he was of the Irish Brigade soldiers and he thanked them for the fine new flags.

Then he startled the assembled company by announcing that although he appreciated the honor the colors represented, he could not accept them because not enough men had survived to keep them safe in battle. He asked the distinguished guests to take the colors back to New York until such time as the Irish Brigade was up to full strength. It never would be—and Meagher would resign from the army only five months later.

After he made an emotional toast to fallen comrades, a soldier serving as a waiter placed a platter covered with a napkin before him. When the general lifted the cover, expecting to find dessert, he saw a cannonball on the plate, a none-too-subtle hint that the brightly lit building was an easy target for Confederate artillery, whose shells were striking in great number all around them.

And so the banquet ended. As the guests left, General Hancock was overheard to remark, "Only the Irish could follow such a fight with such a feast."

At six o'clock on the morning of December 14, Bill McCarter, who had missed the Irish Brigade's banquet, began to believe he might live. Three army surgeons, their clothing splattered with blood and gore from operating all night, walked into his room to see if there was anyone else who needed treatment. One surgeon helped McCarter onto a table, cut away his shirt, and probed the wound with his fingers, searching for the bullet.

Finally the doctor inserted his entire hand into the socket of McCarter's shoulder and located the bullet. He told McCarter to put his own left hand in the wound and feel it for himself. The surgeon then cut the bullet out and swished it in a pail of water. (The bullet was the only thing to be washed during the entire procedure.) The doctor handed the bullet to McCarter.

"I suppose you would like to preserve this relic of the war," he said.

"Yes," McCarter said. He put it in his pocket and kept it for the rest of his life.

Capt. Francis Adams Donaldson, of the 118th Pennsylvania, strolled leisurely through Fredericksburg's streets on the morning of December 14. "It was Sunday," he wrote in a letter to his aunt. "But what does a soldier care about the Lord's day? The streets were lined with wounded and dying men. The ambulances and stretcher bearers were strained to their utmost capacity. The town was actually choked with wounded, every house every room and every nook and corner being filled with the mangled fellows."

Clara Barton worked in one of those houses and had gone without sleep since the battle began. To provide some warmth for the wounded, she and some soldiers had taken apart a chimney, heated the bricks, and packed them around the injured men. One soldier she treated had been shot in the face, which was so clotted and encrusted with his own dried blood that he no longer looked human. Clara paled at the sight but proceeded to cleanse his head, gently wiping the blood away. The outline of a face appeared, greatly disfigured by the impact of the bullet. She gasped as she recognized him—the sexton of her church back home in Massachusetts.

While the wounded Union soldiers clung to life, the magnitude of the losses became known. One regiment numbering more than three hundred before the battle could muster only thirty-six at roll call the next morning. A captain was the highest-ranking officer left. As he stared at what remained of his outfit, he realized that the color-bearers were missing and he asked who would be willing to carry the colors. Two men stepped forward to take them. The captain shook their hands and the regiment silently dressed ranks.

When General Hancock reviewed his division, he noticed three privates from the Irish Brigade standing off to the side.

"Damn it," he shouted. "You there! Close up on your company."

"Sir," one of them said, "we are a company."

"The hell you say!" Hancock returned their salute. "As you were," he told them.

A New Hampshire regiment mustered only seventy men for morning formation. A year before, it had a roster of a thousand. One company consisted of only one sergeant, three corporals, and six privates.

Many of the living remained in danger. The Union infantrymen who had passed the night lying in front of the stone wall, freezing and hungry, menaced by enemy shells and bullets, spent the following day trapped in the same predicament. To try to move, to escape, or even to raise a canteen to take a drink could make them a target.

Two brothers, Robert and Walter Carter of the 22nd Massachusetts, huddled together behind a couple of corpses they had piled up for protection. The bodies had begun to decompose. One brother wrote that the corpses' "fixed and glassy eyes stared at us in the face, and the stench from our comrades became repulsive to the last degree."

The Carters found some rubber ponchos and pulled them over the bodies. "This breastwork of the dead saved our lives more than once during the day, as they were struck several times at least, as denoted by that peculiar dull thud in the dead flesh; and a shiver ran through our spinal columns at every fresh clip."

A true hero of the aftermath of the battle, if not the entire war, appeared among the Union soldiers on the freezing field that day. And he came from behind the stone wall. A nineteen-year-old

Southerner, Sgt. Richard Rowland Kirkland of Company E, 2nd South Carolina, had listened through the night and then well into the day to the wounded Yankees crying out for water. He could stand it no longer. The Union soldiers, trapped on the field, could not help their comrades without risking their own lives, so Kirkland asked his brigade commander if he could go to their aid.

The officer reluctantly granted permission. Kirkland gathered as many canteens as he could carry, climbed over the stone wall, and froze, wondering whether he would be shot. The Union troops opened fire immediately, but Kirkland was not hit. Calmly, slowly, he walked toward the fallen men who had been his enemy the day before. He knelt, in full view of everyone on both sides, and gave a wounded Union soldier a drink of water. The Union soldiers stopped shooting and watched Kirkland in silence as he placed a knapsack under the man's head and spread an overcoat from a dead soldier over him. Then he moved on to the next man.

Kirkland was besieged by injured men begging for water. For an hour and a half, he helped scores of soldiers, frequently returning behind the lines to refill his canteens. No one knows how many lives he saved, but he survived to tell about it. No one could bring himself to fire on such a man as Richard Kirkland, who placed his own life in danger to care for his enemies. (Today, a handsome statue of Sergeant Kirkland—called the "Angel of Marye's Heights"—stands near the stone wall.)

Henry Villard was a determined man. The twenty-seven-year-old German-born writer for the *New York Tribune* wanted to be the first reporter to file the story of the debacle at Fredericksburg. He hoped to scoop all the other reporters who had witnessed the tragic events. To do so, he had to reach Washington as soon as possible and send his story from there to New York.

He began the trip at three o'clock on the morning of December 14 with a twelve-mile ride on horseback to Aquia Creek over rutted roads churned to mud by the heavy rain. The horse threw him once, leaving him covered with muck but no injuries except to his pride. The journey took six hours, twice as long as in daylight over dry roads.

Villard went at once to the quartermaster in charge of the Aquia Creek depot. The man gave him a hearty breakfast, along with disappointing news. Villard had expected to catch the next boat up the Potomac River to Washington. However, General Burnside did not want reporters, or anyone else, leaking word to Washington of his devastating defeat. He had left orders that no one—officer, enlisted man, or civilian, and especially reporters—was to be allowed to board a boat heading north without his permission. A lesser man might have given up, but Villard had arrived in New York nine years before, a penniless ambitious immigrant knowing not a word of English. He was not about to abandon his mission.

He left the quartermaster's office, evaded the armed soldiers guarding the wharf, and strolled down the riverbank. Seeing two black men who were fishing offshore in a little rowboat, he offered them a dollar each to take him out for a ride. Then he promised them an additional five dollars if they would take him out to the steamship channel where the government steamers sailed between Fortress Monroe and Washington. Once aboard, he would be safe, for those boats did not put in at Aquia.

The captain of the first boat he hailed denied Villard permission to come aboard. As a cargo shipper under government contract, the captain was not allowed to carry passengers. That did not stop Villard. He grabbed a rope that was hanging over the side, hauled himself up on the deck, and yelled to the fishermen to row away as fast as they could. Now the captain had no way of refusing Villard passage short of stopping at Aquia Creek, which he was not supposed to do, or throwing him overboard.

Villard wrote, "The captain was at first disposed to be wrathy at my summary proceeding but became mollified on being shown my general army pass, and on my assurance that I commanded enough influence to protect him in case my performance should get him into trouble." The promise of a substantial cash payment may have also helped.

When the steamer docked at Washington, Villard rushed to his newspaper's office on F Street, only to learn that Secretary of War Edwin Stanton had ordered the main telegraph center not to transmit any information about Fredericksburg without his approval.

Villard sent a copy of his story about the battle by courier on the night train to New York, and set out for Willard's Hotel to enjoy a well-deserved meal, confident that his article would be the first news of Fredericksburg to appear in print. He was wrong, but he soon got a chance to make history, as well as to report it.

The War Department did not know much about what had occurred at Fredericksburg, even by the day after the battle. Government officials were aware that heavy fighting had taken place and that the Union army had experienced significant losses. But no one in Washington yet knew the extent of the casualties or how calamitous a defeat the Army of the Potomac had suffered. In the absence of further information about the battle, Stanton had decided to suppress all news.

Secretary of the Navy Gideon Welles heard nothing more than a rumor that the army had done well, and that Burnside and his generals were in good spirits, encouraged by the day's results. But Welles was suspicious of the absence of any definitive reports from the battlefield. He noted in his diary, "When I get nothing clear and explicit at the War Department, I have my apprehensions. Adverse tidings are suppressed with a deal of fuss and mystery, a shuffling over of papers and maps, and a far-reaching vacant gaze."

President Lincoln paced back and forth in the telegraph office of the War Department next door to the White House, waiting anxiously for news. So far he had learned little, but that was about to change, thanks to Henry Villard. While Villard was eating dinner that evening at Willard's Hotel, he was approached by Henry Wilson, the influential senator from Massachusetts, who knew that the reporter had witnessed the fighting at Fredericksburg.

"Have you come from the army?" Wilson asked. "What is the news? Have we won the fight?"

Villard gave the senator his blunt assessment of the situation. He told Wilson that the Union had experienced another staggering defeat. The direct frontal assault Burnside had ordered on Marye's Heights was a murderous blunder, Villard said, and the army was in danger of an even greater disaster if Lee attacked now, while Union forces were in disarray.

Villard was particularly harsh in his judgment of Burnside, an assessment that never softened over the years. Fully three decades later, Villard recalled in his memoirs, "the appalling disaster for which Ambrose E. Burnside will, to the end of time, stand charged with the responsibility."

Villard urged Senator Wilson to go straight to the White House, to describe for Lincoln the crushing defeat, and to urge the president to order the Army of the Potomac to pull back across the Rappahannock River to be safe from a rebel counterattack.

A half hour after Villard finished his dinner, he returned to his newspaper office to prepare his expense account. Senator Wilson arrived to tell him that the president wanted to see him immediately. It was almost ten o'clock. As they approached the White House, Wilson informed Villard that he had not told the president about Fredericksburg. It would be up to Villard.

The newsman disclosed everything he knew about the battle, calling it the worst defeat any American army had ever suffered. Villard told Lincoln that every general he had talked to was convinced that another attack would fail as miserably as the first. He urged the president to order Burnside to withdraw to the north side of the river to avoid further catastrophe.

Lincoln listened to Villard's account and questioned him in detail for almost an hour. Finally he thanked Villard and said, with a sad smile on his face, "I hope it is not so bad as all that."

Before long, Lincoln knew that it was, indeed, as bad as all that. An hour or so after Villard left the White House that night, Pennsylvania's governor Andrew Curtin reached Washington from Fredericksburg. He had also witnessed the battle. Around midnight, Lincoln summoned Curtin to the White House.

"Mr. President," Curtin said, "it was not a battle, it was a butchery."

He described what he had seen—the waves of troops dying at the stone wall—corroborating what Villard had reported. The president looked crestfallen. Curtin apologized for bringing him bad news.

"I'm deeply touched by your sorrow, Mr. President," he said, "and at the distress I have caused you."

Later Lincoln talked with one of his aides about the news from Fredericksburg. The aide noted that the president's despair was reflected clearly on his face and in his voice.

"If there is a worse place than Hell," Lincoln said, "I am in it."

That despair spread quickly in the following days throughout the North as the full extent of the defeat became known. *Harper's Weekly*, an influential magazine, told of the anguish of the people of the Union.

> They have borne, silently and grimly, imbecility, treachery, failure, privation, loss of friends and means, almost every suffering which can afflict a brave people. But they cannot be expected to suffer that such massacres as this at Fredericksburg shall be repeated.

The editor of the *Chicago Tribune* suggested that it might not be possible to defeat the Confederates and predicted that an armistice, leaving the Confederacy intact as a separate nation, would be declared in the coming months. And it was not only civilians who were angered by the tragedy at Fredericksburg. Montgomery C. Meigs, quartermaster general of the Union army, wrote, "exhaustion steals over the country. Confidence and hope are dying." An army lieutenant penned a letter to his mother: "Alas, my poor country! It has strong limbs to march, brave hearts to dare—but the brains, the brains! Have we no brains to use the arms and limbs and eager hearts with cunning?"

Henry Villard's effort to scoop the rest of the press covering the battle at Fredericksburg was scuttled by his own editor, Horace Greeley. When Greeley read Villard's article, he judged it to be far too shocking and demoralizing to the general public to print.

Greeley did publish a piece about the battle under Villard's byline, but not before he softened it considerably, thereby weakening its impact.

Villard's hard day of travel from Fredericksburg to Washington, and his meeting with President Lincoln, ended on a truculent note. He decided to finish his expense account before going back to his hotel. Just as he had completed the work, the *Tribune's* Washington bureau chief, Sam Wilkeson, returned to the office after spending several hours at the bar in Willard's Hotel. He exploded in anger when he read Villard's expense sheet. "Twelve dollars to two Negroes for a ride in a rowboat! Fifty dollars to the captain of a cargo vessel for a trip up the river!"

Wilkeson accused Villard of falsifying the charges and trying to cheat the newspaper out of a considerable sum of money. Then he made the mistake of shoving Villard. "Wearily and methodically, Villard knocked his opponent down, let him get up, and knocked him down again. After repeating this a few times, Villard decided to call it a day, [he] knocked off, as it were, and went back to his rooms."

The dead were buried on December 15. Burnside made a formal request to Lee, and a brief truce was arranged. Several columns of Union soldiers, each containing anywhere from two hundred to three hundred men, moved over the battlefield, along with ambulances to carry the wounded, if anyone was still alive after two days. The nighttime temperature had fallen to zero, killing yet more men, leaving the bodies frozen fast to the ground.

Francis Lawley, a British correspondent reporting the Confederacy's side of the battle, declared himself appalled by the carnage at the stone wall.

> There, in every attitude of death, lying so close to each other that you might step from body to body, lay acres of the Federal dead. I doubt whether in any battlefield of modern times the dead have lain so thick and close. By universal consent of those who have seen all the great battles of this war, nothing like it has ever been seen before.

No one who was there ever forgot what they saw that day, no matter how hard they tried. "I have never seen men lay so thick," said one. "You can't imagine what a horrible spectacle I witnessed. I saw hundreds of men lying dead, shot in all parts and some with their heads, legs, arms, etc. shot off, and mangled in all manner and shapes."

From a field little larger than an acre, the burial detail recovered more than 1,100 corpses—some stacked seven or eight high. Bloated and swollen to grotesque sizes and shapes, their skin had turned black as decomposition set in despite the cold. Rebel soldiers who had long gone without proper shoes, pants, shirts, and overcoats had stripped most Union dead of their clothing. It was a bonanza for them but a depressing sight for the burial detail.

Digging graves in the frozen ground was backbreaking work, and there was neither time nor inclination to show proper respect for fallen comrades. Most bodies were tossed into long, shallow trenches a foot and a half deep. Heros von Borcke said he was shocked at how roughly the Union burial parties disposed of their dead.

He was particularly horrified when he witnessed several hundred bodies being tossed into a hole that had once served as an icehouse.

> The bodies of those poor fellows, stripped nearly naked, were gathered in huge mounds around the pit, and tumbled neck and heels into it; the dull "thud" of corpse falling on corpse coming up from the depths of the hole until the solid mass of human flesh reached near the surface, when a covering of logs, chalk, and mud closed the mouth of this vast and awful tomb.
>
> They were not found for more than three years, not until the war was over.

Some soldiers took advantage of the truce to fraternize with the enemy. At first, officers ordered their men not to talk with those on the other side, but often these self-same officers were the first to break this rule, particularly when they spied an old West Point

Confederate and Union officers met during a truce in the battle in order for each side to collect its dead and wounded. Former colleagues and classmates took the opportunity to have a final toast before resuming their duties. (*Library of Congress*)

classmate or a friend from prewar army days. Quite a few pleasant reunions were held.

Heros von Borcke had long and interesting conversations with a number of Union officers. He was surprised at how openly they admitted to the heavy casualty figures and how intensely they criticized Burnside, blaming him for the defeat. Von Borcke recalled:

> These gentlemen asserted that General Burnside was perfectly incapable of commanding a large army; that his splendid troops had been sacrificed and slaughtered uselessly but that the General himself had taken good care not to endanger his own life, having observed and directed the battle from Phillips House, a point of safety.

Enlisted men of North and South mingled freely and easily, trading coffee for tobacco, reminiscing about the war and their families back home. Some Confederates were still taking advantage of the opportunity to scavenge among the Yankee dead. One rebel began to remove a shoe from a Union body but as it turned out, the man was not dead. He suddenly raised his head and glared at the Confederate soldier.

"Beg pardon, sir," the rebel said. "I thought you had gone above."

Another Confederate soldier found an expensive Belgian rifle. A Union officer upbraided him for stealing. The rebel said nothing until he noticed the Union officer's shiny new boots.

"Never mind," the Southerner said. "I'll shoot you tomorrow and get them boots."

But there was no shooting the next day. Burnside crossed the river to Fredericksburg around noon on December 15 to meet with his commanders, to discuss the painful decision of whether to stay or to go. Should they remain in Fredericksburg, or at least keep a sizable force there, or withdraw completely over the river and go back to Falmouth?

Bull Sumner and Darius Couch urged Burnside to stay on the Confederate side of the river and to keep at least some of his still-powerful army at Fredericksburg. But Joe Hooker argued that the town could not be defended against a determined enemy attack. It would be better to retreat now than to risk being trapped with their backs against the Rappahannock.

Reluctantly, Burnside agreed with Hooker and issued orders to abandon Fredericksburg. The Army of the Potomac would cross back over the river under cover of darkness and pray that Lee would not strike while part of the army was on one side of the river and part on the other.

Among the men who saw Burnside and his staff ride over the bridge away from Fredericksburg that afternoon was Capt. Francis Adams Donaldson of the 118th Pennsylvania. Donaldson wrote:

> The men stood and silently looked upon their commander. They had no bad words to offer him, nothing but pity. There was no soldier more respected in the whole army than General Burnside, but he had now lost the confidence of the men and was of no further use to them. They felt, and, by their silence, showed this. Burnside pulled his hat over his face and looked neither to the right nor the left.

A bit of luck was with the Army of the Potomac that night. A heavy rainstorm blew in, obscuring the sights and sounds of the departing army. Even so, the men did everything possible to move quietly. They poured sawdust over the wooden planks of the bridges to deaden the noise of horses' hooves and heavy wagon wheels. The men were cautioned not to talk among themselves, and to remove their tin cups from their belts so that they would not rattle.

Joshua Chamberlain and the 20th Maine had to cross an open field to reach the town and the two bridges.

> We had to pick our way over a field strewn with incongruous ruin, men torn and broken and cut to pieces in every describable way, cannon dismounted, gun carriages smashed or overturned, ammunition chests flung wildly about, horses dead and half-dead still in harness, accouterments of every sort scattered by the whirlwinds. It was not good for the nerves, that ghastly march, in the lowering night.

By four o'clock in the morning, most of the Federal units had crossed the bridges. There had been no sign that the Confederates had detected their movement. Captain Donaldson was told to take his men to the bridge at the lower end of town, but by the time they got there, the bridge had already been dismantled. Donaldson led his men at double-time march to the other bridge. They reached it just as the engineers were pulling up the planks.

"We lost no time in having them fix them again," Donaldson wrote, "and amid a drenching rain we crossed to the other side. A happier set of men could not well be imagined, to have the river once more between us and the Confederates. It appears we were the last of the Grand Army to leave Fredericksburg."

The Confederate soldiers were dismayed the next morning when the fog lifted to reveal no Union army opposite their positions.

They believed that if they did have to fight the Yankees again soon, it would be better to fight them there, where they held the high ground and where the enemy had to come to them across an empty field.

Now the rebels had lost that advantage. They also understood that once the Union troops had withdrawn across the river, they were not likely to come back the same way. The next fight would be elsewhere, and then the Yankees might gain the advantage.

When Robert E. Lee saw that Burnside had gone, he became depressed. "This morning they were all safe on the north side of the Rappahannock," Lee wrote to his wife. "They went as they came, in the night. They suffered heavily as far as the battle went, but it did not go far enough to satisfy me. Our loss was comparatively slight, and I think will not exceed two thousand. The contest will now have to [be] renewed, but on what field I cannot say."

He was disappointed that he had not been able to strike a more decisive blow against the Union. "At Fredericksburg we gained a battle," Lee explained several months later, "inflicting very serious loss on the enemy in men and material; our people were greatly elated—I was much depressed." He felt that he had accomplished nothing. "We had not gained a foot of ground, and I knew the enemy could easily replace the men he had lost."

Lee's disappointment turned to anger later that afternoon when he rode into Fredericksburg and saw the extent to which the Yankees had vandalized the town. Stonewall Jackson felt the same way when he saw what Union troops had done to the homes, shops, and churches.

"What can we do?" a staff officer asked Jackson as they surveyed the willful destruction.

"Do?" Jackson roared. "Why, shoot them."

General Ambrose Burnside led a futile winter advance in January 1863 in an attempt to outflank Confederate forces following the debacle at Fredericksburg. Known as the "Mud March," the strategy succeeded only in reducing troop morale and confidence in Union leadership. (*Library of Congress*)

THIRTEEN

A Tragic Figure

"This winter is, indeed, the Valley Forge of the war." That was how Maj. Rufus Dawes of the 6th Wisconsin described the period following the army's retreat from Fredericksburg. It was a time of mind-numbing cold, privation, hunger, and despair.

Many units returned to their old camps, and the log huts they had constructed so carefully, only to find them in ruins, completely uninhabitable. What the rains had not destroyed, the camp followers and dog robbers—the scavengers who followed in the army's path—had taken and burned for firewood.

And so the thousands of men of the Army of the Potomac, armed with axes, fanned out over the countryside to lay waste to whole forests of trees that would take many generations to replace. For miles around Stafford Heights and Falmouth, the land was denuded of trees. In their place sprang up vast, ugly, sprawling camps. Log and canvas huts were built large enough to house four men apiece.

Though they were not pretty to look at, and shared a monotonous sameness, the dwellings were functional, able to keep the men tolerably warm and dry. This being the army, there was a system of rules that governed the location of these crude huts: They were neatly arrayed along company and regimental streets, with wider avenues leading to division and corps headquarters. There were also the army's equivalent of public parks—open fields of hard-packed earth to be used for drills.

Once the men had constructed their huts, laid out their streets, and gotten their chimneys working, life settled into a dull and despairing routine. Too much time to remember all the friends they had lost, and to think about how badly the war was going for the Union. So many men killed and wounded, and for what? The army was back where it started, and the Confederates were dug in across the river even stronger than before.

Although Northern soldiers were used to losses, Fredericksburg's casualties were so much more numerous—and all in vain. Nothing had been achieved. "I must say I consider it nothing but a useless slaughter," a New Hampshire boy wrote to his family, "a total sacrifice of thousands of the noblest, bravest hearts that ever espoused our country's cause."

More men died every day, and not just those wounded in the battle. Diseases were rampant in the winter camp and were felling veteran troops and newly arrived replacements alike. Not a day passed without more bodies for the cemeteries that had to be dug in the desolate, treeless landscape.

To add to the misery and the death rate, the Army of the Potomac seemed incapable of feeding its men properly. Lt. Henry Livermore Abbott of the 20th Massachusetts complained in a letter to his mother about the lack of sufficient food: "We haven't been able to get anything from the commissary for four days but hard bread and rice. Men are dying of scurvy because they haven't transportation enough to give us potatoes and onions. Some of my men are in a horrible state."

The army was also incapable of paying its soldiers. Some regiments had not been paid in six months, since the previous summer. Men who had no money could not purchase food to supplement the scant army fare from the sutlers who hovered like vultures around the army camps. Sutlers overcharged, to be sure, but for most soldiers there was no other source of food. Also, men who had not been paid could not send money home to their families, who were often totally dependent on that meager monthly pay.

"Soldiers are all discouraged," Pvt. Henry Matrau of the Iron Brigade wrote to his mother after Fredericksburg. "We think that this war is never going to be ended by fighting for the North and the South are too evenly matched. We are all worn out and tired of bumming around."

A surgeon with the 5th New Hampshire told his wife, "We must prepare for worse times than we have yet seen. There are yet more widows and orphans, more childless fathers and mothers. Death has not yet had a sufficient harvest, though one would think that he must be gutted."

Letters to families and daily newspaper editorials throughout the Union told of pessimism, defeatism, and despair. Joseph Medill, editor of the *Chicago Tribune*, observed that "the feeling of utter helplessness is stronger than at any time since the war began. The terrible bloody defeat of our brave army [at Fredericksburg] leaves us almost without hope. Sometimes I think nothing is left but to fight for a boundary [between United States and Confederate States]."

Other sources echoed Medill's despondent tone. "A seething mass of discontent and demoralization" was how one writer referred to the Army of the Potomac. "The dark days had come when dissatisfaction, discouragement, homesickness, and many other ills of camp life prevailed." A New Hampshire soldier wrote that the battle at Fredericksburg had "depressed the spirit, crushed the hopes and destroyed the effective power of the regiment." Would the army and the nation regain its spirit and the will to continue the fight?

The soldiers of the Army of the Potomac blamed Burnside. "Very little is said about Burnside," Col. Charles Wainwright noted in his diary, "but neither officers nor men have the slightest confidence in him." When Burnside reviewed the 2nd Corps one day after its return across the pontoon bridges from Fredericksburg, the men refused to cheer, as was the time-honored custom whenever the commanding general appeared. Meagher led the Irish Brigade in a rousing hurrah for Bull Sumner, who accompanied Burnside, but kept silent when Burnside passed. The situation was so embarrassing to Old Bull that he privately told his regimental commanders to order the men to cheer for Burnside. They then did so, but with an obvious lack of enthusiasm.

Burnside did not need the open disapproval of his men to remind him that he was at fault for the Union defeat at Fredericksburg. He keenly felt the guilt and the responsibility. However, when his personal physician, Dr. William Clark, returned from Washington with the latest news, Burnside was surprised to learn that Northern newspapers were blaming Lincoln, Stanton, and Halleck for the losses. The papers argued that those leaders had pressured Burnside to make the attack. Burnside grew upset when he realized that others were being blamed for his failure.

"I'll put a stop to that," he told his staff officers, who were horrified when he described what he intended to do. He said he would write an open letter to the press, accepting full responsibility for the defeat. His staff argued that he should not go public with such a statement without first obtaining President Lincoln's permission. Reluctantly, Burnside agreed. He made a hurried trip to the capital, where the president approved of his plan. Indeed, Lincoln may have been relieved to have the onus shifted from himself to Burnside.

Burnside's letter, written on December 17 and formally addressed to Army Chief-of-Staff Halleck, was published in the *New York Times* on December 23, 1862. Burnside praised the officers and men of his command, citing their courage and endurance. "For the failure in the attack, I am responsible," he wrote. "The fact that I decided to move from Warrenton onto this line, rather against the opinion of the President, Secretary [of War] and yourself, and that you have left the whole movement in my hands, without giving me orders, makes me the more responsible."

Ironically, Burnside's openness in taking the blame for the failed assault on Marye's Heights restored public confidence in his abilities. He was lauded for trying to save the reputation of the government by nobly assuming the full mantle of responsibility. Some newspaper editorials, including one in the *New York Times*, even suggested that Burnside was doing so under orders from the Lincoln administration.

In the end, although Burnside's letter enhanced his standing among the general public, it did not do the same among the survivors of the battle. As far as they were concerned, it was Burnside's ineptitude and poor judgment that led to the death of so many soldiers. The majority of the troops in the Army of the Potomac hoped Burnside would be replaced before fighting resumed in the spring, for surely there would be no more campaigning until then.

And so the army settled down in its crude huts and tried to keep warm and dry, secure in the conviction that ice, cold, and snow would keep both armies immobilized for at least three months. They did not know that Burnside was already planning to make another assault across the river in only a few weeks.

On December 21, a poet from New York City arrived in Falmouth to search for his wounded brother. What Walt Whitman saw there would change his life forever. The first place he came to was Lacy House, where Clara Barton and others were working tirelessly to care for the wounded. Whitman did not go inside that day. The sights outside were horrifying enough.

> Outdoors, at the foot of a tree, within ten yards of the front of the house, I notice a heap of amputated feet, legs, arms, hands, etc., a full load for a one-horse cart. Several dead bodies lie near, each covered with its own brown woolen blanket. In the dooryard, toward the river, are fresh graves, mostly of officers, their names on pieces of barrel staves, on broken boards, stuck in the dirt.

He moved on to the makeshift hospitals, where hundreds of wounded men still died every day, even though more than a week had elapsed since the battle. He was appalled at the conditions.

There are merely tents, and sometimes very poor ones, the wounded lying on the ground, lucky if their blankets are spread on layers of pine or hemlock twigs, or small leaves. No cots, seldom even a mattress. It is pretty cold. The ground is frozen hard, and there is occasional snow. I go around from one case to another. I do not see that I do much good to these wounded and dying, but I cannot leave them. Once in a while some youngster holds on to me convulsively, and I do what I can for him; at any rate, stop with him and sit near him for hours, if he wishes it.

Walt Whitman photographed in 1863 at age 44. He wrote of his Civil War experiences as a hospital volunteer in his later poems, newspaper articles, and books. (*Library of Congress*)

Eventually Walt Whitman found his brother George, who had not been hurt, but more than that, he found a calling, a quest. He was not a doctor; he could not remove bullets or patch up maimed bodies, but he could provide solace and comfort. For the rest of the war, Whitman attended to the souls of hundreds of soldiers, and in the process, provided comfort to himself as well.

He wrote to a friend, "What I saw in the war set me up for all time. I never before had my feelings so thoroughly and (so far) permanently absorbed, to the very roots, as by those huge swarms of dear, wounded, sick, dying boys." The experience at Fredericksburg was later reflected in his poems, essays, and books.

Whitman's biographer wrote that at the outset of the war, Whitman had been deeply depressed because of the lack of success of his writing, his economic impoverishment, and his sexual orientation. His life had been described as an "aimless round of bohemian posturing, late-night roistering, and homosexual cruising. He ended the war as 'the Good Gray Poet,' a beloved, almost mystical figure [who] looked back on the Civil War years as the most fulfilling period of his life."

Lacy House was filled to overflowing with wounded. Clara Barton organized a soup kitchen and helped the army surgeons with their operations and amputations. She was quick to push a pillow under the bloody stump of a leg, or rush to a screaming patient with a drink of whiskey. She was particularly moved by the suffering of a young officer from Massachusetts, whose copious bleeding could not be stopped. Clara stayed with him, singing hymns and quoting scripture to comfort him. Toward the end, the poor man hallucinated, believing Clara was his mother. After he died, Clara wrote, "[I] rose from the side of [his] couch and wrung the blood from the bottom of my clothing."

Men wailed and moaned, some died, but others lived, due in great part to Clara Barton's efforts. Wiley Faulkner, of the 7th Michigan, had been shot through both lungs while crossing the river. Given up for dead back on December 11, he was still alive thanks to her. On December 16 he was carried to the railway station for the long, painful train and boat trip to Washington. She described him as "a little white bundle of skin and bones." She stayed with him as long as she could and slipped him a bottle of her milk punch—a mixture of eggnog and rum—which was the only food he had been able to keep down.

Clara slept, when she could, in a freezing tent on the lawn, but she was fast becoming exhausted, mentally and physically. One of her biographers wrote

> At times, in her tent late at night, she did not think she could stand another hour in [Lacy] house. But somehow she always found the strength to go on, drawing on reserves of energy she did not know she possessed. At

dawn, she would suppress her tears, tie her hair up, and go forth again to nurse her dear soldiers.

Even under the best of conditions, and with dedicated aides like Clara Barton and Walt Whitman, medical care was crude, primitive, and often lethal. Writing more than fifty years after the end of the war, W. W. Keen, a Union army surgeon, described the standard surgical treatment offered to wounded soldiers.

> We operated in old blood-stained and often pus-stained coats. We used undisinfected instruments from undisinfected plush-lined cases, and still worse, used marine sponges that had been used in prior pus cases and had been only washed in tap water. If a sponge or an instrument fell on the floor it was washed and squeezed in a basin of tap water and used as if it were clean.
>
> The silk with which we sewed up wounds was undisinfected. If there was a difficulty in threading the needle we moistened it with bacteria-laden saliva, and rolled it between bacteria-infected fingers. We dressed the wounds with clean but undisinfected sheets, shirts, tablecloths, or other old soft linens rescued from the family ragbag. We had no sterilized gauze dressing, no gauze sponges. We knew nothing about antiseptics and therefore used none.

The death rate following surgery was appallingly high. Postsurgery infections ran rampant through the hospital tents. It was surprising when a soldier survived the removal of a bullet or the amputation of a limb. Another Union army surgeon wrote to his wife that he would much prefer to be killed outright than to be treated in one of his own hospitals.

Bill McCarter, Meagher's Irish Brigade adjutant, was among the fortunate. He had lived through the surgery to remove the bullet from his shoulder and had not developed any postoperative infection. On Tuesday morning, December 16, he felt strong enough to explore the hospital complex, which consisted of more than forty tents, eleven of which were devoted to surgery.

The Lacy House at the time of the first battle of Fredericksburg. (*Library of Congress*)

It gave the place the appearance of a little slaughter-house, or, as I then termed it, a "village of butcher shops." Wounded and mangled soldiers laid about in all directions, the hospital tents all being full.

Beyond the surgical tents McCarter discovered huge piles of amputated limbs, which had been tossed out through holes cut in the canvas. He saw a soldier whose stomach had been blown away by a shell. The man was still alive, "but oh, the cries of agony and pain. God keep me from ever witnessing the like again," McCarter wrote.

That was enough for him. He slowly walked down to the rail-road station and joined hundreds of other wounded men waiting in the cold rain. After a delay of many hours a train arrived and McCarter hauled himself aboard a crowded freight car, desperate, as were so many others, to get away from Fredericksburg and seek medical treatment at a hospital in Washington. For most of these soldiers the war was over.

Noah Brooks, the reporter, watched them arrive in Washington and wrote an emotional essay about "the coming of the wounded," for his readers back in peaceful California:

Here they come in squads of a hundred or more, wounded in the face, with fingers gone, armless perhaps, with cruel furrows plowed along their arms by grape or musket ball, with faces grimed and blackened with smoke and powder, ragged, disheveled, and dropping with fatigue and weakness. Here they come creeping, shuffling, limping, and hobbling along, full 1,500 strong, so faint and longing for rest; so weary, oh, so weary, that the heart bleeds at the pitiful sight.

A sadder sight is the unloading at a hospital of the long train of ambulances, which bring up the more severely wounded. There comes a long line of stretchers with men who have left arms, legs, hands, feet, and much blood upon the fatal field of Fredericksburg. Rebel guns have maimed these men for life, and those who went forth full of vigor, hope, and ambition, their hearts beating high with visions of glory and prowess, have returned again—broken, decrepit, useless, and disfigured.

Now and then as a litter is lifted carefully out, an attendant lifts the corner of the covering of the pale, suffering face and directs the burden to a lower room, for the man whom they carry is dead. The passage from the steamer to the hospital is his last, and sisters, mother, and [sweetheart] will weep tomorrow when they see his name in the fatal list of "Since Dead." My peace-blessed California reader, this is war. God help its victims.

Back in Fredericksburg, the men continued with tedious routines, daily formation and drills, and the constant scrounging for food and firewood. It was inevitable that soon the Yankees would begin to trade with the Confederates across the river. The Union soldiers had plenty of real coffee, which the rebels missed, and the Southerners had lots of tobacco, of which the Northerners never had enough.

All this bartering was strictly against regulations, of course, but no matter. The men carried on a lively commerce as long as no officers were present. The exchanges began with toy boats crafted from small tree trunks hollowed out in the center to carry the cargo. About two feet long and six inches wide, the boats were well designed, complete with rudders and sails.

Soldiers from Mississippi dispatched the first boat. It sailed straight and true across the Rappahannock to an outfit from New Jersey. It was loaded with tobacco and contained a note.

> Gents, U.S. Army: We send you some tobacco by our packet [boat]. Send us some coffee in return. Also a deck of cards, if you have them, and we will send you more tobacco. Send us any late [news]papers if you have them.

The little vessel made many trips over the river and back and became so popular that several hundred men would assemble on the shore to greet each new shipment. When officers learned about the trade, they issued stern orders and threats of dire consequences but the men ignored them. The commerce continued not only by toy boat but soon in person as well.

Soldiers began crossing the river to socialize, some on homemade rafts and others clinging to logs as they paddled to the other side. Often the fellowship was enjoyed and appreciated even more than the goods that were exchanged. A story went around that a Confederate general came across several Yankee soldiers who were having a high-spirited visit with his men. He ordered the enemy soldiers arrested and would have shipped them off to Richmond as prisoners of war but for the fervent pleading of his men on the Yankees' behalf.

They told the general that they had given their word of honor that the Northerners would be safe. The general relented; a Southern gentleman, after all, could not go back on his word. He insisted that his men have no more contact with the enemy, however. That agreement lasted about as long as it took for the general to return to his distant headquarters.

If the decision had been left to the soldiers, they would all have gone home and let the politicians straighten things out, but the armies were not about to allow that. Still, relations between the adversaries grew so cordial that one officer was even greeted with cheers by soldiers of the opposing side. Stonewall Jackson was inspecting his troops by the river. As soon as the men caught sight of their beloved Old Jack, they began to cheer. When the Yankee pickets across the river heard the shouts, they yelled across to ask what was happening.

"General Stonewall Jackson," a rebel yelled.

"Hurrah for Stonewall Jackson!" was the reply from the Northern side.

On the night of December 19, a Confederate soldier swam across the Rappahannock and told the pickets on the Union side that he had urgent business with General Meagher. He spoke with a thick Irish brogue and seemed genuine, so he was escorted to the general.

He gave his name as Michael Sullivan, a sergeant in the Confederate army serving with General Cobb's Georgia Brigade at the stone wall. He had taken particular notice of the valiant charge of the Irish Brigade. He did not say whether he had refrained from firing on his fellow Irishmen, but he did indicate that he had marked the spot where one of the brigade's color bearers had been shot down. That night Sullivan had crawled over the wall and retrieved the flag from the dead color bearer.

His reason for crossing the river now was to return the colors. He unbuttoned his coat, pulled out the green flag of the 28th Massachusetts, and handed it to Meagher. An onlooker described Meagher as "deeply moved" by the sergeant's actions.

"You have earned the good will and esteem of the Brigade," Meagher told Sullivan. "You are welcome to stay with us, if you wish."

The sergeant declined the offer and asked permission to return to his regiment. Suddenly he keeled over in a faint from the loss of blood from a flesh wound he had sustained when he left his post earlier that night. Meagher summoned a surgeon to patch up the wound. Two nights later, restored to health, soldiers of the Union's Irish Brigade formally escorted Sgt. Michael Sullivan down to the riverbank, where he was ferried back to his outfit to continue the fight. He would survive the war and later become a successful merchant in Savannah.

The soldiers on both sides took advantage of the winter lull in the fighting to find recreation in a variety of ways. One Texas brigade began each morning with a snowball fight, often throwing perilously close to General Longstreet as he left the house where he was staying with his wife, up visiting from Richmond.

Longstreet endured the joke with his usual imperturbability for several days, until one morning when he saw a line of troops with snowballs in hand. Riding up to them, Longstreet warned, "Throw your snowballs, men, if you want to, as much as you please. But if one of them touches me, not a man in this brigade shall have a furlough this winter. Remember that." Longstreet was left untouched.

Longstreet and many other high-ranking officers—although not General Lee, of course—indulged in a good bit of drinking. Many of the old plantation homes had well-stocked wine cellars. On at least one occasion Longstreet joined in a party of his staff officers and may have imbibed a little too much. He was seen "[riding] around the tent on the back of a staff officer who was on his hands and knees, until both rolled onto the ground."

Some Confederate troops, troubled by the destruction left by the Yankees in Fredericksburg, donated some of their meager pay to help the townspeople. One regiment collected $2,000—a substantial sum from men who had so little themselves. Over several months, a relief effort for Fredericksburg was conducted throughout the South, and eventually donations exceeded $90,000.

The residents needed all the help they could get. Jane Howison Beale, who had fled with her children on December 11—the day the Yankees crossed the river into town—was fortunate in that her house had not been vandalized, whereas her neighbors' homes had suffered considerable damage and pilfering, rendering them almost uninhabitable. "I feel very grateful for all this," she wrote, "and wondered how it had happened, that I should have escaped so much better than anyone else."

On December 17, Lt. Charles Minor Blackford, of the 2nd Virginia Cavalry, rode into town to check on his mother's house, where he had been born and raised.

> Our home was used as an operating hospital and many Yankees were buried in the back yard, one just at the foot of the back steps. In the dining room the huge table was used as an operating table and a small table by its side had a pile of legs and arms upon it. I poured them out into the back yard.

The house had been wrecked, room by room. In the attic Union soldiers had "taken out barrels of old letters which were scattered all over the yard. Among them I found a letter from Light Horse Harry Lee to my grandfather. The whole house was covered with mud and blood and it was hard to realize it was the dear old house of my childhood."

On Christmas Day, Sgt. Thomas Plunkett, of the 21st Massachusetts Infantry, who had lost both arms charging Marye's Heights while carrying the regimental colors, was given a glorious send-off from the train station at Falmouth. The men of his outfit attended, along with Clara Barton. She had witnessed the explosion that wounded Plunkett, had assisted in the amputations, and had nursed and comforted him ever since. Now he was being sent north to a hospital in Washington.

Two days later Clara herself departed for Washington to accompany the last of the wounded. When she reached the capital city, she traveled by streetcar to the boardinghouse where she kept rooms. She was exhausted, barely able to climb the steep steps, and her mind was filled with the suffering she had seen in what she called the "fires of Fredericksburg." Alone and depressed, overtaken by "a new sense of desolation and pity and sympathy and weariness," Clara Barton broke down and cried.

Over the coming days and weeks of winter, she began to realize how much she was beloved by a grateful nation. She had become a celebrity, so idolized that officers whom she did not know saluted when they passed her in the streets. Scores of soldiers came to call, to pay their respects. And, as a true measure of fame, Mathew Brady took her photograph, though Clara remarked to a friend that the picture "looked like death on a pale horse."

Shortly after her arrival in Washington, she received word that some patients at a local hospital had been begging to see her. She went to visit them.

> [S]eventy wounded soldiers saluted her, some standing, others rising feebly from their beds, and gave her three rousing cheers. All of them had left their blood at Fredericksburg, all had been at the Lacy House, all had been bandaged and fed by Clara's hand, and all loved her. For them, Miss Barton was the outstanding nurse of the war, and their hurrahs moved her to her depths. Then a young man with a bright complexion came forward. "I am Wiley Faulkner of the 7th Michigan," he said. "I didn't die and the milk punch lasted all the way to Washington."

Burnside was in trouble. The day after Christmas he received an unpleasant, and certainly unwelcome, message from General Halleck criticizing him for not attacking the Confederates. Halleck referred to the passivity of the Army of the Potomac as "disheartening." Clearly, something had to be done.

Burnside had already begun planning a wide flanking movement against Lee before he received Halleck's scolding. He had sent men to scout the river below Fredericksburg for a suitable place to cross. He selected a spot about seven miles downriver where the main force could ford. He also chose a place some twenty-five miles upriver from Fredericksburg to launch a cavalry raid far behind Lee's line. The goal was to destroy canals, bridges, and railroad lines.

On December 29, Burnside issued orders to his generals to be ready to move their men out on twelve hours' notice. Each soldier was to receive three days' cooked rations and sixty rounds of ammunition. In addition, one week's supplies would be loaded onto wagons that would accompany the main assault force. Burnside looked forward to the opportunity to redeem himself in the new campaign. He was pleased that all seemed to be proceeding well.

But some of Burnside's generals were about to sabotage his plans. Several days before Burnside formulated his latest plan of attack, Generals William B. Franklin and William F. Smith had gone over Burnside's head with their own idea for a new campaign, along with a thinly disguised criticism of Burnside. Franklin and Smith, diehard McClellan loyalists who still resented Burnside for taking Little Mac's place, wrote a letter to Abraham Lincoln.

What they proposed was essentially a rehash of McClellan's failed Peninsular campaign of the year before. In presenting their plan, they implied that someone other than Burnside—who, they declared, was too weak, ineffectual, and indecisive to have the full support of the men—should command the Army of the Potomac. The president rejected their proposal. He had not liked the idea when it came from McClellan and had consented only with reluctance. The dismal failure of that campaign was justification enough for Lincoln to reject it again.

Desperate, Franklin and Smith tried an even more devious route when they received Burnside's orders to advance on twelve hours' notice. The following morning, they approved leaves for two of the brigadier generals in their command—John Newton and John Cochrane—to go directly to the White House bearing a strong message detailing Burnside's incompetence.

Newton was a West Point graduate, a career soldier, and a solid but unimaginative division commander and protégé of Franklin.

He was well versed in the ways of Washington and well known on Capitol Hill as a result of his father's twenty-nine-year service in Congress. Cochrane was a political-appointee general from New York who had served two terms in Congress and had even better government connections than Newton. Their mission was simple—to get rid of Burnside and restore McClellan to command.

Newton and Cochrane later claimed that all they intended to do on their mission to the capital was what every soldier had a right to do—complain to their congressman about conditions in the army. Surely there was nothing sinister in that. They said they were greatly surprised to find that Congress was away on its Christmas recess, which it took without fail every year at that time, as both men well knew.

Since they were unable to see their congressmen, so they later explained, they decided to call on the president. Lincoln listened patiently to their tales of the army's plummeting morale and lack of faith in Burnside, and the weaknesses in Burnside's new plan to outflank the Confederate position. The president was indignant at their disloyalty to their commanding officer and angered by their actions in coming to Washington. Nevertheless, their message apparently had the desired effect. At three thirty that same afternoon, shortly after Newton and Cochrane left, Lincoln telegraphed Burnside: "I have good reason for saying you must not make a general movement of the army without letting me know."

Burnside was shaken and confused. Halleck was pressing him to move against the enemy, and Lincoln was denying him the authority to carry out his plan of attack. Burnside suspended his operations and hurried to Washington to try to clarify the situation.

Lincoln informed Burnside that two of his generals, whom he declined to identify, had said that Burnside's new offensive was bound to lead to disaster, and that none of the senior officers had confidence in the plan—or in him. Burnside, growing visibly upset, said that if his officers had lost confidence in him, then he should resign his command. Lincoln told him to think about the situation and return the next day.

When Burnside returned to the president's office, Secretary of War Stanton and Army Chief-of-Staff Halleck were in attendance. That was an unfortunate, though not entirely unexpected, development. Burnside had brought with him a letter of resignation, which, coincidentally, mentioned both men.

He handed the letter to Lincoln, who read Burnside's offer to resign because of his generals' loss of confidence in him as well as his contention that Stanton and Halleck should also resign for the same reason. Both the army and the nation, Burnside argued, had lost trust in them. Lincoln passed the letter back to Burnside without comment.

Since the president did not choose to reveal the contents of the letter, Burnside did. He told Halleck and Stanton that he had offered his resignation and declared that they should do the same. Lincoln refused to discuss anyone's resignation. Burnside tried another tactic, steering the conversation to the identities of the officers who had visited the president to complain about him. Halleck demanded that they be dismissed from the service, but Lincoln would not reveal their names or consider disciplining them.

The meeting seemed to be increasingly pointless. When Burnside spoke of his intention to attack Lee by crossing the Rappahannock downstream, he received lukewarm responses from Halleck and Stanton and none at all from Lincoln. Burnside asked Halleck and Stanton if they agreed with the plan. They hesitated to commit themselves, saying that the decision was solely for Burnside to make. They supported the idea of offensive action against the Confederates but offered no specific suggestions. Later Burnside wrote bitterly that "No definite conclusion was come to in reference to the subject of a movement."

The meeting adjourned with no agreement about how to proceed against Lee's army at Fredericksburg. Lincoln then wrote a note to Halleck, asking if Burnside's idea had any merit. This was not an unusual request for the president to make of his senior military adviser. Was the plan likely to succeed? Lincoln sounded a bit desperate.

If in such a difficulty as this you do not help, you fail me precisely in the point for which I sought your assistance. You know what General Burnside's plan is, and it is my wish that you go with him to the ground, examine it as far as practicable, confer with the officers, getting their judgment, and ascertaining their temper; in a word, gather all the elements for forming a judgment of your own, and then tell General Burnside that you do approve, or that you do not approve, his plan. Your military skill is useless to me if you will not do this.

Instead of acceding to the president's request for advice, Halleck took offense at what he considered the accusatory tone of the president's letter. He abruptly announced his resignation, arguing that visiting Burnside's headquarters and talking with his subordinate generals would interfere with Burnside's independence as a commander in the field. Lincoln refused to accept Halleck's resignation and said no more about the issue.

After Burnside returned to his headquarters at Falmouth, he felt compelled to talk about his situation. He showed people the letter of resignation that Lincoln had rejected. His openness and honesty may have helped him cope with his own frustration, but it was not good for the morale of the army. After Burnside talked frankly to George Meade, who had lost the battle at Deep Run, Meade wrote an account of the conversation to his wife.

"Finding [Burnside] could get nothing out of any of them, he came back, and thus matters stand. Burnside told me all this himself this morning. God only knows what is to become of us and what will be done." Meade also recounted his own meeting with General Franklin, who had tried to undermine Burnside and his battle plan. "I had a long talk with Franklin yesterday," Meade wrote, "who is very positive in his opinion that we cannot go to Richmond on this line, and hence there is no object in our attempting to move on it."

Rumor, gossip, and some truth about the plot against Burnside filtered through the high-ranking officers of the Army of the Potomac. It was not long before people knew the names of the men who had criticized Burnside to the president. Tension grew between those who supported Franklin and Smith in their effort to bring down Burnside, and those who—while not expressing unqualified confidence in Burnside—were appalled by the back-stabbing tactics of the plotters.

These animosities and intrigues soon became common knowl-edge among the soldiers. Morale plummeted even further and desertions increased as tales about a fight for control of the Army of the Potomac made their way down the chain of command. A soldier from Michigan captured the mood in a letter home.

> We think Burnside "played out." We know he is no gen-eral for such a command. Will the government take warn-ing in time or will they continue as they have begun? Must the Army mutiny before they understand that we are not in "excellent spirits" and "thinking to be led against the enemy" under such men as Burnside? Poor weak-minded fool he!

Ambrose Burnside was nothing if not persistent. On January 5, 1863, he wrote to President Lincoln that he still wanted to cross the river again to pursue the Confederates. He realized that some of his generals disagreed with his plan, he reminded Lincoln, and therefore he enclosed another letter of resignation. This one he left undated, for the president to use any time he saw fit.

Burnside also wrote to General Halleck, telling him that, "in making so hazardous a movement, I should receive some general direction from you as to the advisability of crossing at some point, as you are necessarily well informed of the effect at this time upon other parts of the army of a success or a repulse."

Halleck's reply made it clear that he was not willing to provide any assistance in planning a new campaign. If Burnside's attack failed, then none of the blame could fall on the army's chief-of-staff. Further, Halleck told Burnside, "[I]t devolves on you to decide upon the time, place and character of [any] crossing which you may attempt. I can only advise that an attempt be made, and as early as possible."

The president endorsed Halleck's letter on January 8, adding a lukewarm endorsement of Burnside.

> I approve this letter. I deplore the want of concurrence with you in opinion by your general officers, but I do not see the remedy. I do not yet see how I could profit by changing the command of the Army of the Potomac, and if I did I should not wish to do so by accepting the resignation of your commission.

Thus, despite the dissension and dissatisfaction within his own ranks and the lack of support from Lincoln, Halleck, and Stanton, Burnside retained command of the Army of the Potomac. As usual, he worked day and night, attending personally to the hundreds of details involved in large-scale troop movements, still unable to delegate such tasks to his staff. He even made his own reconnaissance along the banks of the Rappahannock, almost always riding alone, searching for the best place to make the crossing.

By January 15, he had chosen crossing points around Banks Ford, about eight miles upriver from Fredericksburg. Hooker's Center Grand Division would cross just above the ford; Franklin's Left Grand Division would cross a little below. On January 20, the day chosen for the attack, Burnside issued General Orders Number Seven to his men, announcing that "the auspicious moment seems to have arrived to strike a great and mortal blow to the rebellion and to gain that decisive victory which is due to the country." Those words would come back to haunt him.

The vociferous attacks on Burnside continued even as the troops moved out late on the morning of January 20, heading toward Banks Ford. Generals Franklin and Smith and their staff officers were overheard conspiring about how Franklin would assume command once they got rid of Burnside. Col. Charles Wainwright, in command of General Reynolds's artillery, wrote in his diary that Franklin's efforts to undermine Burnside had demoralized the army to such an extent that the failure of the new assault was inevitable.

Fighting Joe Hooker told a *New York Times* reporter that Burnside's strategy was absurd. Hooker referred to Burnside as incompetent, and to the Lincoln administration as imbecilic. "Nothing would go right," Hooker predicted, "until we had a dictator, and the sooner the better." And Hooker was more than ready to assume that role himself. Who else could lead the nation to victory? "It had become virtually open rebellion in the high command," Hooker contested. "Nothing like this had ever happened before in the Army of the Potomac."

It was not only the high command that was disenchanted with Burnside. On the night prior to the attack, Capt. Henry Livermore Abbott, of the 20th Massachusetts, wrote to his father.

> Tomorrow, we shall again meet the foe. There is serious disaffection through the army, not among the men merely, but just as bad among their officers. I am terribly afraid that the army is going to disgrace itself. Nobody has the slightest confidence in Burnside.

Lt. Henry Roper, also of the 20th Massachusetts, recalled how "the utmost dissatisfaction, almost insubordination, was shown here at the prospect of an attack. Regiments openly said they would not cross the bridge. The 42nd New York of our Brigade hooted at the order, even the 15th Massachusetts. [They] cheered for Jefferson Davis and groaned for President Lincoln."

In the 5th New Hampshire, Pvt. Miles Peabody wrote in a letter home: "It does not seem possible that our Generals think of attacking [Fredericksburg] again after such a lesson as they received there before. This Regiment feels rather downhearted at the prospect. Many of them say that they will not go into another fight." Lt. James Larkin expressed his feelings to his wife on the morning of the attack: "I am fearful it will be a sorry job."

"We struck tents about one p.m. Tuesday, January 20th and started off to the tune of 'The Girl I Left Behind Me,'" wrote Capt. Francis Adams Donaldson.

> Every face was bright with the 'devil-[may]-care' look of soldiers, perfectly indifferent to destination, nature of movement, or fate. No one cared, no one had confidence, and it made not the slightest difference whether they stayed in camp or inaugurated a campaign, it was all one and the same thing to them. The army had settled down into perfect indifference.

They marched about five miles that afternoon. By the time the sun was setting, they were making camp for the night. That was when the storm struck. For weeks the weather had been dry, even warmer than usual, but that evening wind and rain slashed through the piney woods like icy, stinging needles. In no time at all, the men were drenched. They fought to erect their pup tents in the roaring winds and to coax their campfires to life, but it was hopeless. The canvas tents were too fragile, the wood too wet to burn. There was no warming coffee that night, and little shelter.

To make matters even worse, the supply wagons that contained all the food and other provisions were lost somewhere to the rear. The only men who ate that night were those who had carried food in their haversacks. Most men went hungry, and few got any sleep. Captain Donaldson, of the 118th Pennsylvania, recalled that his men "stood up all night with muskets and cartridge boxes held close to their persons to keep dry, and just took the pelting, pouring rain as it came along."

In the morning, conditions worsened as the troops attempted to move out, beginning what reporters inevitably called the Mud March. The world was reduced to a sea of thick brown paste, the kind of mud that entrapped a man or horse or wagon with every step or turn of the wheel. The Northern Virginia soil was a mixture of clay and sand. When so much water was added so suddenly, the soft, sticky ground rendered the roads impassable and left the army helpless.

The men toiled throughout the day in the torrential, wind-driven rain, trying miserably to move forward a few yards at a time, ultimately making no progress. Mules and horses disappeared, sucked into the mud. Hundreds had to be shot to keep them from strangling; a quick death by gunshot was better than drowning, inch by inch, in the muck. Cannon and heavy wagons sank to their axles. Teams of twenty horses and three hundred men pulling on ropes could not budge them.

Colonel Wainwright watched his exhausted men, and then made his way to headquarters. He found Generals Franklin and Smith, along with their staff officers "in quite a comfortable camp; doing nothing to help things on, but grumbling and talking in a manner to do all the harm possible."

Burnside, on the other hand, spent the day with his men, out in the mud, encouraging them to push on. He scouted new routes to get the pontoons down to the river, but the wagons transporting the boats were the heaviest of all. Despite intense efforts, they made little progress. One wagon driver who saw Burnside ride by shouted an angry reminder of his General Orders Number Seven: "General, the auspicious moment has arrived." An army surgeon recalled Burnside as a tragic figure, "virtually alone and covered with mud."

Confederate troops watched from across the river, enjoying the Yankees' predicament. They yelled advice, offering to ride over in the morning to haul the Union guns out of the mud. The rebels posted handmade signs pointing the way to Richmond. Other placards noted the obvious, that Burnside's army was "stuck in the mud." The Southerners had themselves a grand time watching the Federal troops work so hard all day to achieve so little.

The storm showed no signs of easing. The mud grew thicker and deeper, and the soldiers' spirits plummeted as the long day ended. The rain continued throughout the night. Some men became so discouraged they decided to quit. They gathered their belongings, slipped out of camp, and headed north, only to be rounded up and brought back by the cavalry units Burnside had sent to find them. The rest resigned themselves to another night without sleep or food, hoping that even so stubborn a man as

Ambrose Burnside would realize that there was no point in continuing. Surely he would lead them all back to Falmouth in the morning.

They were wrong. Burnside's orders remained unchanged, even though the storm was as fierce as the day before. The soldiers were told to keep the pontoons and equipment moving down to the river. Not until midday did Burnside finally abandon the effort and order his army to turn around. But going back was no less a nightmare than going forward, and it took almost two days before the first of the troops reached Falmouth.

Col. Zenas Bliss, of the 7th Rhode Island, was among the men who had stayed in Falmouth to guard supplies. He was horrified at the condition of the returning troops.

> They were the worst lot of men I ever saw together. Many of them had thrown their arms away, and the hill[s] between the station and their camps were covered with men; some very drunk straggling toward their camp, and cursing Burnside and everybody else, I guess. It looked as though the enemy could have crossed the river at that time, and captured the whole Army.

The men returned, broken in spirit, to camps that were no longer habitable. When they had left on the Mud March, they had been ordered to systematically destroy everything they had so carefully built and accumulated for their comfort. And so they came back to campsites that lay in ruins. That was the final insult. Many decided then that they were through with the war. By the end of January, roll calls revealed that fully 27 percent of the Army of the Potomac—more than 86,000 men—had deserted. Although some of them were caught, large numbers were never seen again.

No one knows the total losses from the Mud March. Some Union soldiers became so infirm in the storm that they lay down in the mud and died. Others contracted pneumonia and other respiratory illnesses shortly after their return to Falmouth. Historians estimate that as many men died from the Mud March as had been killed in some of the previous battles.

Morale, low enough before the storm, fell even lower. One enlisted man wrote that he had never seen such a high level of discontent as following the Mud March. Brig. Gen. Marsena Patrick wrote in his diary on the night of January 23.

> It is said that a very bad feeling has sprung up in the Army against Burnside, growing out of his Fredericksburg failure and this last sad attempt, which is, perhaps, more disastrous to him than the first. The officers at headquarters are much disgusted at a certain want of decision, even in small matters. We are now without wood and without water. We are all disgusted.

William Child, a surgeon with the 5th New Hampshire, returned to Falmouth and wrote to his wife:

> Will fortune ever favor us? Oh, Carrie, why don't those at home who have been so fiery and furious against any compromise [with the Confederates] come out here and learn what it is to be a soldier? Let them come here away from wife and children and every thing that makes life sweet. Let them march through snow and rain, through mud and hot burning sun, the ground for a bed, the sky for a covering. Where are those in New Hampshire who had talked so bravely? Let them walk up to the Fredericksburg batteries. We need all their aid.

The men were tired of war, but even more, they were tired and angry at what their leader had done to them. What would Burnside do next?

On January 23, while his army was making its way back to Falmouth, Burnside invited Smith and Franklin, two of his strongest critics, to lunch. "I shall never forget the boned turkey, which for awhile drove out all memory of our hard camp fare," wrote Maj. Gen. William Smith of their lunch. "General Burnside was very variable in spirits, at times almost gay and then relapsing into moodiness; from one of these fits he started up saying, 'In a day or two you will hear of something that will surprise you.'"

Burnside was about to strike back against his detractors, those who, in his view, were responsible for the Union army's defeat of December 13 at Fredericksburg. When the meal was over and the guests had left, Burnside launched a new campaign by issuing General Orders Number Eight, asking the president to approve the dismissal from the service of four generals, and the transfer of five others out of the Army of the Potomac. Joe Hooker was on the list, as were his luncheon guests, Smith and Franklin. Others to be disciplined included John Newton and John Cochrane, who had visited Lincoln to complain personally about Burnside.

At 8:50 that night, Burnside telegraphed the president. "I have prepared some very important orders, and I want to see you before issuing them. Can I see you alone if I am at the White House after midnight?" Lincoln agreed. Burnside departed immediately, but his transport got bogged down in the mud, so he missed the train. He did not reach Washington, DC, until seven o'clock in the morning. He went straight to the White House and presented Lincoln with General Orders Number Eight—and an ultimatum. The president had to choose: Either endorse Burnside's request to sack those who had spoken against him, or finally accept Burnside's resignation.

Burnside received Lincoln's answer at ten o'clock the next morning. Lincoln relieved Burnside of command of the Army of the Potomac. To replace him, Lincoln selected Fighting Joe Hooker. When Maj. Henry Livermore Abbott, of the 20th Massachusetts, learned of his new commanding officer, he wrote to his father about the army's expectations: "We all expect Hooker will soon make his grand failure and [we] patiently wait for it." They would have to wait only four months for Hooker's downfall.

By January 26, the change of command was complete. Burnside took his leave at a reception in Falmouth with some of the officers he liked. "Farewell, gentlemen," he told them. "There are no pleasant reminiscences for me connected with the Army of the Potomac."

Sgt. Thomas Plunkett was unable to go home. He was well enough to do so, and his brother had come to Washington to accompany him, but they were unable to break through the War Department's red tape. Nobody there would even take the time to hear their story.

Clara Barton was incensed when Plunkett told her of the situation, and she immediately brought him to see Henry Wilson, the powerful senator from Massachusetts.

"Mr. Wilson," she said, "permit me to introduce you to Sergeant Plunkett of the Massachusetts Twenty-First."

"How do you do, Sergeant?" Wilson said, automatically extending his hand.

"You will pardon the Sergeant for not offering you his hand," Clara said. "He has none."

"No hands!" Wilson said. "No hands! My God; where are they?"

When Clara explained that Plunkett had no arms, either, and how he had lost them through his heroic actions, Wilson asked what he could do to help the sergeant.

"He wants to go home," Clara told him. "His brother is here waiting to take him [but] they cannot reach the War Department."

Plunkett needed a furlough instead of a discharge, so that he could continue to receive his pay until his pension as a disabled veteran would start. Senator Wilson promised to take care of everything. At ten o'clock that night, he called on Clara at her boardinghouse to announce that the matter was settled. Plunkett could go home the next day.

Wilson was highly distraught about Sergeant Plunkett's plight. He paced the room and finally slumped in a chair and held his head in his hands.

"What a price," he muttered. "What a price! And where and what will be the end?"

Such is the fate of war.

FOURTEEN

AFTERMATH

After his failure at Fredericksburg, Burnside was sent far enough away from the Army of the Potomac to ensure that he would not be involved in any major campaign. In late March 1863, he took command of the Department of the Ohio, which included Michigan, Ohio, Indiana, Illinois, and most of Kentucky.

Although Burnside no longer went to war, the war came to him in several ways: Southern sympathizers in Illinois and Indiana, raids by the Confederate cavalry leader John Hunt Morgan in Kentucky, and Northern dissidents called the Copperheads who were trying to sabotage the Union war effort in order to bring about peace with the South. If the president thought he was sending Burnside where he could not get into more trouble, he was wrong.

Morgan's raiders were beaten back quickly, but Burnside had a greater problem with citizens he considered disloyal to the Union. He cracked down harshly and ordered the arrest of anyone who criticized the government.

He was not alone in taking such punitive measures to crush opposition to the war. Lincoln had issued a proclamation subjecting any person considered disloyal to martial law. The president had suspended habeas corpus for those arrested. They were stripped of their rights and tried by the army rather than by a civilian court. In his new command, Burnside declared that any statement of sympathy for the enemy or in opposition to the war would not be tolerated.

Clement Laird Vallandigham, a former Ohio congressman who opposed Lincoln's draconian war powers against civilians, decided to test Burnside's zeal. On May 1, 1863, Burnside sent two officers in civilian clothes to take notes at Vallandigham's speech to a public antiwar rally. Three days later, soldiers broke down the door of Vallandigham's house and arrested and imprisoned him in a military jail. The charge was urging people to resist Burnside's order.

Protests erupted throughout Ohio. During Vallandigham's two-day trial by military commission, which imposed a prison sentence for the duration of the war, Burnside arrested newspaper editors for criticizing the government's actions. The protests spread nationwide. Lincoln wisely banished Vallandigham to the Confederate States and reminded Burnside that although he and the cabinet supported Burnside's actions in arresting the congressman, they questioned the need to do so.

In September, Burnside was given the opportunity to return to the war by leading an army south into Tennessee. He captured Knoxville and helped Grant win his victory at Chattanooga by drawing Longstreet's troops away so that Grant did not have to contend with that major force. Historians agree that without Burnside's bold and risky maneuver, Grant might well have lost that battle.

Burnside believed that he had redeemed himself for his failure at Fredericksburg. In January 1864, both houses of Congress passed a joint resolution praising Burnside for his service to the Union. Secretary of War Stanton gave Burnside command of his old 9th Corps, with which he had achieved such success in North Carolina. It was an independent command of 50,000 men—the largest single corps in the Union army—and it was attached to the Army of the Potomac, which he had so recently led. This time Burnside was to operate independently and take orders only from Grant, who now commanded all the Union armies.

In May 1864, Grant ordered the Army of the Potomac south through the densely forested area known as the Wilderness of Spotsylvania, where Lee held it in check. Then, in a brilliant series of marches around Lee's forces, the Union troops moved steadily southward, fighting bloody battles through Spotsylvania, Hanover Court House, and the Cold Harbor crossroads. By June, Grant, Meade, and Burnside held Lee's Army of Northern Virginia under siege outside Petersburg, Virginia, where both sides remained in place, facing each other across the miles of trenches that scarred the countryside. The war had reached a stalemate; there seemed no way to break it.

One of Burnside's officers, Lt. Col. Henry Pleasants, had been a mining engineer before the war and many of his men of the 48th Pennsylvania had been coal miners. Pleasants proposed digging a tunnel five hundred feet long, packing the end with explosives, and blowing up a portion of the Confederate line. This would leave a gap large enough for Burnside to pour troops through so they could go on to capture Petersburg.

Burnside was so confident of success that he had all of his baggage packed in advance. He expected to move his headquarters into Petersburg right behind his victorious troops. The mine explosion tore a large chunk out of the rebel line, as Pleasants had intended, leaving the way open to Petersburg. But the aftermath was a disaster. Not all of this was Burnside's fault, but, as was his custom, even when the battle was obviously lost he obstinately stuck to his original plan. A court of inquiry would later place the blame for the failure primarily on Burnside.

He was sent home on leave to await further orders, which never came. He offered to serve as a subordinate officer to Grant or Sherman, or as an aide or even a bearer of dispatches, but the War Department no longer wanted him in any capacity. Burnside resigned from the army on the day before Lincoln was shot. Less than a year later, he was elected to the first of three terms as governor of Rhode Island. He later served as a US senator and died in 1881, at the age of fifty-seven.

Fighting Joe Hooker replaced Burnside as commander of the Army of the Potomac after Fredericksburg and was a great success—for a while. He thoroughly revamped the army; set up a leave program; fired incompetent and corrupt quartermasters so that the men were provided with better food, uniforms, and equipment; and set about cleaning up the camps. Those important changes, together with designing distinctive badges for each corps, greatly enhanced spirit and morale. The desertion rate fell sharply.

Having rebuilt the army, Hooker then devised a brilliant plan for defeating Lee and bringing the war to an end. "May God have mercy on General Lee," he boasted, "for I will have none." In late April, with 40,000 men in place at Falmouth feigning another assault on Fredericksburg, thus forcing Lee to keep troops there, Hooker quietly marched his remaining 70,000 troops nine miles upriver. There they crossed, still unbeknownst to Lee, and headed south. It appeared that Hooker would be successful in outwitting Lee, just as Burnside had done early in his command.

All went well until Hooker's troops reached the Wilderness, near the Chancellorsville crossroads. It was there that Lee daringly divided his army and let Stonewall Jackson attack the Union right flank. Hooker promptly lost all of his initiative, daring, and aggressiveness, and retreated in disorder. Years later, Hooker said that he had simply lost confidence in himself. Once again, Lee had defeated the Army of the Potomac.

A month later, when Lee audaciously invaded Maryland and Pennsylvania, Lincoln replaced Hooker with George Meade, whose understrength division had fought tenaciously in Franklin's wing at Fredericksburg. Hooker was sent west, where he served under Grant at Chattanooga, and then under Sherman during the Atlanta campaign. Hooker resigned in July when another general was given command of the Army of the Tennessee, a job he thought should be his. He finished out the war serving in the upper northwest states, far removed from the fighting fronts. He remained in the army after the war until a stroke forced him to retire in 1868. He died eleven years later in New York.

The Joint Committee on the Conduct of the War found William B. Franklin to be responsible for the disaster at Fredericksburg. The Committee's conclusion, reached four months after the battle, in April 1863, was that if Franklin had made use of all the troops available to him, then Burnside's plan would have been successful and victory achieved.

While the report may have been too optimistic with regard to the probable success of Burnside's attack, the result was devastating to Franklin's career and his ego. Furious, he wrote a pamphlet defending his conduct at Fredericksburg. He paid for the cost of printing one thousand copies, which he sent to congressmen, newspaper editors, and others in positions of power.

The pamphlet did not change the low opinion of him held by the War Department, which sent him far away from Washington. He was ordered to report to Maj. Gen. Nathaniel Banks, commanding the Department of the Gulf, headquartered in New Orleans. "I am convinced now," Franklin wrote to his wife on arrival there, "that I was only sent here to get rid of me. There are more generals than are needed." He was right on both counts.

Given command of a corps, Franklin was ordered to launch an amphibious assault on the Texas coast to capture Sabine City and its forty thousand bales of valuable cotton. His boats got lost and ran aground far from their destination. The troops sank in the mudflats up to their waists and the element of surprise was lost. Franklin was blamed for the debacle. A century later, a Civil War historian wrote, "Had justice been done, Major General Franklin would have been broken to the ranks for incompetence and shot for cowardice." The affair hardly improved Franklin's tarnished reputation.

Franklin next led his corps on the ill-fated Red River campaign, an overland invasion of Texas. The attack failed and the army retreated to southern Louisiana. Although Franklin was not blamed for this failure, he did receive a minor leg wound that festered. Declared unfit for duty after this injury, he went to Maine on medical leave to stay with his wife.

In the summer of 1864, during the siege of Lee's army outside
Petersburg, Franklin went to visit his old friend, Maj. Gen.
William F. "Baldy" Smith. While returning from Virginia by train,
Franklin was captured by a Confederate cavalry patrol north of
Baltimore. He escaped and spent three days eluding his captors
with no food and little sleep, limping on his bad leg until he was
rescued.

He returned home and waited six months—with growing
impatience, frustration, and anger—for a new command. Word
finally came from the War Department in December 1864, when
he was ordered to report to Wilmington, Delaware, to preside over
the board established to consider the retirement of disabled officers. Franklin's war was over, and so was his military career.

He resigned from the army after the Confederate surrender and
began a new career as vice president and general manager of the
Colt Firearms Manufacturing Company in Hartford, Connecticut.
He became immensely wealthy and died in 1903, shortly after his
eightieth birthday.

Edwin Vose "Bull" Sumner asked to be relieved of his command
after Fredericksburg to avoid serving under Joe Hooker. He was
reassigned to St. Louis to head the Department of the West, but
before assuming command he stopped in Syracuse, New York, to
visit his family. There he fell ill, but was determined to proceed to
his new command. Duty called, and Old Bull was not about to be
delayed by sickness.

"Everybody could see that he was a sick man," his biographer
wrote, "everybody but Sumner. He insisted [on being allowed to
leave]; [he] pleaded, begged, and put on a front as if he were not
at all sick." His doctor told his daughter to keep her eye on him
and not to let him leave the house. They knew that if he went out,
he would head for the railway station and the next train west.

Sumner's condition worsened and he began to ramble, sometimes incoherently, about his duty to his country and how he had
to report to St. Louis because a soldier's place was with his com-

mand. On Friday afternoon, March 13, 1863, he asked for a glass of wine. He raised it in a toast and spoke in a clear, strong voice: "God save my country, the United States of America." And then, one of his biographers wrote, "His arm weakened, the glass tilted and the contents fell on the bedspread. The glass fell on the bed. The general went into a coma. A few hours later he was dead."

Thomas Francis Meagher was worried that he would be out of a command because there were so few men left in the Irish Brigade after Fredericksburg. He secured a twenty-day medical leave for his knee injury and went home to New York City to muster new recruits. He found that there were very few volunteers left, even among the Irish. He asked the War Department to return his brigade to New York to help encourage recruitment, but the request was denied.

Meagher overstayed his leave, and when he finally returned to Falmouth he had to face a military commission. Somehow he was able to explain away his unauthorized absence, but the incident furthered the decline of his reputation in the Union army.

He tried for another leave, this time to go to Washington to enlist the aid of influential political contacts to help him keep his command, but that request, along with yet another to release his brigade to return to New York, was rejected. While waiting for his fortunes to change, he organized a steeplechase in Falmouth for St. Patrick's Day.

Everyone had a grand time at the horse races, wheelbarrow races, and the greased-pig chase, while consuming a punch made from eight baskets of champagne, ten gallons of rum, and twenty-two gallons of whiskey. No one ever accused Meagher of not knowing how to put on grand entertainment or of not drinking more than anyone else.

After the steeplechase, Meagher persuaded the brigade surgeon to certify that he had a severe attack of rheumatism, requiring medical leave. This was granted, and Meagher returned to New York. He rejoined the army in time for the disastrous defeat at

Chancellorsville. He tried again to persuade the War Department to let his men go home for rest and recruitment duty, but once again he was refused.

By May, he was so desperate that he offered his resignation from the Irish Brigade. To his surprise and chagrin, his resignation was accepted. Meagher went home in despair to his father-in-law's house on Fifth Avenue in New York, wondering what to do next. He tried to withdraw his resignation with appeals to both the War Department and the State Department, but neither succeeded. The war, as well as chances for promotion, glory, and a general's salary, was passing him by.

Finally in December 1863, a year after the battle at Fredericksburg, he was reinstated as a brigadier general of volunteers but was not given a command. He stayed in New York, keeping busy by giving inspirational talks and attending lavish banquets. Nine months later he was ordered to Nashville, Tennessee, to General Sherman's army, but no one seemed to want him there, either. He was passed along from one outfit to another until he was given his own command—several brigades of convalescents assigned to guard duty around Chattanooga.

Meagher was then ordered to take a provisional division, composed of drunken officers and undisciplined troops, to Savannah, Georgia. Along the way, in an alcoholic haze of his own, he lost many of his men, though not to battle. They simply wandered away and most of them never came back. General Halleck wrote that Meagher's command was in a state of utter confusion and that Meagher had no idea how many troops he had or where they were. Grant was furious when he learned of the situation. He said, "If [Meagher] has lost his men it will afford a favorable pretext for doing what the service would have lost nothing by having done long ago—dismissing him."

On February 20, 1865, Meagher was relieved from active duty. On the Fourth of July, the proud remnants of the Irish Brigade marched smartly down Fifth Avenue in New York. Few people in the crowd noticed Thomas Francis Meagher in civilian clothes, walking along the sidewalk with the rest of the spectators.

After the war he went west, becoming acting governor of Montana Territory. In 1867, he fell overboard from a river steamer tied up at a dock at the town of Fort Benton and drowned. He had been ill, had no future employment prospects, was out of money and deeply in debt, and was drinking heavily and taking a number of medications, including opium pills. His body was never found and no one knows whether his death was an accident or a suicide.

Clara Barton was so exhausted after Fredericksburg that in April 1863 she joined her brother at his post at Hilton Head, South Carolina, for a much-needed rest. She promptly found herself assuming the role of nurse again, attending to the chief quarter-master, Lt. Col. John Elwell, who had broken his leg. He had been a physician, a lawyer, and a college professor before the war and Clara was immediately attracted to him. Unfortunately, he was already married.

They lived next door to each other and Clara's affection grew. When Elwell contracted yellow fever, her care most likely saved his life. They began a love affair. He called her "Birdie," and "My Pet," asking to visit her "nest." "I did have a fine sleep last night," he wrote to her one morning. "How could it be otherwise? That was one of the golden hours of life to me."

She wrote equally passionate notes to him, but they both accepted the fact that he would remain married to his wife, and that their love could not last beyond the idyllic time together at the beach at Hilton Head. She imagined the waves themselves telling her, "This far shall thou go and no farther!"

Growing apace with her love for Elwell was a gnawing sense of guilt over spending her days in such bliss while Union soldiers were fighting and dying without her comfort and aid. In July, having missed the battle at Gettysburg, Clara joined a Union expedition against the Confederate-held Fort Wagner, some four miles north of Charleston.

She watched, spellbound, as the black soldiers of the 54th Massachusetts, led by their twenty-five-year-old colonel, Robert

Gould Shaw, were cut to pieces by the deeply entrenched rebels. And to her greater horror, she saw her lover, Colonel Elwell, ride toward the fort, shouting that the men were being slaughtered. As a quartermaster, he was not supposed to take part in the fighting.

Clara saw him fall from his horse, wounded, and she braved a hail of shells and bullets to reach him. She brought him back to the Union lines, bandaged his wound, and demanded that he stay alive. He was sent back to the hospital at Hilton Head while Clara stayed to nurse the rest of the wounded.

After six strenuous weeks at the front, Clara was stricken with dysentery. She was so ill that she was certain she would not survive. She was brought to Hilton Head, where her brother, John Elwell, and other friends cared for her around the clock. But the day after Christmas, 1863, she decided to return to the war.

In Washington, however, there seemed to be no work for her to do. The Army of the Potomac was in winter quarters and there would be no fighting until spring. Dorothea Dix was now in charge of the army nurses, and she did not want to share the glory and publicity of her efforts with the well-known Clara Barton. "It was a painful irony that Clara had cleared the way for other women to serve in field hospitals, only to find herself excluded from them," one of her biographers wrote.

Her old friend Senator Wilson could not help, for General Grant had ordered all women and civilians to leave the Army of the Potomac. She became so depressed that she wished she were dead. "I cannot raise my spirits," she wrote. "I want to leave all."

She wrote to Secretary of War Stanton asking for a pass to enable her to rejoin the army but received no reply. Finally, in May 1864, after the battle at the Wilderness, she was given another chance. More than eight thousand casualties from that battle had been sent, ironically, to nearby Fredericksburg, but there were no medical facilities for them there. The army needed Clara Barton to return to the very place where she had witnessed so much suffering two years earlier. By the end of the war she was considered a national heroine, the "angel of the battlefields."

She went to Andersonville, the notorious Confederate prisoner-of-war camp in Georgia, on a mission authorized by Lincoln before his assassination. Her job was to search for missing Union soldiers, to identify and mark their graves. She lectured on her war work, and in the course of her travels she met many of the men whose lives she had saved. While in Cleveland, she saw John Elwell with his wife. In later years, he wrote tender letters to her, reminiscing about their love affair, but she never saw him again.

In 1870, Clara Barton served at the front with the International Red Cross during the Franco-Prussian War. She helped establish the American Red Cross and served as its president from 1881 until 1904. At the age of seventy-seven, she was still nursing wounded soldiers, this time in Cuba during the Spanish-American War. She died in 1912 at the age of ninety. Her final words were "Let me go; let me go!"

Sgt. Thomas Plunkett saw Clara Barton in New York City four months after he was wounded. He told her he had received donations totaling four thousand dollars to provide for his care. Two weeks later, when he arrived home in West Boylston, Massachusetts, a thousand people greeted him as a hero. On March 30, 1866, he was awarded the Medal of Honor for saving the colors at Fredericksburg. In 1869, the state of Massachusetts gave him a job as a messenger at the State House. He married, had two children, and died in 1885 at the age of forty-five. At his funeral service, the battle-scarred flag he had saved from touching the ground at Fredericksburg was placed next to his casket.

The town of Fredericksburg lay in ruins after the battle. Photographs taken at the time look like those of European cities at the end of World War II. Bare chimneys, remnants of walls, and rubble-strewn streets marked its sorrowful appearance. Even those buildings that remained standing wore battle scars. The townspeople who returned after the fighting were ruined. Wealthy men became paupers. Women and children faced starvation. Stonewall Jackson urged his men to take up a collection for their relief. The soldiers raised the staggering sum of $30,000. Trainloads of food and clothing were also collected throughout the South, along with another $170,000.

As stories of starving refugees and pictures of the destruction spread throughout the South, the Confederates' anger grew. This was the first time that war's awesome power had been visited on a town of that size. It would not be the last. Southerners would soon have reason to lament the destruction of Atlanta, Georgia; Columbia, South Carolina; and the Confederate capital at Richmond itself.

Fredericksburg today is an attractive, charming town. The Park Service maintains part of the battlefield much as it was in 1862. A portion of the stone wall and the sunken road can be seen, as well as part of the open field over which so many Union troops marched and died. At one end of the wall is an excellent visitor's center and museum. In the town itself, the Fredericksburg Area Museum, opened in 1992 at 907 Princess Anne Street, contains many artifacts of the battle and of the Civil War in general.

Across the river, Bull Sumner's headquarters at Chatham can be visited. From the porch, one can look across the river at the town and the hills beyond. The Phillips House, where General Burnside once had his headquarters, burned to the ground sometime after the battle.

In town, at least one house along the riverfront, 1312 Sophia Street, remains the same as it was at the time of the battle. Nearby are the sites of the pontoon bridges. Behind the town, at Lee's Hill, one can see the remains of trenches and gun emplacements. Lee Drive, now a tree-shaded road, contains breastworks, trenches, and gun positions used by Jackson's troops as they faced Franklin's wing of the Union Army.

I lived in Fredericksburg for three years, a few blocks from the canal that the Union troops had to cross. I taught at Mary

Washington College, then the women's branch of the University of Virginia. Situated northwest of the stone wall, Brompton, the mansion atop Marye's Heights, was the home of the college's president. Its white pillars and redbrick walls still bore the signs of the fighting, and the stairs inside were scarred by spur marks. For a time after the battle, Brompton served as a military hospital.

If you stand on the sunken road early of a foggy winter morning and look across the open ground, it is easy to imagine the ghosts of the soldiers who fought there in 1862, to imagine them still trying to reach the stone wall that called so many to their death.

NOTES

PROLOGUE

"Don't let it fall" (Oates, 113)

"a great slaughter pen" (W. Jones, 161)

"It can hardly be in human nature for men to show more valor" (Pride and Travis, 176)

"If there is a worse place than Hell" (McPherson, 574)

"Oh, those men, those poor men over there" (Foote, 42)

"All that day we watched the fruitless charges" (Warren, 8)

CHAPTER ONE: ALAS FOR MY POOR COUNTRY

"So it is called, but that is a mistake" (Nicolay and Hay, 175)

"The change in his personal appearance was marked and sorrowful" (Brooks, *Washington*, 9)

"cross the Potomac and give battle to the enemy" (Nicolay and Hay, 175)

"Will you pardon me for asking what the horses of your army have done?" (Nicolay and Hay, 177)

"By direction of the President it is ordered that Major-General McClellan be relieved" (Johnson and Buel, *Battles and Leaders*, 103)

"Late at night I was sitting alone in my tent" (Johnson and Buel, *Battles and Leaders*, 104)

"I am sure that not a muscle quivered" (Sears, 340)

"Well, Burnside, I turn the command over to you" (Johnson and Buel, *Battles and Leaders*, 104)

"That, sir, is the last thing on which I wish to be congratulated" (Nichols, 624)

"Poor Burn feels dreadfully, almost crazy" (Sears, 341)

"He is very slow" (Sandburg, 625)

"The army is filled with gloom and greatly depressed" (Meade, 325)

"One could not help feeling a certain tenderness" (Sandburg, 625)

"How can I describe it, how can I tell the utter despondency of the soldiers" (Donaldson, 162, 163, 165)

"Today we have been on review" (Carter, 159)

"The army is in mourning" (Patrick, 173)

"A sadder gathering of men" (Donaldson, 164)
"I heard [Humphreys] say that he wished" (Donaldson, 164)
"One word [from McClellan], one look of encouragement" (Johnson and Buel, *Battles and Leaders*, 104)
"It can be safely said that from the hour" (Nicolay and Hay, 197)

CHAPTER TWO: MARKED FOR GREATER THINGS

"simple, honest, loyal soldier" (Catton, vol. 1, 256)
"He seemed dashing and brave" (T. H. Williams, 180)
"knowledge and judgment" (Meade, 351)
"when once convinced of the correctness of my course" (O'Reilly, *The Fredericksburg Campaign*, 53)
"intense stubbornness which sometimes takes hold of weak minds" (W. Smith, 59)
"Burnside turned to me"; "would have willingly laid down his life" (W. Smith, 63)
"But for your great powers of endurance" (Marvel, *Burnside*, 174)
"We shall see what we shall see" (Sandburg, 625)
the "leading beau" in all of Centreville (Poore, 29)
"You should be a cadet at West Point!" (Poore, 31)
"Benny Havens, Oh!" (Poore, 41)
"finest looking and most soldier-like of the corps" (Poore, 44)
"sufficient self-denial to stop" (Poore, 57)
"remained a blight on his reputation" (Marvel, *Burnside*, 11)
Another tale is told about Lottie Moon (Poore, 74)
"My dear, you have shocked me by swearing" (Poore, 74)
"I met a man tonight," (Poore, 87)
"The General is a man of action" (Marvel, *Burnside*, 38)
"By Jove, I'll send one of these to my wife" (Marvel, *Burnside*, 81)
"If there is an honest man on the face of the earth" (Marvel, *Burnside*, 92)
"a pretty young woman asked if she could kiss him" (Marvel, *Burnside*, 115)

CHAPTER THREE: HE WAS SIMPLY ELEGANT

"political Hell" (Leech, 185)
"bulging eyes, his flabby cheeks, his slack-twisted figure" (Catton, vol. 1, 196)
"Halleck was buttoned up tight" (Leech, 180)
"a typical old-line government-service hack" (Catton, vol. 1, 197)
"he rubbed his elbow first" (Catton, vol. 1, 196)

"a military imbecile, though he might make a good clerk" (Musicant, 190)

"I am not fit for it"; "It will succeed, if you move rapidly" (Ambrose, 95)

"The first duty of a soldier is to obey his orders" (Stanley, 68)

"His soldiers used to tell with great relish" (Stanley, 299)

"He seemed to be always on the defensive" (Stanley, 178)

"Draw sabers! Charge!" (Stanley, 210)

"I have belonged to the general government over forty years." (Stanley, 236)

"It is a damned piece of cowardice" (Stanley, 237)

"Sumner at least was one man we could always rely on." (Stanley, 238)

"Steady, men, steady! Don't be excited." (Stanley, 262)

"very picture of a veteran soldier" (Villard, 349)

"Like many officers in this army" (Marvel, "The Making of a Myth," 3)

"lacked the boldness or creativity" (O'Reilly, *The Fredericksburg Campaign*, 138)

"I have thought so much of leaving the Army" (Snell, 34)

"I was kept back by Franklin" (Snell, 61)

"skillful at following his commander's orders" (Snell, xii)

"stubbornly methodical commander" (Snell, 168)

"beautiful cadet" (Hebert, 20)

"a model of a war-god" (Villard de Borchgrave and Cullen, 207)

"What a handsome fellow he was!" (Hebert, 23–24)

"is aware that I know some things about his character" (Hebert, 41)

"Here's a thousand, Captain" (Hebert, 45)

"I was at the battle of Bull Run" (Hebert, 49)

"Joe Hooker is our leader/He takes his whiskey strong" (Furgurson, 25)

"I suppose we shall have one more blunder" (Hebert, 151)

CHAPTER FOUR: NO PONTOONS, NO CROSSING

"You [will] be there hanged by the neck until you be dead" (Athearn, 13)

"I am here to regret nothing I have ever done" (Athearn, 12)

"Worst of all,[Meagher] had no audience" (Athearn, 20)

"He is a fine, military looking young gentleman" (Athearn, 29)

"handsome, daring, reckless of consequences" (Wylie, 32)

"It was a moral certainty that many of our countrymen" (Beller, 21)

"YOUNG IRISHMEN TO ARMS!" (P. Jones, 35)

"fox hunters; a class of Irish exquisites good for a fight" (McCormack, 2) "suffered desperately, their red dress making them a conspicuous mark" (Beller, 26)

"bore himself with distinguished gallantry" (Athearn, 97)

"It is as well to keep up our spirits by pouring spirits down" (McCormack, 2)

"sad, most unfortunate, intemperate habits"; "He was very drunk, looked strangely wild" (McCarter, 70)

"Three minutes later, to my horror" (McCarter, 71)

"The line of march was seven miles long"; "It makes my heart ache to see the devastation" (Teall, 22–23)

"There are but few able bodied men left." (Pettit, 36)

"This vast army, with its three heads pushing out" (Child, 146)

"That's all right. I was afraid you had stolen them." (Nolan, 169)

"My orders were to advance" (Stanley, 283)

"His mind had been made up to cross the river" (Stackpole, 86)

"No, Sumner. Wait for the pontoons." (Howard, 317)

"As it required thirteen days" (Howard, 319)

CHAPTER FIVE: THE MAN WHO COULD DO NO WRONG

"At heart Robert E. Lee is against us"; "General Lee will surely be tried" (Chesnut, 70, 71)

"General Lee in the streets here bore the aspect of a discontented man" (W. Jones, 58)

"We always understood each other so well" (Freeman, *R.E. Lee*, 428)

"It is plain that the enemy is abandoning his position" (Lee, *Wartime Papers*, 337)

"that Burnside's whole army had marched for Fredericksburg"; "send a daily detail to gather sassafras buds" "I think Burnside is concentrating" (Lee, *Wartime Papers*, 341)

"Quiet days interrupted only by soldiers begging for food" (Light, 48)

"I fear that our men with insufficient clothing" (Lee, *Wartime Papers*, 328)

"Anything that Lee had was sacred"; "Lee commanded the souls of his men" (G. Smith, 181)

"birth defect" (Thomas, 17)

Always at the top of his class (G. Smith, 25)

"I am conscious of having lost a great deal" (Anderson and Anderson, 169)

"rent by a thousand anxieties" (Anderson and Anderson, 203)

"Lee, you have made the greatest mistake" (Freeman, *R.E. Lee*, 615)

"The army of General Lee [is] collecting around us" (Beale, 123)

CHAPTER SIX: WE ARE IN THE HANDS OF THE PHILISTINES

"We hear of stormy conflicts" (Light, 11)

"I cannot believe that our glorious land" (Light, 13)

"the great excitement prevailing"; "Now there is but one topic of thought" (Light, 16–17)

"April 18, 1862. Good Friday." (Light, 27–28)

"We are in the hands of the Philistines" (Happel, 37)

"a generous man and a kind, humane officer" (Quinn, 75)

"Fredericksburg is a captured town." (Beale, 62)

"Never mind, General, if you will write the decline and fall of this rebellion" (Happel, 49)

"The Secesh people were very indignant" (Patrick, 73–74)

"The boys looked on and enjoyed the scene" (Herdegen, 54)

"The enemy are in full possession of the country" (Light, 32–33)

"Since my last entry, my heart has been crushed" (Beale, 72)

"We can hear nothing from our army or our friends"; "It strikes at the root of those principles" (Beale, 73)

"[A] thundering sound shook the house"; "I went out feeling a good deal of indignation" (Beale, 109–110)

"[We] watched with trembling hearts" (Beale, 122)

"Longstreet is a capital soldier." (Wert, 131)

"the staff in my right hand,"; (Wert, 152)

"my old war horse" (Wert, 200)

"Wouldn't it be nice for you to be here again?" (Vandiver, 415)

"I have written that he was ambitious"; "You say that I must live on [fame] for the present" (Vandiver, 289–290)

"The revolution has at last found a great Captain" (Vandiver, 414)

"The coat is much too handsome for me (Vandiver, 409)

"dressed up as fine as a Lieutenant"; "Come here, boys. Stonewall has drawed his bounty" (Douglas, 205)

"Young gentlemen, this is no longer the headquarters" (Vandiver, 418)

"Maybe I ought to, ma'am, but I am not going to." (Vandiver, 6)

"I am very ignorant" (Vandiver, 13)

"That fellow looks as if he had come to stay." (Vandiver, 14)

"talked back to him, contradicted him, derided him." (Vandiver, 79)

"If the culprits expected a reaction" (Vandiver, 79)

"Then, sir, we will give them the bayonet!" "Look! There is Jackson standing like a stone wall." (Chambers, 377)

"My Own Dear Father" (Vandiver, 418)

CHAPTER SEVEN: LET THE YANKEES COME

"Headquarters of the Army of the Potomac, November 21st, 1862"
(Johnson and Buel, *Battles and Leaders*, 70–71)
"Many were almost destitute" (Johnson and Buel, *Battles and Leaders*, 71)
"It was a pitious sight" (Lee, *Wartime Papers*, 343)
"Yes they must fear the worst." (Light, 48)
"I am as yet unable to discover what may be the plan" (Lee, *Wartime Papers*, 344)
"I think from the tone of the Northern papers" (Lee, *Wartime Papers*, 345)
"that his new Army commander seemed no faster" (Marvel, *Burnside*, 168)
"Could you, without inconvenience, meet me" (Stackpole, 102)
"everybody concerned would have been much better off" (Catton, vol. 2, 28)
"if we could throw a bridge across the river"; "We were ordered back to camp" (Johnson and Buel, *Battles and Leaders*, 121–122)
"two more weeks looking down on the town" (Foote, 21)
"We had a dinner of hard tack and salt pork," (Adams, 1)
"I began my search for a hotel" (Wightman, 84)
"Now for the butter" (Wightman, 85)
"The canvasback ducks were the *piece de resistance*" (Wainwright, 129–30)
"We settled down in earnest," (Corby, p. 130)
"We have been here two nights" (Carter, 169)
"You have no idea what it is, this winter campaign" (Carter, 170, 171)
"Breakfast: Coffee, Hardtack, Pork." (Nolan, 169)
"I thought we should all starve." (Carter, 170)
"The village of Falmouth is a wretched straggling old place" (Wainwright, 131)
"one of the most Godforsaken places" (Moe, 207)
"Here was a good opportunity for target practice" (McCarter, 93)
"I frequently stood near the bank of the river" (McCarter, 94)
"There is constant badinage." (Coffin, 140)
"The men anticipated spending what many of them termed 'a gay and happy winter'" (McCarter, 83)
"I am at a loss to understand why we are here" (Carter, 169)
"I deem it my duty to say that I cannot make the promise" (Foote, 24–25)
"I've pretty much made up my mind" (Catton, vol. 2, 32–33)
"The men in the old regiments" (Marvel, *Burnside*, 190)

"I don't think we can ever conquer them," (Pride and Travis, 163)

"I am no prophet, nor the son of a prophet" (Donaldson, 172)

"It looks to me as if we were going over there to be murdered" "I am sure we cannot take those hills." (O'Reilly, *The Fredericksburg Campaign*, 375)

"Father, they are going to lead us over in front of those guns" (O'Reilly, *The Fredericksburg Campaign*, 121)

"General Burnside's whole army is apparently opposite Fredericksburg" (Lee, *Recollections and Letters*, 85–86)

"I am opposed to fighting here" (Vandiver, 420)

"The road was filled with rebel troops perfectly protected" (Haupt, 183)

"Well! If they wait for me to fall back" (M. Perry, 183)

They rang out "Hail Columbia" (Johnson and Buel, *Battles and Leaders*, 86)

"Major, I never permit the unnecessary effusion of blood" (Goolrick, 170)

"a giant in stature, blond and virile" (J. Perry, 189–190)

"sweetly ornamented with a half-a-bushel of artificial flowers" (J. Perry, 194)

"ample proof of the excellent spirits of our troops" (Von Borcke, 85)

Chapter Eight: Bring the Guns to Bear

"What do you think of [my plan]?"; "made a remark about my readiness" (Johnson and Buel, *Battles and Leaders*, 126)

"All the orders have been issued to the several commanders of the grand divisions"; "If the General-in-Chief desires it"; "I beg of you not to telegraph details of your plans" (United States War Department, *Official Records*, 64)

"preposterous to talk about our crossing"; "General Burnside closed the conference" (Johnson and Buel, *Battles and Leaders*, 129)

"Tomorrow, if our present plans are carried out" (Johnson and Buel, *Battles and Leaders*, 126)

"small, slender, and striking" (Oates, 3)

"Where other little girls listened to fairy tales"; "I don't know how long it has been" (Oates, 8)

"one-woman relief agency" (Oates, 17)

It is the night before a battle. (Carroll, 78)

Every time a sound was answered with a minié ball (Freeman, *Lee's Lieutenants*, 335)

"Bring the guns to bear"; "roofs collapse, walls and chimneys cave in"

(Oates, 107)

"The town caught fire in several places." (Johnson and Buel, *Battles and Leaders*, 75)

"my youngest son, a boy of ten years" (Beale, 129)

"I beheld, it seemed to me, the most brilliant light" (Goolrick, 42)

"[Mother] had just reached the door opposite" (Goolrick, 44)

"You have enough to do to watch the Yankees"; "She apparently found the projectiles very interesting"; "For God's sake, Madam"; "Tell General Lee that if he wants a bridge of dead Yankees" (Freeman, *Lee's Lieutenants*, 336–337)

"Those people delight to destroy the weak" (Freeman, *R.E. Lee*, 446)

"Get out. You can't go." (Coffin, 149)

"Can't you go forward, Lieutenant Adams?" (Adams, 1)

"He found the door locked," (Adams, 1)

"Mr. Abbott, you will take the first platoon forward." (Abbott, 16)

"The end was distant only a few seconds" (Abbott, 18)

"That was enough for Brandon" (Freeman, *Lee's Lieutenants*, 338)

"echoed in our ears" (Beale, 132)

"truly felt that praise for our deliverance" (Beale, 134)

"What a scene met our eyes" (Goolrick, 44)

"And so great was our relief" (Goolrick, 46)

"Come to me. Your place is here."; "the water hissing with shot"; "Oh what a day's work was that" (Oates, 108–109)

"Still, it would have been better had Burnside crossed" (Marvel, *Burnside*, 178)

CHAPTER NINE: A CITY GIVEN UP TO PILLAGE

"We could distinctly see the enemy's earthworks" (Donaldson, 177)

"Shit. They want us to get in." (Foote, 39)

"We cover the ground now so well" (Johnson and Buel, *Battles and Leaders*, 79)

"If the straggler would not go back into the fight" (Freeman, *Lee's Lieutenants*, 341)

"I must confess I felt extremely nervous" (Von Borcke, 110)

"I shall try to do them all the damage in our power" (Freeman, *R.E. Lee*, 451)

"When I went into town, a horrible sight presented itself" (Patrick, 188, 189)

"a carnival night" (Coffin, 150)

"Boys came into our place loaded with silver pitchers" (Freeman, *Lee's Lieutenants*, 344)

"With tobacco for their clay pipes" (P. Jones, 152)

"whatever I may witness in the future" (Baxter, 115)

"a blamed rebel" (Moe, 211)

"I tried to get you some memento of Fredericksburg" (Abbott, 155)

"the men were motivated by a bitterness" (Baxter, 116)

"Yes! Yes!" Burnside replied. (Smith, 61)

"Would Burnside adopt our plan" (Johnson and Buel, *Battles and Leaders*, 133)

"It is a pitiful picture" (K. P. Williams, 824–825)

"I will do no such thing" (Ambrose, 97)

"composed by a man with an enormous sleep deficit" (Marvel, *Burnside*, 180)

"keep his whole command 'in position'"; "Already disturbed by the lateness of the hour" (O'Reilly, *"Stonewall" Jackson at Fredericksburg*, 32, 33)

Chapter Ten: There Was No Cheering

"There was something eerie about the morning" (Catton, vol. 2, 49)

"I expect to be sacrificed" (O'Reilly, *The Fredericksburg Campaign*, 59)

"We are in a house abandoned by Mr. Knox"; "You will have a stone wall to encounter"; "Now I fear you more than ever" (Howard, 327, 328)

stepped upon the gallery (Johnson and Buel, *Battles and Leaders*, 97)

"Thus glorified, 'Old Jack' was dazzling to the eye"; "Are you scared by that file of Yankees"; "Sir, we will give them the bayonet" (Freeman, *Lee's Lieutenants*, 346, 348)

"I opened little Mary's box of delicious fruit"; "You saved my life"; (Oates, 111)

"Major, my men have sometimes failed to take a position" (Freeman, *Lee's Lieutenants*, 349)

"You are alone and in great danger" (Oates, 112)

"Cheer up, my hearties!" (Marvel, *The Battle of Fredericksburg*, 37)

"several shells bursting in the ranks" (Lauvaas and Nelson, 105)

"It is not every man that can face danger" (Marvel, *The Battle of Fredericksburg*, 37)

"It was magnificent, but it was not war." (Freeman, *R.E. Lee*, 459–460)

Riamh Nar drhuid O sbairn Lan. "Never retreat from the clash of spears." (McCormack, 1)

"I know this day you will strike a deadly blow" (Beller, 75–76)

"the clink, clink, clink of the cold steel" (McCarter, p.vi)

"Shoulder arms. Left face. Forward, march." (McCarter, 167)

"They presented to us, who were just about to go into it" (McCarter,

171)

"Lay him down and cut the leg off at once" (McCarter, 171)

"Irish Brigade, advance! Forward, double-quick, guide center!" (P. Jones, 154)

"There are those damned green flags again" (Beller, 75)

"Oh God, what a pity! Here comes Meagher's fellows!" (McCarter, p.vi)

"On they came in beautiful array" (Johnson and Buel, *Battles and Leaders*, 98)

"filled with wonder and a pitying admiration" (Linderman, 62)

"Line after line of our men advance in magnificent order" (P. Jones, 154)

"simply melted away before the grape and cannister" (Corby, 131–132)

"concealed and bore up against for days" and "much to his embarrassment" (Athearn, 120)

"His retreat across the river without orders" (Villard, 371)

"I laid disabled, disheartened, hope a mere shadow" (McCarter, 180–181)

"Bill, I see the bastard that laid you there." (McCarter, p. 182)

"The prospect of death now seemed to increase." (McCarter, 182–183)

"Caldwell, you will forward your brigade at once"; "Attention! Every man is expected to do his duty today"; "The tattered colors of my regiment"; "many acts of cowardice and bravery" (Child, 153–155)

"the rapid disintegration of our troops" (Villard, 371)

"Had not the smoke of a terrific battle screened it" (Goolrick, 51)

"It's very painful" (Freeman, *Lee's Lieutenants*, 361)

"stayed all day giving the wounded drink"; "I wish those people would let Mrs. Stevens alone." (Goolrick, 51)

"I remember that the whole plain was covered with men"; "would do its duty and melt like snow"; "Oh, great God!" (Johnson and Buel, *Battles and Leaders*, 113)

"General, they are massing very heavily" (Johnson and Buel, *Battles and Leaders*, 81)

"Led by our gallant Captain Weymouth we moved up the bank" (Adams, p. 2)

"This was Clara Barton's war"; "literally obliterated the stripes" (Oates, 114)

"the noise was deafening" (McCarter, 184)

"The poor animal presented an appearance wild" (McCarter, 185)

"They might court martial me" (Moe, 213)

"Hooker has been ordered to put in everything"; "I can't carry that hill by frontal assault"; "Well, Couch, things are in such a state" (Johnson and Buel, *Battles and Leaders*, 113, 114)

"a torrent of vituperation [that] made the air blue" (Furgurson, 29)

"That was just what we wanted." (Alexander, 179)

"No one lives who goes there" (Perry, 187)

"General, a battery can't live there." (Johnson and Buel, *Battles and Leaders*, 115)

"God help us now"; "We reached the final crest" (M. Perry, 187)

"The attack of our division closed a battle" (Johnson and Buel, *Battles and Leaders*, 127)

"Finding that I had lost as many men as my orders required" (Hebert, 159)

Chapter Eleven: Death Has Been Doing Fearful Work

"And now the thick veil of mist" (Von Borcke, 116–117)

"A star this morning, William?" (O'Reilly, *"Stonewall" Jackson*, 64)

"[Pelham was] a very young looking, handsome, and attractive fellow" (Alexander, 174)

"Tell the General I can hold my ground"; "It is glorious to see such courage" (Freeman, *Lee's Lieutenants*, 350)

"The air warmed steadily and the ground became disagreeable" (O'Reilly, *"Stonewall" Jackson*, 48)

"Hold your fire, boys, until the command is given" (O'Reilly, *"Stonewall" Jackson*, 77)

"General Meade has just moved out." (Coffin, 162)

"Meade advanced half a mile" (Coffin, 162)

"But he *must* advance" (Marvel, "The Making of a Myth," 18)

"1.25 o'clock P.M. Meade is in the woods" (Coffin, 163–164)

"almost made the stones creep" (Nichols, 153)

"I assume the authority of ordering you to the relief" (Cleaves, 92)

"was almost wild with rage" (O'Reilly, *"Stonewall" Jackson*, 126)

"My God, General Reynolds, did they think my division could whip Lee's whole army?" (Nichols, 153)

"were driven back over me in disorder" (Marvel, "The Making of a Myth," 25)

"Mr. Smith, had you not better go to the rear?" (Freeman, *Lee's Lieutenants*, 357)

"It was useless. They went right through us." (O'Reilly, *"Stonewall" Jackson*, 148)

"It is well that war is so terrible." (Freeman, *R.E. Lee*, 462)

"felt he was outnumbered" (Marvel, *Burnside*, 192)

"All of my troops are in action" (K. P. Williams, 332)
"I put in all the troops I thought it proper and prudent" (Nichols, 155)
The testimony of all the witnesses before [this] committee (Snell, 263)
"I want to move forward"; "countenance glowed as from the glare of a great conflagration" (Freeman, *Lee's Lieutenants*, 369)
"so completely swept our front" (Chambers, 299)
"nothing could have lived while passing over that plain" (Freeman, *Lee's Lieutenants*, 373)
"hardened soldiers' hearts" (O'Reilly, *"Stonewall" Jackson*, 166)
"fiery lances and banners of blood and flame" (Trulock, 100)
"The sky flashed and grew dark again"; "Of course we enthusiastic young
fellows" (Freeman, *Lee's Lieutenants*, 374)

Chapter Twelve: Alone with the Dead

"It's all arranged" (Johnson and Buel, *Battles and Leaders*, 127)
"General, I hope you will desist" (Johnson and Buel, *Battles and Leaders*, 41)
"With this reluctant admission" (Marvel, *Burnside*, 298)
"cheerful in his tone" (Johnson and Buel, *Battles and Leaders*, 117)
"Oh, those men! Those men over there" (Foote, 42)
"I expect the battle to be renewed at daylight." (Lee, *Wartime Papers*, 359)
"The night was bitter cold" (Johnson and Buel, *Battles and Leaders*, 116)
"in every conceivable posture" (Oates, 114)
"seemed to be burned on my brain"; "the cries of the wounded rose up" (Reardon, 98–99)
"A burning, raging fever now attacked me." (McCarter, 191)
"We sneezed, coughed, choked, spluttered and spit"; "My hand had plunged in to the wrist" (Carter, 198)
"a wail so far and deep and wide"; "the living and the dead were alike to me" (Trulock, 97–98)
"Only the Irish could follow such a fight with such a feast" (P. Jones, 159)
"I suppose you would like to preserve this relic" (McCarter, 199)
"It was Sunday" (Donaldson, 89)
"Damn it. You there! Close up on your company." (P. Jones, 157)
"fixed and glassy eyes"; "This breastwork of the dead" (Carter, 201)
"The captain was at first disposed to be wrathy" (Villard, 388)
"When I get nothing clear and explicit" (Leech, 221)

"Have you come from the army?" (Villard, 389)

"the appalling disaster for which Ambrose E. Burnside will stand charged" (Villard, 393)

"I hope it is not so bad as all that." (Villard, 391)

"Mr. President, it was not a battle, it was a butchery" (Sandburg, 631)

"If there is a worse place than Hell, I am in it" (McPherson, 305)

"They have borne, silently and grimly, imbecility, treachery, failure, privation" (McPherson, 306)

"exhaustion steals over the country" (McPherson, 206)

"Alas, my poor country!" (Sandburg, 631)

"Twelve dollars to two Negroes for a ride in a rowboat!"; "Wearily and methodically, Villard knocked his opponent down" (Villard de Borchgrave and Cullen, 217)

"There, in every attitude of death" (Hoole, 40–41)

"I have never seen men lay so thic." (O'Reilly, *The Fredericksburg Campaign,* 458)

"The bodies of those poor fellows" (Von Borcke, 149)

"These gentlemen asserted that General Burnside was perfectly incapable" (Von Borcke, 141)

"Beg pardon, sir, I thought you had gone above"; "Never mind. I'll shoot you tomorrow and get them boots." (Freeman, *R.E. Lee,* 471)

"The men stood and silently looked" (Donaldson, 192)

"We had to pick our way over a field" (M. Perry, 188)

"We lost no time in having them fix them" (Donaldson, 193)

"This morning they were all safe on the north side" (Lee, 365)

"At Fredericksburg we gained a battle" (Gallagher, *The Fredericksburg Campaign,* 131)

"What can we do?"; "Why, shoot them." (Foote, vol. 2, 45)

Chapter Thirteen: A Tragic Figure

"This winter is, indeed, the Valley Forge" (Greene, 175)

"I must say I consider it nothing but a useless slaughter" (Pride and Travis, 185)

"We haven't been able to get anything from the commissary" (Abbott, 158)

"Soldiers are all discouraged" (Matrau, 39)

"We must prepare for worse times" (Pride and Travis, 192)

"the feeling of utter helplessness is stronger"; "depressed the spirit, crushed the hopes"; "A seething mass of discontent and demoralization" (Greene, 174)

"Very little is said about Burnside" (Wainwright, 149)

"I'll put a stop to that" (Marvel, *Burnside,* 207)

"For the failure in the attack, I am responsible" (United States War Department, *Official Records,* 67)

"Outdoors, at the foot of a tree"; "There are merely tents" (Whitman, 41–42)

"What I saw in the war set me up for all time." (Morris, 100–101)

"aimless round of bohemian posturing" (Morris, 6–7)

"[I] rose from the side of [his] couch"; "a little white bundle of skin and bones"; "At times, in her tent late at night" (Oates, 117–119)

"We operated in old blood-stained and often pus-stained coats" (Morris, 96)

"It gave the place the appearance of a little slaughterhouse" (McCarter, 206)

"but oh, the cries of agony and pain" (McCarter, 207–208)

"Here they come in squads of a hundred or more" (Brooks, *Mr. Lincoln's Washington,* 45)

"Gents, U.S. Army: We send you some tobacco" (Catton, vol. 2, 71)

"General Stonewall Jackson," a rebel yelled. (Chambers, 313)

"You have earned the good will and esteem of the Brigade" (P. Jones, 162)

"Throw your snowballs, men"; "[riding] around the tent on the back of a staff officer" (Wert, 225)

"I feel very grateful for all this" (Beale, 140)

"Our home was used as an operating hospital" (C. Blackford, 150)

"a new sense of desolation and pity" (Oates, 117–118)

"[S]eventy wounded soldiers saluted her" (Oates, 121)

Halleck referred to the passivity as "disheartening." (Marvel, *Burnside,* 208)

"I have good reason for saying you must not make a general movement of the army" (Sandburg, 632)

"No definite conclusion was come to" (Sears, 138)

"If in such a difficulty as this you do not help" (Nicolay and Hay, 215)

"Finding [Burnside] could get nothing out of any of them" (Sears, 149–150)

"We think Burnside 'played out.'" (Sears, 151)

"in making so hazardous a movement, I should receive some general direction"; "[I]t devolves on you to decide upon the time" (Ambrose, 100, 101)

"I approve this letter." (Nicolay and Hay, 217)

"the auspicious moment seems to have arrived" (United States War Department, *Official Records,* 127)

"Nothing would go right until we had a dictator"; "It had become virtually open rebellion in the high command" (Sears, 152)
"Tomorrow, we shall again meet the foe." (Abbott, 162–163)
"the utmost dissatisfaction, almost insubordination" (Greene, 197)
"It does not seem possible that our Generals think of attacking again"; "I am fearful it will be a sorry job." (Pride and Travis, 193)
"We struck tents about one p.m. Tuesday"; "Every face was bright with the 'devil-[may]-care' look"; "stood up all night with muskets" (Donaldson, 206)
"in quite a comfortable camp" (Wainwright, 159)
"General, the auspicious moment has arrived." (Catton, vol. 2, 89)
"virtually alone and covered with mud" (Greene, 201)
"They were the worst lot of men" (Greene, 203)
"It is said that a very bad feeling has sprung up" (Patrick, 207–208)
"Will fortune ever favor us?" (Pride and Travis, 194)
"I shall never forget the boned turkey" (Smith, 65–66)
"I have prepared some very important orders" (K.P. Williams, 544)
"We all expect Hooker will soon make his grand failure" (Abbott, 165)
"Farewell, gentlemen. There are no pleasant reminiscences" (Greene, 215)
"Mr. Wilson, permit me to introduce you to Sergeant Plunkett" (Oates, 122, 123)

CHAPTER FOURTEEN: AFTERMATH

"May God have mercy on General Lee" (McPherson, 639)
"had the attack been made upon the left" (Snell, 263)
"I am convinced now that I was only sent here" (Snell, 278)
"Had justice been done" (Snell, 285)
"Everybody could see that he was a sick man"; "God save my country"; "His arm weakened" (Stanley, 289)
"If [Meagher] has lost his men" (Athearn, 137)
He called her "Birdie," and "My Pet" (Oates, 149)
"This far shall thou go and no farther!" (Oates, 151)
"It was a painful irony that Clara had cleared the way" (Oates, 213)
"I cannot raise my spirits" (Oates, 221)
"What a price" (Oates, 222)
"Let me go; let me go!" (Epler, 433)

BIBLIOGRAPHY

Abbott, Henry Livermore. *Fallen Leaves: The Civil War Letters of Major Henry Livermore Abbott*. Edited by Robert Garth Scott. Kent, OH: Kent State University Press, 1991.

Adams, John G. B. *Reminiscences of the Nineteenth Massachusetts Regiment*. Boston: Wright, Potter Printing Co., 1899.

Alexander, Edward Porter. *Fighting for the Confederacy: The Personal Recollections of General Edward Porter Alexander*. Edited by Gary W. Gallagher. Chapel Hill: University of North Carolina Press, 1989.

Ambrose, Stephen E. *Halleck: Lincoln's Chief of Staff*. Baton Rouge: Louisiana State University Press, 1990.

Anderson, Nancy Scott, and Dwight Anderson. *The Generals: Ulysses S. Grant and Robert E. Lee*. New York: Alfred A. Knopf, 1987.

Athearn, Robert G. *Thomas Francis Meagher: An Irish Revolutionary in America*. New York: Arno Press, 1976.

Barton, William E. *The Life of Clara Barton: Founder of the American Red Cross*. Boston: Houghton Mifflin, 1922.

Baxter, Nancy Niblack. *Gallant Fourteenth; The Story of an Indiana Civil War Regiment*. Traverse City, MI: Pioneer Study Center Press, 1980.

Beale, Jane Howison. *The Journal of Jane Howison Beale: Fredericksburg, Virginia, 1850–1862*. Fredericksburg, VA: Historic Fredericksburg Foundation, 1979.

Beller, Susan Provost. *Never Were Men So Brave: The Irish Brigade During the Civil War*. New York: Margaret K. McElderry Books, 1998.

Berkeley, Henry Robinson. *Four Years in the Confederate Artillery: The Diary of Private Henry Robinson Berkeley*. Edited by William H. Runge. Chapel Hill, NC: University of North Carolina Press (for the Virginia Historical Society), 1961.

Blackford, Charles Minor. *Letters from Lee's Army, Or Memoirs of Life in and Out of the Army in Virginia During the War Between the States*. New York: Charles Scribner's Sons, 1947.

Blackford, W. W. *War Years with Jeb Stuart*. Baton Rouge: Louisiana State University Press, 1993.

Brooks, Noah. *Mr. Lincoln's Washington: Selections from the Writings of Noah Brooks, Civil War Correspondent*. Edited by P. J. Staudenraus. New York: Thomas Yoseloff, 1967.

————. *Washington, D.C. in Lincoln's Time*. Edited by Herbert Mitgang. Chicago: Quadrangle Books, 1971.

Carroll, Andrew, ed. *War Letters: Extraordinary Correspondence from American Wars*. New York: Scribner, 2002.

Carter, Robert Goldthwaite. *Four Brothers in Blue; Or, Sunshine and Shadows of the War of the Rebellion: A Story of the Great Civil War from Bull Run to Appomattox*. Norman: University of Oklahoma Press, 1999.

Catton, Bruce. *The Army of the Potomac*. Vol. 1, *Mr. Lincoln's Army.;* and Vol. 2, *Glory Road*. New York: Doubleday, 1951, 1952.

Chambers, Lenoir. *Stonewall Jackson*. New York: William Morrow, 1959.

Chesnut, Mary Boykin. *Mary Chesnut's Civil War*. Edited by C. Vann Woodward. New Haven: Yale University Press, 1981.

Child, William. *A History of the Fifth Regiment New Hampshire Volunteers*. Earlysville, VA: Old Books Publishing, 1996.

Cleaves, Freeman. *Meade of Gettysburg*. Norman: University of Oklahoma Press, 1960.

Coffin, Charles Carleton. *Four Years of Fighting: A Volume of Personal Observation with the Army and Navy from the First Battle of Bull Run to the Fall of Richmond*. Boston: Ticknor & Fields, 1866.

Conyngham, David. *The Irish Brigade and Its Campaigns*. New York: Fordham University Press, 1994.

Corby, William. *Memoirs of Chaplain Life: Three Years with the Irish Brigade in the Army of the Potomac*. Edited by Lawrence Frederick Kohl. New York: Fordham University Press, 1992.

Donaldson, Francis Adams. *Inside the Army of the Potomac: The Civil War Experience of Captain Francis Adams Donaldson*. Edited by J. Gregory Acken. Mechanicsburg, PA: Stackpole Books, 1998.

Douglas, Henry Kyd. *I Rode with Stonewall*. Chapel Hill: University of North Carolina Press, 1940.

Dowdey, Clifford. *Lee*. Boston: Little, Brown, 1965.

Epler, Percy H. *The Life of Clara Barton*. Whitefish, MT: Kessinger Publishing, 2006.

Foote, Shelby. *The Civil War, a Narrative:* Vol. 2, *Fredericksburg to Meridian*. New York: Random House, 1963.

Freeman, Douglas Southall. *Lee's Lieutenants; A Study in Command*. Vol. 2, *Cedar Mountain to Chancellorsville*. New York: Charles Scribner's Sons, 1943.

————. *R. E. Lee: A Biography*, Vol. 2. New York: Charles Scribner's Sons, 1936.

Furgurson, Ernest B. *Chancellorsville 1863: The Souls of the Brave*. New York: Alfred A. Knopf, 1992.

Gallagher, Gary W., ed. *The Fredericksburg Campaign: Decision on the Rappahannock*. Chapel Hill: University of North Carolina Press, 1995.

Goolrick, John T. *Historic Fredericksburg: The Story of an Old Town.* Richmond: Whittet & Shepperson, 1922.

Greene, A. Wilson. "Morale, Maneuver, and Mud." In *The Fredericksburg Campaign: Decision on the Rappahannock,* edited by Gary W. Gallagher, 171–228. Chapel Hill: University of North Carolina Press, 1995.

Happel, Ralph. *Chatham: The Life of a House.* Philadelphia: Eastern National Park & Monument Association (for Fredericksburg & Spotsylvania National Military Park), 1984.

Haupt, Herman. *Reminiscences of General Herman Haupt.* New York: Arno Press, 1981.

Hebert, Walter H. *Fighting Joe Hooker.* Lincoln: University of Nebraska Press, 1999.

Herdegen, Lance J. *The Men Stood Like Iron: How the Iron Brigade Won Its Name.* Bloomington: Indiana University Press, 1997.

Hoole, William Stanley. *Lawley Covers the Confederacy.* Tuscaloosa, AL: Confederate Publishing Company, 1964.

Howard, Oliver Otis. *Autobiography of Oliver Otis Howard, Major-General United States Army.* New York: Baker & Taylor, 1907.

Johnson, Robert Underwood, and Clarence Clough Buel, eds. *Battles and Leaders of the Civil War.* Vol. 3, *Retreat from Gettysburg.* Whitefish, MT: Kessinger Publishing, 2004.

Jones, Paul. *The Irish Brigade.* Washington, DC: Robert Luce, 1969.

Jones, Wilmer. *Generals in Blue and Gray.* Vol. 1, *Lincoln's Generals.* Mechanicsburg, PA: Stackpole Books, 2006.

Luvaas, Jay and Harold W. Nelson, eds. *U.S. Army War College Guide to the Battles of Chancellorsville and Fredericksburg.* Carlisle, PA: South Mountain Press, 1988.

Lee, Robert E. *Recollections and Letters of General Robert E. Lee.* Edited by Capt. Robert E. Lee. Old Saybrook, CT: Konecky & Konecky, 1992.

———. *The Wartime Papers of R. E. Lee.* Edited by Clifford Dowdey & Louis D. Manarin. New York: Bramhall House, 1961.

Leech, Margaret. *Reveille in Washington, 1860–1865.* New York: Harper, 1941.

Light, Rebecca Campbell, ed. *War at Our Doors: The Civil War Diaries and Letters of the Bernard Sisters of Virginia.* Fredericksburg, VA: American History Company, 1998.

Linderman, G. *Embattled Courage: The Experience of Combat in the American Civil War.* New York: Free Press, 1989.

Longstreet, James. *From Manassas to Appomattox.* Philadelphia: Lippincott, 1895.

Marvel, William. *The Battle of Fredericksburg.* National Parks Civil War Series, Fredericksburg & Spotsylvania National Military Park, 1993.

———. *Burnside.* Chapel Hill: University of North Carolina Press, 1991.

———. "The Making of a Myth." In *The Fredericksburg Campaign: Decision on the Rappahannock,* edited by Gary W. Gallagher, 1–25. Chapel Hill: University of North Carolina Press, 1995.

Matrau, Henry. *Letters Home: Henry Matrau of the Iron Brigade.* Edited by Marcia Reid-Green. Lincoln: University of Nebraska Press, 1993.

McCarter, William. *My Life in the Irish Brigade: The Civil War Memoirs of Private William McCarter, 116th Pennsylvania Infantry.* Edited by Kevin E. O'Brien. Campbell, CA: Savas Publishing, 1996.

McCormack, John F., Jr. "Never Were Men So Brave." *Civil War Times,* December 1998.

McDonald, Cornelia Peake. *A Woman's Civil War: A Diary with Reminiscences of the War from March 1862.* Edited by Minrose C. Gwin.Madison: University of Wisconsin Press, 1992.

McPherson, James M. *Ordeal by Fire: The Civil War and Reconstruction.* New York: Alfred A. Knopf, 1982.

Meade, George. *The Life and Letters of George Gordon Meade, Major-General United States Army.* New York: Charles Scribner's Sons, 1913.

Moe, Richard. *The Last Full Measure: The Life and Death of the First Minnesota Volunteers.* New York: Henry Holt, 1993.

Morris, Roy, Jr. *The Better Angel: Walt Whitman in the Civil War.* New York: Oxford University Press, 2000.

Musicant, Ivan. *Divided Waters: The Naval History of the Civil War.* New York: HarperCollins, 1995.

Nash, Eugene Arus. *A History of the 44th Regiment, New York Volunteer Infantry, in the Civil War, 1861–1865.* Dayton, OH: Press of Morningside Bookshop, 1988.

Nichols, Edward J. *Toward Gettysburg: A Biography of General John F. Reynolds.* University Park: Pennsylvania State University Press, 1958.

Nicolay, John G., and John Hay. *Abraham Lincoln: A History.* New York: Century, 1890.

Nolan, Alan T. *The Iron Brigade: A Military History.* New York: Macmillan, 1961.

Oates, Stephen B. *A Woman of Valor: Clara Barton and the Civil War.* New York: Free Press, 1994.

O'Reilly, Francis Augustín. *The Fredericksburg Campaign: Winter War on the Rappahannock.* Baton Rouge: Louisiana State University Press, 2003.

———. *"Stonewall" Jackson at Fredericksburg: The Battle of Prospect Hill, December 13, 1862.* Lynchburg, VA: H. E. Howard, 1993.

Palfrey, Francis W. *The Antietam and Fredericksburg.* New York: Scribner's, 1882.

Patrick, Marsena. *Inside Lincoln's Army: The Diary of Marsena Rudolph Patrick, Provost Marshal General, Army of the Potomac.* Edited by David S. Sparks. New York: Thomas Yoseloff, 1964.

Perry, James M. *A Bohemian Brigade: The Civil War Correspondents—Mostly Rough, Sometimes Ready*. New York: John Wiley, 2000.

Perry, Mark. *Conceived in Liberty: Joshua Chamberlain, William Oates, and the American Civil War*. New York: Viking Press, 1997.

Pettit, Frederick. *Infantryman Pettit: The Civil War Letters of Corporal Frederick Pettit*. Edited by William Gilfillan Gavin. Shippensburg, PA: White Mane Publishing, 1990.

Poore, Benjamin Perley. *The Life and Public Services of Ambrose E. Burnside: Soldier, Citizen, Statesman*. Providence, RI: J. A. & R. A. Reid, 1882.

Pride, Mike, and Mark Travis. *My Brave Boys: To War with Colonel Cross and the Fighting Fifth*. Hanover, NH: University Press of New England, 2001.

Quinn, Silvanus Jackson. *The History of the City of Fredericksburg, Virginia*. Richmond: Hermitage Press, 1908.

Reardon, Carol. "The Forlorn Hope." In *The Fredericksburg Campaign: Decision on the Rappahannock*, edited by Gary W. Gallagher, 80–112. Chapel Hill: University of North Carolina Press, 1995.

Sandburg, Carl. *Abraham Lincoln: The War Years*. Vol. 3. New York: Charles Scribner's Sons, 1939.

Sears, Stephen W. *Controversies and Commanders: Dispatches from the Army of the Potomac*. Boston: Houghton Mifflin, 1999.

Simpson, Tally. "Fredricksburg [*sic*] Letter, Christmas, 1862." Accessed online at awod.com/gallery/probono/cwchas/fredxmas.html.

Smith, Gene. *Lee and Grant: A Dual Biography*. New York: McGraw-Hill, 1984.

Smith, William F. *Autobiography of Major General William F. Smith, 1861–1864*. Edited by Herbert M. Schiller. Dayton, OH: Morningside, 1990.

Snell, Mark A. *From First to Last: The Life of Major General William B. Franklin*. New York: Fordham University Press, 2002.

Stackpole, Edward J. *The Fredericksburg Campaign*. Harrisburg, PA: Stackpole Books, 1957.

Stanley, Francis. *E. V. Sumner, Major-General, United States Army (1797–1863)*. Borger, TX: Jim Hess Printers, 1969.

Stuart, J.E.B. *The Letters of General J.E.B. Stuart*. Edited by Adele Mitchell. Stuart-Mosby Historical Society, 1990.

Stern, Madeleine B. *Louisa May Alcott: A Biography*. Boston: Northeastern University Press, 1996.

Stone, Sarah Katherine. *Brokenburn: The Journal of Kate Stone, 1861–1868*. Edited by John Q. Anderson. Baton Rouge: Louisiana State University Press, 1995.

Swinton, William. *Campaigns of the Army of the Potomac: A Critical History of Operations in Virginia, Maryland and Pennsylvania from the Commencement to the Close of the War, 1861–5*. New York: Charles B. Richardson, 1866.

Tate, Thomas K. "The Delicate and Dangerous Work of Placing Pontoon Bridges Fell to the Corps of Engineers." *America's Civil War*, May 1993, pp. 8 ff.

Teall, William C. "Ringside Seat at Fredericksburg." *Civil War Times Illustrated*, May 1965, pp. 17–34.

Thomas, Emory M. *Robert E. Lee: A Biography*. New York: Norton, 1997.

Trulock, Alice Raines. *In the Hands of Providence: Joshua L. Chamberlain and the American Civil War*. Chapel Hill: University of North Carolina Press, 1992.

United States War Department. *The War of the Rebellion: A Compilation of the Official Records of the Union and Confederate Armies, Series 1*. Official records, 1880–1901.

Vandiver, Frank E. *Mighty Stonewall*. New York: McGraw-Hill, 1957.

Villard, Henry. *Memoirs of Henry Villard, Journalist and Financier, 1835–1900*. Boston: Houghton Mifflin, 1904.

Villard de Borchgrave, Alexandra, and John Cullen. *Villard: The Life and Times of an American Titan*. New York: Doubleday, 2001.

Von Borcke, Heros. *Memoirs of the Confederate War for Independence*. New York: Peter Smith, 1938.

Wainwright, Charles S. *A Diary of Battle: The Personal Journals of Colonel Charles S. Wainwright, 1861–1865*. Edited by Allan Nevins. New York: Harcourt Brace, 1962.

Walker, Francis A. *History of the Second Army Corps in the Army of the Potomac*. New York: Charles Scribner's Sons, 1887.

Warren, Jack D., Jr. "Hallowed Ground: Should the Historic Sunken Road Be Closed?" *The Free Lance-Star* (Fredericksburg), April 7, 2001.

Wert, Jeffry D. *General James Longstreet*. New York: Simon & Schuster, 1993.

Whitman, Walt. *Specimen Days & Collect*. Philadelphia: Rees Welsh, 1882.

Wightman, Edward King. *From Antietam to Fort Fisher: The Civil War Letters of Edward King Wightman, 1862–1865*. Edited by Edward G. Longacre. Rutherford, NJ: Fairleigh Dickinson University Press, 1985.

Williams, Kenneth P. *Lincoln Finds a General: A Military Study of the Civil War*. Vol. 2. New York: Macmillan, 1949.

Williams, T. Harry. *Lincoln and His Generals*. New York: Alfred A. Knopf, 1952.

Wren, James. *Captain James Wren's Civil War Diary: From New Bern to Fredericksburg; B Company, 48th Pennsylvania Volunteers, February 20, 1862–December 17, 1862*. Edited by John Michael Priest. New York: Berkley Books, 1990.

Wylie, Paul R. *The Irish General: Thomas Francis Meagher*. Norman: University of Oklahoma Press, 2007.

INDEX

ACKNOWLEDGMENTS

Anyone attempting to tell the story of an event long past owes a debt of gratitude to many individuals and organizations, to the witnesses who wrote letters and kept diaries, to the archivists and editors, to the researchers and authors. All writers on the Civil War draw on the massive collection of papers and reports from the United States War Department, *The War of the Rebellion: A Compilation of the Official Records of the Union and Confederate Armies.*

In addition, it is a pleasure to acknowledge special assistance from the personnel and the publications of the Virginia Historical Society, the Historic Fredericksburg Foundation, and the Fredericksburg & Spotsylvania National Military Park.

I thank Bruce H. Franklin of Westholme Publishing for his enthusiasm and his dedication to the book, Trudi Gershenov for her striking book jacket, and Rachelle Mandik for her thoughtful and meticulous editing. Thanks also to my literary agent, Robin Rue, of Writers House, for her persistence and counsel. As always, I thank my wife, Sydney Ellen, who continues to make everything better, including this book.